The

ANATOMY

of RICHES

The
ANATOMY
of RICHES

SIR ROBERT PASTON'S
TREASURE

Spike Bucklow

REAKTION BOOKS

To Tara, Ella and Izzy

759. 2 BUC

Published by
REAKTION BOOKS LTD
Unit 32, Waterside
44–48 Wharf Rd
London N1 7UX, UK

www.reaktionbooks.co.uk

First published 2018
Copyright © Spike Bucklow 2018

Supported by the Paul Mellon Centre for Studies in British Art

Additional support from the Marc Fitch Fund

Printed and bound in China by 1010 Printing International Ltd

A catalogue record for this book is available from the British Library

ISBN 978 1 78023 979 8

Contents

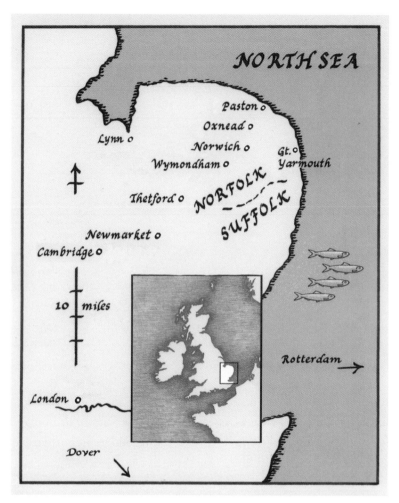

East Anglia; the Pastons' world.

Prologue

This book uses a very large but little-known still-life painting as a window on to a world of momentous change and it explores events that helped shape today's world. I first became aware of the painting when five men cautiously manoeuvred a very heavy crate into our conservation studio one damp winter afternoon. The crate was left to allow its contents to acclimatize to our studio's environment, then unpacked to reveal a much bigger than usual still-life, which stayed untouched while money was raised for its conservation. During that time, while working on other paintings, I glanced at it most days and gradually adjusted to its oddities. Eventually, the painting's physical needs were assessed and it disappeared off to London for a second opinion. It then reappeared to undergo an intensive treatment that took over four years. When it first arrived, the painting was called the *Yarmouth Collection*. By the time it left its name had been changed and it is now known as the *Paston Treasure*. Whatever the name, I found it fascinating. And it became even more intriguing after scientific investigation revealed a number of changes, including, hidden under the visible paint, a mysterious woman wearing a red laced bodice and ribbons in her hair.

The hidden woman was just one of the things that made me want to know more about the people and the things that lay behind the painting. Before I came to work in conservation I used to make props and special effects for films and TV, in the days before computer-generated imagery. Looking back, surrounded by Old Master paintings, I began to feel that my time in the film industry was like a modern version of medieval cathedral building. Both involved different craftspeople coming together for one project and then moving on to other projects as their particular stage in the process ended. Through the 1980s I worked with a constantly changing stream of art directors, designers, illustrators, sculptors, mould-makers, painters and mechanics, moving round London from studio to studio. Similarly, in the cathedral-building tradition of journey-men, the *Paston Treasure*'s seventeenth-century painter moved around Europe from patron to patron. I imagined parallels between my own life as part of the enormous teams of people who made films like *Star Wars* and *Indiana Jones* and the lives of the many people involved in the making of this painting.

Yet 350 years have passed since it was painted and I knew that tracing those people would be a challenge. Since the *Yarmouth Collection* had turned into the *Paston Treasure* in just a few years, track-ing the people who had contributed to it over the centuries would not be easy. It might not seem like a good start, for example, that art historians are still unable to agree about exactly who painted the *Paston Treasure*. All that can be said is the artist was probably Dutch and probably male.[1] Luckily, however, there are clues about many of the other people behind the painting and about many of the things it depicts. Some of those people are named but some are unnamed and their contributions are just evident from their work. This book tries to follow their trails using well-known historical events, literature in the patron's library, surviving personal letters and the painting itself. The painting will be considered as both a visible image – a still-life – and as a physical object, a 247 × 165 × 5 cm-sized thing made of wood, iron, canvas, oil and pigment.

This book enters into the world of a seventeenth-century English country gentleman, Sir Robert Paston (1631–1682), the man who oversaw the *Paston Treasure*'s creation. It is a story of one man and the things he held dear at a time of rapidly shifting values, a time very much like our own. Sir Robert's world was troubled by political upheavals, wars and strange diseases, and he had to negotiate his way through radical social and technological changes, the difficult birth-pangs of the modern world. The book explores the origins of our world through the experience of Sir Robert and the fate of his family and its wealth. Some parts of his painting are now quite faded, but it is nonetheless still a faithful record of how the whole world's destiny changed in the course of his lifetime. Sir Robert's treasures came from all over the world, and as his fortunes reversed, they continued their journeys elsewhere.

Like anything else, a painting comes into existence when all the things it needs are ready. For any cultural artefact, those things include ideas, materials, time and, usually, money. The particular shape a painting takes is determined by a patron's wishes and an artist's skills, with the artist sometimes having more influence over the outcome and the patron sometimes having a greater say. In the case of the *Paston Treasure*, the dominant creative force was undoubtedly Sir Robert. The highly skilled painter was used as a humble scribe, to whom Sir Robert dictated the composition. While there are plenty of seventeenth-century still-life paintings that feature exotic domestic goods, there are very few 'group portraits' of one person's exotic possessions. And, of those few, the *Paston Treasure* is the only one in which their owner had the upper hand in its creation. The painting is unique.

Of course, paintings are conceived in the imagination. They are the fruit of thoughts and feelings that are painted, not written. So, to understand the *Paston Treasure*, analysis of the available historical evidence needs to be complemented with sympathy, empathy and speculation.[2] For a traditionally inclined man like Sir Robert, speculation meant considering everything as a mirror that reflected, in its own way, an aspect of God. According to many – including his close family friends Thomas Browne and Thomas Henshaw – anything at all could be such a mirror or 'hieroglyph'. As this book will show, those hieroglyphs included loved ones, music, paintings and even things as apparently worthless as pigeon droppings. In other words, every single thing on earth had its own inherent meanings but also reflected, or pointed to, other things with other meanings.

The book's title is a nod towards a book that Sir Robert had in his extremely well-stocked library – Richard Burton's extraordinarily popular *The Anatomy of Melancholy*, which was first published in 1621. Burton described his book as a river that was 'sometimes precipitate and swift, then dull and slow; now direct, then [meandering];

now deep, then shallow; now muddy, then clear; now broad, then narrow'.[3] Burton's book was about much more than just melancholy, and, likewise, this book is about more than just Sir Robert's picture or his treasures. It is also about the concept of richness, and it acknowledges that no rich thing can be appreciated adequately from a single point of view.[4] The book tracks the *Paston Treasure*'s creation and the journeys taken by the people associated with it, as well as the things it depicts, in the manner of Richard Burton's river. It follows them like tributaries that flow from the hills to join, travel together and then split apart into a delta that dissolves into the sea. The book acknowledges that the many tributaries which make up works of art are shaped by money, materials and skills, guided by visions of politics and religion. The book also acknowledges that, if a historic work of art manages to come down to us, then it has a life of its own, the trajectory of which once again depends on money, materials, skills, politics and religion.

Works of art are interwoven with people's lives and political events. For example, when I worked in the film industry, my personal experience of the extra-terrestrials I helped make included shelves of chemicals, fibreglass moulds and the overpowering stench of ammonia. Outside the studio, my journey to work on a satirical TV show was complicated when the police shut down parts of London to protect newspaper offices while Margaret Thatcher confronted the miners. The studio was a converted banana warehouse in long-derelict docklands, now completely obliterated under a rash of skyscrapers. At the time of writing, it is an international centre of finance.

Back in the painting conservation studio, after funding for the *Paston Treasure*'s treatment had been found, my relationship with the painting deepened. I was part of a team of four who spent nearly a thousand hours working on it, and when the painting left to go back to its owner, it was like saying goodbye to a family member.[5] Little did I then know, but ten years later the Yale Center for British Art in New Haven would become interested in the painting and we would be reunited. And, as if to underline how lives can be entwined with art, a key member of the Yale team, Jessica David, had studied the painting when she was training in our studio.

This book uses the *Paston Treasure* as a lens to explore seventeenth-century events and objects, treating them as hieroglyphs and examining the sometimes otherworldly things to which they allude. It attempts to see as if through the eyes of Sir Robert, a loving family man who raised his children through the great plague, in the aftermath of civil war, and who sought solace in seashells and an alchemical laboratory.

To do justice to the painting, and the ways it reflects the birth of the modern world, each chapter adopts a different perspective. The opening chapter looks at where the money came from to pay for the painting and the objects it depicts. Chapter Two considers Sir Robert's formative years to try and understand why he chose to create such an unusual painting. Chapter Three explores the circumstances surrounding the painting's commission as well as the experience of being intimately involved in a painting's creation. Chapter Four investigates the journeys that some of the spectacular objects took in order to reach Sir Robert's home in Norfolk in the east of England. Chapter Five outlines the potentially world-changing research in which Sir Robert was engaged as the painting took shape on the canvas. Chapter Six looks at what happened to his family's vast collection of curiosities, rarities and riches before the paint even had a chance to dry. The closing chapter considers the most profound personal meanings that such a strange painting could have held for Sir Robert and his closest friends. Finally, an epilogue speculates on why a family's trajectory may have changed so suddenly through the course of one man's life.[6]

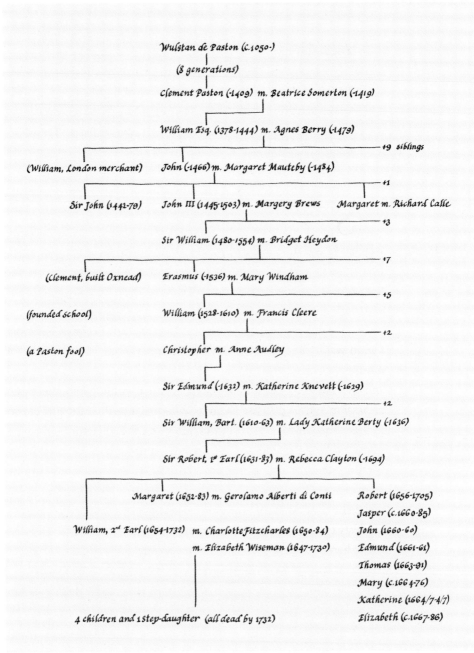

Wulstan de Paston (c.1050-)

(8 generations)

Clement Paston (-1409) m. Beatrice Somerton (-1419)

William Esq. (1378-1444) m. Agnes Berry (-1479)

+9 siblings

(William, London merchant) — John (-1466) m. Margaret Mauteby (-1484)

+1

Sir John (1441-79) — John III (1445-1503) m. Margery Brews — Margaret m. Richard Calle

+3

Sir William (1480-1554) m. Bridget Heydon

+7

(Clement, built Oxnead) — Erasmus (-1536) m. Mary Windham

+5

(founded school) — William (1528-1610) m. Francis Cleere

+2

(a Paston fool) — Christopher m. Anne Audley

Sir Edmund (-1632) m. Katherine Knevett (-1629)

+2

Sir William, Bart. (1610-63) m. Lady Katherine Berty (-1636)

Sir Robert, 1st Earl (1631-83) m. Rebecca Clayton (-1694)

Margaret (1652-83) m. Gerolamo Alberti di Conti | Robert (1656-1705)

Jasper (c.1660-85)

William, 2nd Earl (1654-1732) m. Charlotte Fitzcharles (1650-84) | John (1660-60)

m. Elizabeth Wiseman (1647-1730) | Edmund (1661-61)

Thomas (1663-91)

Mary (c.1664-76)

Katherine (1664/7-4/7)

4 children and 1 step-daughter (all dead by 1732) | Elizabeth (c.1667-86)

The Paston family tree.

one

Ancestors

The Peasants' Revolt – Norfolk's insurrection – Judge William Paston – the Paston letters – John Paston – John Amend-All – Sir John Fastolf – the Wars of the Roses – Margaret Paston – Margery and Richard Calle – the Tudors – Clement Paston – William and Katherine Paston

Sir Robert Paston's treasures were a family affair. He was very proud of his ancestors and managed to trace them all the way back to a man called Wulstan, who allegedly came over from France following William the Conqueror.[1] However, when we sift through the evidence today, the trail seems to go cold somewhere in the fourteenth century.

One day in the late fourteenth century, not far from London, a man was struck so hard that his 'brains fell out'.[2] This was not a random act of violence – the victim had indecently assaulted a girl and was killed by her father. Yet the murder was not a simple crime of passion, either, because the man who had assaulted the girl did so in the course of his official duties. He was a tax collector, assessing a household for the Poll Tax, which, according to law, was payable by 'all those that were undergrown'.[3] In modern terms, the tax was due from everyone with pubic hair. The tax collector 'turned her up' to see if she should pay, and his murder by a man defending his daughter's modesty caught the public's imagination. The father instantly became a folk hero but within months he too was dead, stabbed in the street by the Mayor of London.

The short-lived hero was Wat Tyler. Hard facts about him are difficult to disentangle from the myths, but he was a key figure in the Peasants' Revolt of June 1381.[4] This well-organized insurrection involved fairly restrained and selective violence. The action was carefully co-ordinated so that, for example, while the king, Richard II, was confronted by one group of rebels at Mile End, another group successfully attacked the Tower of London, seizing royal officials.[5] However, the violence was not directed at the king, who was barely older than Wat's own daughter. Richard II's own pubic hair had probably grown only a year or so before he had to face down the angry mob.

The Peasants' Revolt came in the wake of the worst natural disaster ever to hit England. One generation earlier, the Black Death had wiped out nearly half the population in the space of just a few years. Those who survived struggled to restore normality as every conceivable social structure had been utterly decimated in its wake. The Peasants' Revolt erupted after a decade of oppression and punitive taxation brought on by domestic and foreign policy failures as, adding political to natural problems, England was constitutionally ill-prepared for a child king. The peasants' anger was directed at the child king's corrupt ministers and officials or, more specifically, 'all lawyers and men of the Chancery and the Exchequer'. For example, a Marshal of the King's Bench who sought refuge in Westminster Abbey was dragged out of its sacred precincts and beaten to death.[6] Traditionally, fugitives from the law or the mob could claim sanctuary in church, which was rarely violated from without; more often, the fugitive escaped when the guard relaxed. The mob's act was a sign of their anger and desperation. And it was counterproductive, since storming the Abbey weakened the protection they themselves could receive from the many officials who routinely abused the law.

The Revolt collapsed quickly, and while ringleaders were executed, most rebels received relatively lenient sentences. However, the injustices continued, discontent simmered and, in its aftermath, court judgements hardened, so those who would earlier have been treated as mere felons became traitors. Despite, or possibly because of, this clamp-down, tensions mounted and violence erupted once more. The following year, in 1382, about one hundred miles northeast of London, an alleged conspiracy to murder the Bishop of Norwich was uncovered across the county of Norfolk. Bishop Despenser's response to the Revolt had been particularly despised. He was the only loyalist in the whole country to have put it down with force and he had pursued a ruthless campaign of vengeance, putting rebels to death without due process of law. Uncovering this particular conspiracy led to the execution of ten men, but records of their trial do not exist. Perhaps records have been lost or perhaps these were yet more summary executions. Such extra-judicial killings smacked of anger and desperation in at least some of the governors, as well as in the governed.[7]

The Norfolk-wide conspiracy had planned to mobilize re-inforcements at the great fair held at Horsham St Faiths, six miles north of Norwich.[8] The fact that the alleged conspirators were caught before they could act suggests – if they were indeed guilty – the presence of an active surveillance network across rural Norfolk. Under Bishop Despenser, through the 1370s and '80s, the people of Norfolk evidently lived in a climate of rumour and fear. Most of the executed conspirators were poor but at least one, a spice merchant, was apparently quite prosperous. Two of them came from Wymondham, a small town about fifteen miles from Horsham St Faiths, and at a similar distance in the opposite direction lay the tiny village of Paston.

At that time, a man called Clement lived in Paston. He was a 'good plain husbandman' who worked about one hundred acres of land. He had a single plough, rode bareback to the mill with his corn under him, and bought back the corn-meal 'as a good husband ought'.[9] One of his local markets was the very same Horsham St Faiths, which lay directly between his fields and Norwich, England's second city. Clement may have worked the land, but he would have been relatively well off and he probably enjoyed a status similar to Wat Tyler, a skilled labourer who could afford servants. Like Wat, Clement was a peasant making good. His farm was relatively large, in a – for the times – densely populated part of the country and one of the most productive areas of England. The village of Paston was on the northern edge of east Norfolk, the region with the highest land valuations in the whole country.[10]

We know nothing of Clement's political views or whether he had any involvement in the uprisings of 1381 and 1382. However, we do know that he had married Beatrice about five years earlier. She was a 'bondwoman', meaning that she was also a peasant, bound to the land. Her brother, Geoffrey, however, had raised himself from those same humble beginnings to become a local solicitor. So, while the Peasants' Revolt targeted 'all lawyers', some peasants evidently saw a future in the law. After all, along with the Church and the military, the law was one of the few options that offered peasants the chance to escape a life of servitude or working the land.

Beatrice and Clement had a son, William, who would have been about four years old when the uprising on the family's doorstep was so brutally suppressed. Beatrice's solicitor brother must have seen William's potential since he paid for him to go to school and then the Inns of Court. Thanks to a well-inclined uncle, the family had a chance to move away from labouring on the land, which they grasped with both hands. Education and circumstance turned the clever boy into a young man with steely intelligence and driving ambition.

Over time, William built a successful legal career, the bread-and-butter of which involved negotiating land transactions. In the late fourteenth century, Norfolk had relatively few large landholders but many peasant smallholdings of five acres or less. The pattern for the next century was one of small landlords like Clement buying out individual peasant farmers, enlarging their farms and consolidating their fields. William's legal skills would have given the family a distinct advantage in acquiring neighbouring peasants' fields as the old feudal system crumbled in the wake of the Black Death. As the family grew, they took the name Paston from the village at the centre of their network of farms, which spread from gently undulating woodland in the west to broadlands cut through with rivers and lakes in the east. Their little world was bounded to the north by the sea and by swampy fens and exposed heaths to the south.

Back in London, Richard II died in 1400. He was the last Plantagenet, usurped by Henry IV, the first Lancastrian. Henry eventually managed to gain control of the divided country after eight years of fighting, but he died, exhausted, in 1413. He was succeeded by Henry V, who reigned until succeeded in turn by Henry VI in 1422. Meanwhile, unnoticed by history, William's mother, Beatrice, had died in 1409 and his father, Clement, died in 1419 when William was 41. Rather than being buried in the churchyard, both were buried inside the church of St Margaret's, Paston. This was a mark of achieving some status in the local community.

Meanwhile, William's forceful and uncompromising legal skills were winning wider recognition. By 1411 he had become a legal counsel for Norwich city and Norwich Cathedral and by 1415 he was a steward of several estates. He became a Justice of the Peace in two significant Norfolk towns, Great Yarmouth and Bishop's Lynn, later to become King's Lynn, then JP for Norfolk in 1418. William earned £70 per annum as a judge, which he supplemented with very significant legal fees from clients, an income which was far higher than most minor gentry and completely dwarfed his peasant father's income of perhaps £3 a year.[11]

William focused all his considerable energies on building a lucrative career that put him in a position to buy bigger and bigger properties. In 1419 he bought woods and clearings on the gently sloping banks of the River Bure at Oxnead. This was about ten miles inland from the village of Paston, about halfway between their ancestral origins and the fair at Horsham St Faiths, just north of Norwich. The following year, at the age of 42, he inherited all Clement's properties, and it was only at this point, relatively late in life, that he considered marrying. With much land to his name, he successfully negotiated marriage to a girl less than half his age. Agnes Barry was the daughter of Sir Edmund Barry and she stood to inherit three estates upon her father's death. Since William was the son of a peasant she was marrying well beneath her station, but her gentry connections brought a degree of respectability to the Paston name.

As a lawyer, William left a professional paper trail, but unusually he also left personal correspondence. In fact, the Paston letters are the earliest collection of English family letters, many of which were found in several sacks at Oxnead in the eighteenth century.[12] Not all survived, because writers often asked recipients to burn them after reading, but those that did throw light on everyday life and offer insights into the people behind the events. Together they constitute the earliest biography of an English family. Coincidentally, the earliest English biography of an individual was left by William's close neighbour and almost exact contemporary Margery Kempe. Margery was born around 1373, the daughter of a mayor and JP of Bishop's Lynn. She bore fourteen children, had a series of spiritual visions, vowed a life of chastity and then made pilgrimages around Europe and the Holy Land. William does not mention Margery, but he would certainly have known of her – either through business connections in Lynn or because of her famed mystic devotion, which was often expressed in uncontrollable weeping and wailing.[13]

The Paston family letters suggest that William's character was much more materialist than mystic. In fact, his transactions indicate a ruthlessly acquisitive nature which was assisted by significant personal courage, as he was prepared to use force to get his way. For example, William presided over probably the last trial by combat held in England. He represented a knight who had brought a case against an earl, and rather than opt for the usual trial by jury, the case was to be settled by armed combat between two champions, with God deciding the outcome. In the event, the earl's champion failed to appear and the knight won by default, but since technically William's client won, it enhanced his reputation as a tough lawyer who would balk at nothing. He continued to acquire land for the family and at least twice took advantage of rich and recently widowed women.[14] It was alleged that he imprisoned one unfortunate widow in a pit beneath Norwich Castle for three years as part of his campaign to get his hands on her property.[15] He had little interest in the spirit of the law and, when it suited him, little interest in its letter either.

The calculating, single-minded and unscrupulous William had turned into exactly the kind of lawyer that the Peasants' Revolt had targeted only a generation earlier. Unfortunately, taking advantage of the vulnerable was a common, and apparently timeless, legal practice. As the Bible said, lawyers 'devour widows' houses' (Mark 12:40). Of course, not everyone was taken in by such heavy-handed abuses of the law and responses varied. After one particularly unpleasant business transaction with the Pastons, the aggrieved Prior of Bromholme sinisterly declared: 'since you are thus cruel and inexorable to us . . . you shall henceforth always have one of your own family a fool, till it is become poor.'[16] Whether this was a prophecy or a curse, the passage of time did indeed reveal a succession of Paston 'fools'. William's shrewd and pitiless behaviour had consequences that hung heavily over the family's heads for many generations.

The next generation came in 1421 when William and Agnes had a son, John, rapidly followed by three more sons and a daughter. All were born at Oxnead, which quickly became the family's favourite home and would remain so for centuries. In due course, John followed his father's example and entered the law, being educated at Cambridge and then admitted to the Inner Temple in 1440. That same year William arranged a marriage between John and Margaret Mauteby. She was another heiress and an extremely good catch for the son of a mere lawyer. Success seemed assured.

Four years later, though, in 1444, the grand architect of the family's success died. William was buried in the lady chapel of Norwich Cathedral, a posthumous honour far greater than his parents had achieved when they were laid to rest in Paston parish church. Critically, however, he had failed to demonstrate any of his characteristic legal skill when it came to disposing of his possessions. In good time, he had written a will leaving most property to his wife, who was in her early forties, and enough money to pay for a monk to sing prayers for his soul every day for seven years. (As a sharp lawyer who had doggedly pursued money, William probably expected his soul to occupy the fourth circle of Upper Hell. Upper Hell was where the 'sins of incontinent appetites' were cleansed. The circles of Lower Hell were reserved for souls that indulged in the worse 'sins of malice'.[17]) Yet, closer to death and witnessed only by his wife and daughter, William had revised his will. Amongst other details, the chantry changed from seven years to perpetuity, and his eldest son was even further disadvantaged.

When he discovered this, John was furious. In a rage, he seized the family's portable valuables and used his legal training to force probate on the original will's terms, which were still far from generous towards him. In turn, John was far from generous to his siblings and even appropriated the money ring-fenced for William's chantry. William had thought that some of his worldly goods would ensure balm for his soul, easing his sufferings in the Inferno and assisting progress through Purgatory. Instead, they were diverted to bolster his eldest son's worldly ambitions. John proved to be like his father – single-minded and driven by an ambition that knew no limits. John's decision to ignore his father's final wishes may have been strategically shrewd, but not surprisingly it caused deep rifts in the family.

William's ruthlessness had made many enemies, and internal divisions did not help when it came to deflecting external threats. Several neighbouring families were competing for land and status since others had followed the same strategy as Clement and William – they too were steadily acquiring and consolidating Norfolk's many peasant smallholdings. For example, William had been in conflict with one particular family for ten years over the purchase of a manor. Crisis struck when John had just taken over the helm in 1445. Since William had put his legal career first and delayed marrying, John was young and inexperienced when his father died. He was only 22 and very vulnerable to those with eyes on the family estates. William had been extremely tough and overbearing, but John was as yet unproven – he certainly had his father's ambition, but only time would tell if he also had his skills. In the twists and turns of the family's history, some of his father's unsavoury tactics were now being used against him. John had to fight to defend the Paston lands and in this, his very first test, he lost and the manor went to his opponent.

Three years later, in 1448, another Norfolk neighbour – also an ambitious lawyer, who was probably bolstered by John's earlier failure – came after another Paston property. John's purchase had been completely above board and he negotiated for eight months, even going so far as to petition the king. Eventually, he lost patience and sent his wife – with their six- and four-year-old sons – to occupy a house on the disputed property. This was a very risky move. While John was away in London, Margaret wrote telling him that she had barred the doors and built defences but asked him to send body armour, pole-axes and crossbows, since her handbows could not be fired from the windows. In the same letter she also asked him to buy one pound of almonds, one pound of sugar and a yard of very expensive black broadcloth (costing between 44d. and 48d.) for a hood, since there was no 'good [dyed] cloth . . . in this town'. Margaret not only brought connections, land and money to the Pastons, she also brought true grit and style. The house, which was defended by Margaret and twelve men, was besieged for three months and eventually taken by an army of a thousand heavily armed mercenaries employed by the rapacious neighbour. The house was practically demolished and men on both sides were hurt, but Margaret and the children were unharmed and sought shelter with a brave Paston ally. After three more years of harassment and battling through the courts, John finally managed to reclaim the estate. The house, however, was never repaired.[18]

Private armies rampaging around the countryside were a side effect of the complete breakdown of the feudal system. It turned out that the very thing that had earlier enabled the Pastons to grow now threatened to cut them down. As the feudal system crumbled, John – who was to prove as self-serving as his father – nailed his colours to the forces of law and order because he saw that what was good for the county would also be good for him. He was conscientious in his civic duties, knowing that he was simultaneously serving his family's interests. Sometimes, however, duty or self-interest put him – as well as his wife – in grave danger, and shortly after petitioning the sheriff about one particular marauding gang, an attempt was made on his life in Norwich Cathedral. Such was the life of a medieval lawyer. John would have witnessed it all before as a child and would have remembered his father having been threatened with dismembering as part of one legal dispute. His father had only felt relatively safe after being made a judge.[19] Violence was a much more common response to the Pastons' business methods than the prior's prophecy, or curse, of congenital mental frailty.

Down on the farm – or, rather, the ever-increasing number of farms – life was not necessarily too much easier. Money was scarce and landlords like the Pastons often took much of their rent in kind, in barley, malt, sheep or wool. Farmers' fortunes have always fluctuated and in the mid-fifteenth century prices were dropping, rents were falling and many tenant farmers were deeply in arrears. Whereas his grandfather Clement could simply ride to local fairs like Horsham St Faiths, John had to ship his produce as far as Newcastle, London or Flanders to get a good price. In bad years, the Pastons' agents seized crops from their tenant farmers, either straight from the field or by sealing barns after the harvest. Conflicts of ownership between landlords further complicated the picture since tenants did not always know who had the right to their rents.[20] Even when there was no dispute about legal ownership, there was always the danger of blatantly illegal rustling. In a single year, John estimated that over six hundred of his sheep were taken in raids by the Duke of Norfolk, and another year he lost eleven hundred sheep and four hundred lambs in raids by the Duke of Suffolk.[21]

Actually, it would probably be more accurate to say the raids were instigated by Elizabeth, Duchess of Norfolk, and Alice, Duchess of Suffolk, since it has been said that the region was really ruled by women.[22] Certainly, Elizabeth and Alice featured regularly in the Paston correspondence. Together with Margaret Paston, who was prepared to defend the family property against armed men, it seems that these East Anglian women were forerunners of the royal household. After all, Henry VI's wife would prove to be the power behind the throne. Clearly, the Pastons' Norfolk could be like Hollywood's Wild West, only colder and wetter, with more strong women and a wider variety of weapons.

The Pastons' Norfolk even had its own Robin Hood figure, an outlaw called Roger Church, alias 'John Amend-All', whom Margaret thought might have been secretly supported by someone of high birth. His band of outlaws protected peasants against a wide range of Norfolk nobility and gentry, including, at times, the Pastons themselves. Over four hundred years later, in 1883, Robert Louis Stevenson's novel *The Black Arrow* drew heavily on events described in the Paston family's letters. Stevenson based his fictional rebel leader on John Amend-All, although he called the character Ellis Duckworth, the real name of another outlaw also mentioned in the Paston letters.[23]

Margaret had been prepared to sell barley, collect rents and defend property from armed men. Yet she came from a securely established family, so in his more optimistic moments John probably thought all his difficulties – outlaws, his father's will, competition from others and the agricultural depression – would not unduly affect his family's progress. Margaret brought nine manors into the Paston family and, even more importantly, she had very good connections since she was related to the great Sir John Fastolf. Locally, Fastolf had lots of land, but nationally he had made his name fighting for Henry V.

Fastolf had served in Ireland and France and, following Henry V's death in 1422, became a lieutenant in Normandy and continued to serve in France, being honoured with the Order of the Garter in 1426. Later, however, a charge of cowardice was made against him and although he was eventually vindicated, the case had dragged on and his military reputation had been tarnished. He returned to England in 1439, rich and successful, but because of extremely fluid and unpredictable domestic politics was greeted with hostility. While fighting in France he had bought more land, from France to Yorkshire, and he also purchased a small tavern, the Boar's Head, in Southwark, London. He owned many estates, manors and castles, yet by a strange quirk of fate this modest pub had the biggest impact on how he came to be remembered. It became significant because, about 150 years after Fastolf's death, William Shakespeare was writing his *Henry V* while frequenting south London pubs. In the play's original draft, Prince Hal's companion was the historically correct Sir John Oldcastle, but in the final draft Shakespeare took the old pub landlord's name and adapted it to 'Falstaff' for the prince's drunken and cowardly companion. Shakespeare's Falstaff bears little relation to Sir John Fastolf, but the late sixteenth-century fictional character served to reflect and reinforce prejudices against the real mid-fifteenth-century military hero.

Yet, worse than a damaged reputation, Fastolf had no obvious heirs. Intrigue swirled around him, and for an opportunistic, land-hungry, ambitious lawyer like John Paston, he was irresistible. This was the point, two generations after Wat Tyler and Clement Paston, at which the family had the chance of playing on a national, as opposed to a merely regional, stage. Following in his father's footsteps, John was starting to get a formidable legal reputation, and through Margaret he had become engaged in Fastolf's business. The two men became firm friends, and although they were not related by blood, Fastolf called John his 'right trusty and well-beloved cousin'.[24]

The Pastons had every expectation of further advancement but they knew it would not be plain sailing. John knew that having land or money was not enough in such turbulent times – he had to find a patron to help protect him, his family and his properties. They had a skeleton in their cupboard and desperately needed to hide it: if Clement had indeed been an 'unfree' peasant, then William – and, in turn, John – would have inherited few legal rights but many legal restrictions. As lawyers, they knew that vicarious gentrification through marriage changed nothing. In fact, the only details we have about Clement come from one of the Paston's adversaries, and they were published with the express intention of undermining the family. The Paston's legally disadvantaged position could only be maintained with the threat or exercise of force. And worse than the now shameful grandfather Clement, in 1262 a slightly more distant ancestor had lived off fifteen acres, which he rented for the modest sum of 36*d*. plus one hen per annum.[25] The even more distant – and possibly fictitious – ancestor Wulstan was extremely important to the Pastons, because as a follower of William the Conqueror, his Norman stock would have offered their family tree a respectable root.[26] However, the current Pastons knew that nothing could beat a powerful living patron who might actively help erase the family's unfortunate past, stabilize their precarious present and promise a more prosperous future.

As Margaret was fighting off mercenaries, John's would-be protector, Fastolf, was building his own magnificent castle at Caister on the Norfolk coast. Trouble threatened from every direction. Depressed rural England was verging on lawlessness and when the war with France reignited, the ripples were even felt in deepest Norfolk. In 1450, for example, John's mother, Agnes, wrote a letter describing her fear of French pirates on the local beach. Pirates had stolen ships and attacked several people, releasing them only after being convinced they were pious pilgrims on their way to venerating a piece of the True Cross held at the church in the neighbouring village of Bacton. In France Joan of Arc led the French to victory, and by 1453 the English had lost all but Calais. Meanwhile, back in England, the Wars of the Roses were brewing as the ruling Lancastrian dynasty was challenged by the House of York.

Sir John Fastolf died in 1459 and on his deathbed he made John Paston his sole heir. Not surprisingly, existing executors questioned the will. Countless minor and not-so-minor gentry wanted a slice of Fastolf's enormous estate. John doubtless had bitter memories of his father's untidy will and the way it had divided his family just fifteen years earlier, and those memories probably coloured his response to Fastolf's will. He was not going to yield. The mad scrabble for riches involved numerous legal hearings in the Norwich court, the Westminster court, the Ecclesiastical court, and in many smaller manor and county courts. In order to defend the massive inheritance, John attended every hearing he could, but it took at least two and a half days on horseback to get between Norwich and London.[27] His litigants ran him ragged, attending one court after another across the whole southeast of England. Just one man was desperately galloping from court to court trying to defend the whole Fastolf inheritance, and it was an impossible task given the number of others who also had eyes on the prize.

While John was trying to protect his right to Fastolf's lands, he rather rashly ignored a command from the king. He was severely rebuked and immediately sped to London, where he was instantly thrown into Fleet Prison. His enemies were triumphant, but when the king heard the catalogue of harassment he had suffered, he was released. Quite soon though, double-booked in different courts, he once again found himself in contempt and in gaol.[28]

However, things were not all bad, because John Paston had, after all, come to the personal attention of the king. He had even been offered a knighthood. He must have considered himself to be far too busy to undertake all the duties of a knight – which included an obligation to fight – because he turned it down, preferring instead to pay a fine. Also, he knew that the king – Henry VI, a Lancastrian – was himself weak and under threat from Yorkist pretenders so might not have been able to offer much effective security as a patron. Nonetheless, John was fully aware that some formal connection to the court would offer his family a degree of protection and might help open doors, so he arranged for his eldest son to take the honour. Arranged marriages were a good way to link families who enjoyed roughly similar status, but trying to forge bonds with families of much higher status needed different approaches.[29]

John and Margaret had five sons and two daughters. Confusingly, they chose to call both the first two boys John. The eldest son was knighted and placed in the royal household. We will call him Sir John. John Paston also used his second son, whom we will call John III, to try and win protection. At the age of seventeen, he was found a position in the household of the new Duke of Norfolk, who was about the same age. (He was the son of Elizabeth, the duchess whose men had earlier stolen the Pastons' sheep.) The intention was for their sons to form friendships that might eventually convert into networks of influence. Unfortunately, at home there had been very serious personality clashes between John and his eldest son, who was thrown out in 1464 and only grudgingly readmitted six months later after repeated pleading by his mother. So it is perhaps not surprising that he disappointed his father when placed in the king's household, where he failed to network effectively. He returned home and was, for a while, at a loose end. Luckily, John III was more successful with the young Duke of Norfolk.[30] The two brothers had quite different characters but they got on well, through thick and thin. Meanwhile, their proud father was still stubbornly negotiating Fastolf's disputed will. The multiple forces ranged against them were getting the upper hand, and in 1464 the whole family met to hold crisis talks. By this time, the Paston estates were extensive, but the family's finances were spread extremely thinly and they were very vulnerable. It was make or break time.

Throughout most of 1465 John was tied up in hearings at various London courts. Meanwhile, the fearless Margaret was again defending assaults on their properties in Norfolk. As the Duke – or, more probably, Duchess – of Suffolk amassed men on one side of a river, Margaret gathered her men on the other with 77 head of cattle. The stand-off continued for weeks as both sides used the law, threats and violence as they saw fit. Margaret eventually won the day. Such victories were sweet, but within the year John was dead. He had been worn out by the fight. The Bishop of Norwich wrote a letter of condolence to Margaret, admitting that he himself could not have withstood 'the sorrow and trouble' that John had born 'to win Sir John Fastolf's goods'.[31]

At John's death, absolutely nothing had been resolved, and who knows whether he ultimately regretted his apparently futile pursuit of Fastolf's estate? If he had not obstinately chased the elusive inheritance, then he and his family would have been rich enough to live comfortably but modest enough to avoid too much attention from other predatory aspiring families. As it was, he chose to pursue the prospect of even greater riches and set in train a torturous series of events with which the next generations had to grapple.

The die had been cast and the family's prospects looked bleak – they had powerful enemies but no powerful allies. Worse still, it was widely thought that the new head of the family, Sir John, was rather ineffectual. Sir John's grandfather William had been a ruthless lawyer and his father, John, had proved equally ruthless in time. In fact, his father's tenacious refusal to compromise over Fastolf's will undoubtedly cut short his life. Sir John, on the other hand, was very different – he preferred play to work. As the rest of the family struggled on in Norfolk, Sir John was happily haemorrhaging money, living the high life in London. He was the head of the third generation of Pastons to have escaped toiling the land but he seemed to lack his father's and grandfather's single-minded drive.

The many court cases rumbled on, but possibly because of Sir John's less than whole-hearted participation, a compromise was eventually found. It involved the family splitting Fastolf's lands in Norfolk, Suffolk, Essex and Surrey with a co-executor and surrendering all title deeds except for Caister, which the Duke, or Duchess, of Norfolk attempted to seize in 1461 and then besieged for five weeks in 1469. In 1470, after eleven years of fighting over Fastolf's will, the family theoretically won the battle for Caister. But they had effectively lost the war. Just as John had overruled his mother's version of his father's will, the courts eventually overruled his version of Fastolf's will. With the young Sir John at its head, the family was seriously divided and under attack.

The untidy division of wealth in grandfather William's will and the loss of most of Fastolf's lands meant that money was exceedingly tight, and the family would have floundered were it not for history repeating itself. Just as the ancestral William had benefited from a benevolent uncle, so too did Sir John. Some may have been tempted to dismiss Sir John as a 'Paston fool'; however, an estranged uncle – who happened to be a wealthy London-based businessman, also called William – genuinely appreciated Sir John's company and connections. In fact, Sir John's easy-going attitude turned out to be exactly what the family needed as it navigated the crisis of his father's death. Uncle William chose to bankroll his fun-loving nephew.

Thanks in large part to support from Uncle William, Sir John lived well and even found time to write a bestseller. He described his book as a guide to knighthood, and it included diverse subjects from 'the manner and form of coronations of kings and queens', through sailing directions, weather prognostications and astrological diagrams, to a 'secret of secrets'.[32] Sir John was evidently interested in the blurred boundary between the natural and supernatural worlds. In this he was not alone – hence the book's popularity – and numerous copies were made for various members of the gentry, with slight variations to suit each patron.[33] Sir John also had Ovid's *Art of Love* transcribed for him.[34] And he had at least one servant who was also engaged in the arts, because in 1473 he complained that he had been deserted by his servant William Wood, who left to play Robin Hood in the May festivities. Robin Hood was first mentioned in a ballad of 1377 – on the eve of the Peasants' Revolt and the year before grandfather William was born – but Sir John's letter mentioning his servant's departure is the first evidence of Robin Hood as a subject for the stage.[35]

Sir John knew how to enjoy life. He could be both relaxed and happy, apparently unlike his obsessive father and grandfather. However, even for Sir John, it was not all fun and games and it took another six years of negotiation before he could eventually move into Caister Castle. He was not able enjoy it for long because by 1479 he was dead, probably brought down by a wave of plague that swept through London that year. Much to his mother's disappointment, he had never married, so Sir John's younger brother, John III, became the next head of the family. John III was neither ruthless like his father nor reckless like his brother; instead, he seemed practical, efficient and responsible as well as socially adept.

While Sir John had played in London, John III and their mother, Margaret, had been engaged in the day-to-day business of running the farms in Norfolk. In this task the Pastons were assisted by servants like Richard Calle, who arranged leases, collected rents, organized the sale of produce, drew up accounts and generally advised on commerce, agriculture and politics. Calle was loyal and courageous and was actively involved in some of the paramilitary showdowns that threatened the family. At the same time he was evidently also rather more intimately involved in the family than either John III or his mother knew. Richard was deeply in love with Margery, one of the Johns' sisters, and, scandalously, they eloped. The family responded by forcing them apart. In letters, Richard wrote plaintively about the 'painful life that we lead' and complained that it seemed 'a thousand years ago since that I spoke with you'.[36] Margery was not forgiven, but Richard was too valuable to lose for long and after three years he was back with the Pastons. He eventually earned enough money to buy a farm in Bacton, a village right next to Paston, where he and Margery lived and brought up three sons. Yet despite being tough and pragmatic, John III and his mother were not hard-hearted. Margaret remembered Richard and Margery's eldest son in her will and left money for Sir John's illegitimate daughter, while John III accepted a marriage proposal from Margery Brews, who took advantage of a Valentine's Day tradition.[37] It seems that John III embodied a mix of both his father's and his elder brother's best attributes.

Uncle William's friendship with playboy Sir John had saved the family, but his relations with the younger nephew John III were much frostier. When John III became the Paston patriarch, Uncle William went to court to fight for estates that he claimed had been bequeathed to him in grandfather William's contentious will. The case dragged on for a decade or so, but by that time the balance of power across the nation was starting to turn in a direction that would eventually favour John III's branch of the family.

For decades the Pastons had sought the protection of a patron. Sir John Fastolf, kings Edward IV and Henry VI, the young Duke of Norfolk and others had all proved unwilling or unable to provide the family with much protection for long. This was due in large part to widespread strife during the turmoil that followed the collapse of feudalism. In the 25 years after Fastolf's death, England had six monarchs – a Lancastrian, a Yorkist, a Lancastrian, then three more Yorkists, with internal Yorkist tensions erupting around Richard III. With repeated rapid and violent change at the top, the chains of allegiance upon which patronage depended kept breaking, and new bonds were constantly being forged as everyone tried to reposition themselves in the hope of gaining some semblance of security. Getting close to people in power could bring great rewards but it also entailed great risk, since political fates became entangled. Luckily, John III's character helped him read the signs and allowed him to skilfully negotiate the ever-changing landscape. He was neither too assertive nor too reticent with any protagonists, and his actions seemed measured and balanced, making him acceptable to both Lancastrian and Yorkist factions.

In 1485 the Lancastrian Henry VII, who had won the throne on the battlefield, healed the Lancastrian–Yorkist rift by arranging a marriage with Elizabeth of York. In so doing he created a new dynasty, the Tudors. And in the wake of this marriage, a new set of locals became empowered as chains of authority percolated down to country squires and their tenant farmers. John III was an ardent supporter of Henry VII and had fought bravely at the Battle of Stoke, in the thick of a fight in which thousands died. He was knighted on the field for his valour. In that moment, the Pastons emerged from crisis. John III developed a close relationship with Tudor favourite John de Vere, who was destined to become the arbiter of power across East Anglia until beyond John III's death in 1503. A century after Clement and Beatrice, the Pastons were finally secure in their lands and in their status. The once upstart family had become an unquestionable part of the establishment.

The Tudors stayed in power throughout the sixteenth century, and as far as the Pastons were concerned, the lands enjoyed relative economic stability. The family enjoyed a slow consolidation of properties and connections which turned them into one of the richest and most respected families in the region. By the end of the century, their wealth was proverbial and it was said that 'There never was a Paston poor.'[38] After a rollercoaster century followed by a period of steady growth, the family was in a position to be grateful to their hard-working ancestors. Each new generation duly honoured their ancestors by constantly reusing their names, repeating them as if in a slow chant down the centuries. By calling their children Clement or William or Margaret, numerous Paston parents expressed the hope that future generations might grow up to embody some of the qualities shown by past generations.

For example, at the end of the sixteenth century, another Clement Paston became a sea captain, commanding a 250-ton trading vessel, the *Hone of Hamburgh*, as well as the *Pellican of Dansick* and the *Anne Gallant*. With this last ship he captured the French *Mermaid*, kept most of its goods and imprisoned its commander, whom he eventually ransomed for £1,600. He became a soldier, an MP and an Elizabethan courtier.[39] This wayfaring Sir Clement was a contemporary of Sir Francis Drake and Sir Walter Raleigh, and the details of his life were a long way from the Clement who rode his corn to market. Yet his courage, industry and investment for future generations were the same.

The Pastons' interests now spread well beyond Norfolk, but their hearts remained near the village from which they took their name. The intrepid Sir Clement valued his Norfolk roots and – funded, in true Paston style, largely by the money his heiress wife brought him – he built a vast mansion on the shallow terraces of the gently meandering River Bure, right next to the old family home at Oxnead. It was as if, even after sailing the high seas, he was invisibly bound to the same soil that the first Clement had worked. He died in 1598, aged 83, leaving no heirs, and Oxnead was inherited by Sir Clement's nephew, another William. This particular William was one of many Pastons to succumb to the lunacy predicted by the Prior of Bromholme.[40]

The house was inherited by Sir Edmund in 1610, just after marrying Katherine Knevett. That same year, Sir Edmund and Katherine's eldest son, yet another William, was born. At the age of fourteen, this particular William was sent to the University of Cambridge, where he became accomplished in several languages and, to his mother's great relief, did not overly exert himself with tennis. Or, at least, so it would seem from their letters. This William was well liked across Cambridge and he returned to Oxnead three years later 'furnished with graces', according to his mother, 'as a bee comes laden to the hive'.[41] Sadly, just two years later, in 1629 when he was only nineteen, William's mother died. Meanwhile, his father's health had declined so William effectively became the head of the house, and it was he who had to commission his mother's monument for the Paston church. It was a marble and alabaster ensemble that cost an extraordinary £340 and included an epitaph attributed to John Donne. The sculptor, Nicholas Stone, had just been appointed master mason at Windsor Castle and he regularly worked for King Charles I. This seventeenth-century William Paston wanted only the best, and Nicholas Stone became part of his growing circle of artistic and intellectual friends.[42] A beacon nestling between fields and woodlands, Oxnead rapidly became famed for its hospitality.

In some profound ways, this seventeenth-century William was very different from his fifteenth-century namesake. The fifteenth-century William had been obsessively acquisitive, hungering for status in the eyes of others. He had further disrupted an already hostile landscape by aggressively carving out his own uncompromising path. On the other hand, the seventeenth-century William took pleasure in providing lavish hospitality. He contributed to a much more benign environment by generously sharing out his family's magnificent riches. Of course, the scale of his largess depended upon his forebears' gains, but the disposition to give, rather than take, was his alone. Over the centuries that separated these two Williams, the Pastons had changed their ways. They ceased to be the self-serving family that rapaciously exploited their neighbours and matured into a family that open-handedly enriched the various communities of which they were part. For example, they had endowed a school in neighbouring village of North Walsham, which is now a sixth-form college and still bears their name.[43] The seventeenth-century William lived well and spent extravagantly on a collection of treasures for his Oxnead home and its gardens, which was open to all comers. Their not-so-small patch of the kingdom seemed perfect and complete.

William married Lady Katherine Berty, daughter of the Earl of Lindsey, a well-known soldier and courtier. Their first child, Robert, was born in 1631, seemingly destined for a charmed life. He certainly arrived in the lap of luxury. It was only ten miles as the crow flies from where the first Clement had worked the land, but Robert's Norfolk was a completely different world. In due course, Robert would become the head of the family and achieve a degree of aggrandizement beyond his ancestors' wildest dreams. King Charles II would create a brand new position specifically for the family and Robert would become the first Earl of Yarmouth.

In time, Robert would also celebrate the family's accumulated treasures in a monumental still-life painting. That painting, the *Paston Treasure*, is now ten miles from Oxnead, at the very heart of the city of Norwich. It hangs on the walls of the great castle founded by William the Conqueror, with whom Robert's distant ancestor, Wulstan, had supposedly come to England.

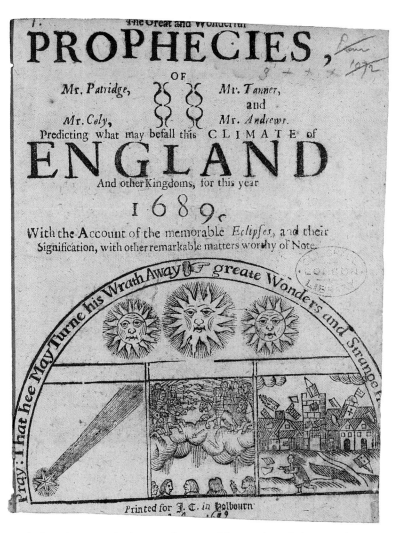

The Great and Wonderful

PROPHECIES,

OF

Mr. Patridge,   Mr. Tanner,
and
Mr. Coly,   Mr. Andrews.

Predicting what may befall this CLIMATE of

ENGLAND

And other Kingdoms, for this year

1689

With the Account of the memorable *Eclipses*, and their
Signification, with other remarkable matters worthy of Note.

Pray: I that hee May Turne his Wrath Away Of greate Wonders and Strange

Printed for J. C. in Holbourn

The heavily trimmed title page of a copy of the astrological almanac *The Great
and Wonderful Prophecies of Mr Partridge, Mr Coly, Mr Tanner and Mr Andrews . . .* (1689).

two

Growing Up

Oxnead, Norfolk – the Court of Charles I – Westminster School – civil war
– the Cavalier winter – Trinity College, Cambridge – Robert Paston's gap year –
the body politic – the execution of Charles I – the weather – Oliver Cromwell's
death – the coronation of Charles II – Cromwell's head

The previous chapter galloped across several centuries, keeping up with the Pastons' swelling coffers. This chapter slows
the pace to accompany the young Robert Paston as he was being
prepared to take his turn shouldering responsibility for the family's
fortunes. For a long time there had been plenty of 'Paston fools' but no
'Paston poor'. Every Paston child had been born with a roof over its
head, but what went on in the wider world changed radically. A couple
of centuries before Robert was born, Paston children had grown up
in houses besieged by mercenaries, in farms harassed by malicious
duchesses and in a country split by warring dynasties. By contrast, in
1631, Robert was born into a house that thronged with well-wishers,
in an estate at peace with its neighbours and in a country that enjoyed
stability and prosperity. Inevitably, this would have influenced how he
grew up.[1] The range of childhood experiences then was much as it is
now, and as a little boy Robert was blissfully unaware of the reasons
why, but his earliest years were as close to idyllic as is possible.[2]

The Oxnead that his father presided over was a hub of fashionable society, a beacon of refinement and a cultural oasis in peaceful rural
Norfolk. Sir William's son grew up in benign and opulent surround-
ings famed for their hospitality. The young Robert would have enjoyed
playing in the terraced pleasure grounds and the south-facing gardens
that sloped gently down to the banks of the River Bure. He could have
played hide-and-seek amongst manicured topiary, in a garden populated with gods – Nicholas Stone's statues included a Venus and Cupid
(extraordinarily expensive at £30), a Jupiter, Juno, Apollo, Hercules,
Mercury, Diana (£25 apiece) and more, all guarded by a three-headed

37

Cerberus (costing £14).[3] In the grand, sprawling Elizabethan house, he had been surrounded by hundreds of great paintings.

Living in peace – as opposed to living through war – may seem much more important than being surrounded by art. But the peace and the art were connected, because historic links between art and politics were much stronger than we find easy to imagine today. For example, when the fifteenth-century Paston servant absconded to play Robin Hood on stage, we might think he was interested in the arts, not politics. Yet attempts by sixteenth-century Scottish authorities to suppress Robin Hood plays were met with riots in Edinburgh, during which gaols were stormed and prisoners freed. And in seventeenth-century England, Robin Hood 'unequivocally dominated' May Day festivals, which became 'a saint's day for the canonized outlaw'.[4] Robin Hood's influence was everywhere and shades of him have even been glimpsed in Shakespeare's exiled Duke Senior. The Globe's audience would have seen clear parallels between *As You Like It*'s Forest of Arden and England's Sherwood Forest.[5] For Robert's family, the annual Robin Hood plays might even have stirred ancestral memories of rural Norfolk under the dreaded Bishop Despenser or encounters with John Amend-All and Ellis Duckworth.

Yet relationships between art and politics change constantly. When Robert was growing up, it was evolving from the relationship that Queen Elizabeth had established while Sir Clement rebuilt Oxnead.[6] Elizabeth's favoured political art form had been painting, and she chose to be portrayed as a vestal virgin, a divine judge and an impartial heroine in a never-ageing, ever-youthful programme of timeless icons. Of course, this was propaganda, but not as we know it. Modern propaganda is the cynical manipulation and misrepresentation of facts, whereas late sixteenth- and early seventeenth-century propaganda concerned itself with branding and spin. There was no centralized, top-down propaganda machine – image-making was flexible and it reflected, as well as helped form, public opinion.[7]

Charles I, who ascended to the throne six years before Robert was born, was one of England's greatest patrons of the arts, a fact acknowledged even by the Puritan poet Lucy Hutchinson from the opposite end of the political spectrum. She said men of 'learning and ingenuity in all the arts' were honoured at court and that Charles was 'a most excellent judge and great lover of paintings'. Charles employed Continental painters like van Dyck and Rubens, whose styles were sometimes disconcertingly new to the English eye, but their various propaganda functions remained essentially the same. Together, the king and his painters vastly extended the iconography of royal art. Van Dyck's portrait of *Charles I on Horseback* depicted him as emperor, knight, lover and even warrior-saint. His radical and completely unprecedented royal family portraits celebrated Charles's emotional and domestic life.[8] According to Lucy Hutchinson, the king also ushered in a new 'temperate, chaste and serious' morality at court.[9] In Norfolk William Paston copied this court art and ethos. The first ever folio English dictionary was dedicated to 'the truly Noble, and Perfect Lover and Encourager of Arts and Sciences, Sir William Paston' and called Oxnead a 'Centre of Hospitality to Strangers and Ingenious Persons'.[10] All these early cultural experiences steadily percolated into the young Robert's very core and, in the fullness of time, would eventually help shape his monumental painting, the *Paston Treasure*.

In setting the scene for the world which influenced Robert Paston, it is important to recognize that Charles's actions suggest he saw painting, poetry, music and theatre as powers that could actively create the harmony and balance he wanted for his realm. It was as if he saw art as a kind of white magic, like that exercised by Shakespeare's Prospero in *The Tempest*.[11] It seemed the king was attempting an almost supernatural politic of beauty, using the arts to build not a passing illusion, but a means of glimpsing true reality. By imitating the harmony of the spheres, it was thought that painters, poets, musicians and actors were able to draw the perfection of the heavens all the way down to earth.[12] Such ideas were completely in tune with much contemporary scientific thinking. After all, just a few years earlier Johannes Kepler, the German astronomer, had attempted to express planetary motion in terms of musical notations.[13]

Charles may have loved painting, but his favourite and most extravagant art form was the 'masque', a court theatre. His most sumptuous dramas unfolded in the Banqueting House in the Palace of Whitehall, which architect Inigo Jones had modelled on classical ideas of cosmic harmony. It was the king's sophisticated vision of himself and his country, cast in stone. The process of building the Banqueting House was overseen in part by Nicholas Stone, one of Sir William Paston's circle of artistic friends and a regular visitor to the young Robert's Oxnead. The Banqueting House's exterior and interior were conceived as being completely complementary so that, together, outside and inside provided a balance of inclusion and exclusion or, more accurately, relative exclusion, since Charles lived most of his life on public display. Its outer dignity was complemented by inner opulence, its outer decorum with inner licence, and outward gravitas with inward fantasy.[14] Those who participated in these spectacular theatrical rituals knew that they did not reflect life outside, but by consciously acting as if they did, each person could adopt perspectives that differed from their day-to-day points of view. Repeated often enough, these shifts in perception altered behaviours in the outside world and, Prospero-like, their fictions could transform reality.[15]

Inside the Banqueting House, Charles commissioned Rubens to paint an exuberant ceiling that celebrated his father, James I, in heaven. Its design was based on his father's vision of union, and spectacular masques were performed immediately below this image of heaven.[16] Inigo Jones also worked as a set designer, making innovative single-point perspective stage sets which, of course, could only be appreciated fully from a single position in the auditorium. That unique position was taken by Charles, and those further from the king – in a hierarchical audience, ever more distant both spatially and politically – enjoyed an ever more distorted view of the depicted reality. The spectacle, which included hymns of praise to the king, was thoroughly Neoplatonic, with everything invisibly emanating from, and visibly returning to, the king at the centre.[17] They reinforced the idea of Charles – according to Jones, this time in the role of playwright – as one who 'transcends as far common men as they are above beasts [and who embodies] all the virtues joined together'.[18] The visually opulent displays were created with the intention that, to again quote Jones's masque, 'Corporeal beauty . . . may draw us near to . . . the beauty of the soul, unto which it hath analogy.'[19]

The courtly arts were amply nourished by roots sunk deeply into Greek philosophy and the Christian tradition. They also had a profoundly patriotic strand, and in Rubens's Banqueting House ceiling Charles's father, James I, was accompanied by Brutus, the legendary Trojan ancestor of the kings of Britain. Ideas of art and magic entwined in the service of God, king and country were shared by scholars, diplomats and artists – like Dr John Dee, Sir Henry Wotton and Giovanni Lomazzo – because the court's aesthetic applied equally to theatre and to statecraft. The other arts also benefited from the political and intellectual value placed on beauty, and the practice of painting flourished in London and the court. At the same time, demand for pictures rose across the whole country.[20] In Norfolk Sir William Paston's Oxnead basked in the same philosophy of beauty, harmony and balance, and the impressionable young Robert would have innocently absorbed its peaceful, benevolent atmosphere. Surrounded by beauty, all would have seemed right in the world.

But the balmy days were not to last. Tragically, when Robert was just five years old, his mother died in childbirth. For months he had seen his mother's belly slowly swell and, as an only child, would have looked forward to the arrival of a playmate. Instead, the heart of the family was suddenly snatched away. Oxnead changed overnight, its tranquillity shattered. As High Sherriff of Norfolk, Robert's father had civic duties to fulfil, but as soon as he could, he left Oxnead. Sir William went on a more than usually adventurous Grand Tour, getting as far as the Middle East, and would, in due course, return with traveller's tales and great treasures. Meanwhile, however, at the tender age of nine and having lost both parents, Robert was sent off to school. He went knowing that the future burden of family responsibility would fall on his shoulders alone.

School was at Westminster, 130 miles and a ride of two and a half days away. Westminster School worked their pupils hard and Robert attended under the direction of Dr Richard Busby, whose harsh discipline was to become legendary. Their seven-hour days started with Aesop on Mondays and Ovid on Tuesdays. Aesop dominated the pupils' early years and Ovid their middle years, while Homer and Virgil became the focus for later years. The children left being able to read and write poetry in Latin and, unlike children from other schools, also in Greek.[21] Twenty years after Robert's arrival there, John Evelyn said that pupils as young as twelve or thirteen were fluent in Latin, Greek, Hebrew and Arabic.[22]

The wider world's harsh realities had tragically intruded on Robert's home in Oxnead and it did not take long for them to overshadow his school in Westminster. A decade is an extremely long time in politics and one of the things that changed between the 1630s and the 1640s was attitudes towards the arts. In a Protestant country still smarting from religious conflict a century earlier, one of the problems with Charles's patronage of painting and theatre was that it smacked of Catholicism. The previous century had been torn apart by discord between Protestants and Catholics, part of which involved the wholesale destruction of not just churches, but also art. (Sir Henry Wotton still feared that his collection of paintings could be seen as 'morally corrupt'.[23]) Charles's championing of the arts had a very benign influence on Robert's 1630s childhood of Oxnead, but as the pendulum swung in the 1640s, Robert witnessed a bewildering backlash.

Across East Anglia, the regional figurehead for this extreme backlash was a Puritan member of the minor gentry called Oliver Cromwell. As a young boy, Robert would not have understood the ideological fine points that underlay the political and religious shift. But he didn't need to – he would have felt a very visceral change in the atmosphere. He would have overheard his father's conversations and sensed the change of tone and mood that came with the mention of increasingly hostile neighbours' names. Each of those neighbours' names would have been associated with another – Cromwell, a name that evoked fear and loathing. Cromwell, the young Robert would have concluded, was a sinister figure who lay spider-like at the middle of an invisible web threatening everything he held dear. For him, Cromwell would have been all the more forbidding for being unseen, a malevolent force that, at a distance, was able to control feelings even within the heart of what had once been a secure family home.

When Robert was sent off to school, mainly Puritan Parliamentarians accused mainly Anglican Royalists of 'popery', and Parliament repeatedly legislated against a wide variety of the arts, including painting, sculpture, music and theatre. Puritans paraded and burned religious vestments, prayer books and 'scandalous pictures' on vast public bonfires in acts of high public theatre, orchestrated much like the earlier Royalist rituals, though pursuing very different policies. The destruction of art went hand in hand with legislation that imposed strict new codes about blasphemy and sexual morality as well as banning superstitious festivals such as May Day and Christmas.[24] One iconoclast argued that the insides of churches should be painted a uniform black to remind members of the congregation of the 'blacknesse and darknesse that is within them'.[25] However, much of the religiously motivated disruption and destruction had a quite familiar feel about it, at least for the majority of less hard-line Puritans for whom one form of theatre was simply swapped for another.[26]

Westminster School included children from Puritan backgrounds, like Robert's exact contemporary the future poet John Dryden, but critically for Robert the headmaster was Anglican and so were his family. Tensions between Anglicans and Puritans mounted to the extent that, in 1641, the school felt it necessary to purchase forty pounds of musket shot and gunpowder to defend itself. The following year, when Robert would have been about eleven, the schoolboys were assembled to help defend Westminster Abbey against 'a mob of Puritans'.[27] That same year, the theatres were closed and the Civil War erupted. Westminster's headmaster, Richard Busby, did not hide his loyalties but was a wily operator. For example, a few years later, when everyone was required to sign up to legislation he disliked, his strategic absence was recorded with a single word, 'sickly'. The authorities did not pursue his compliance.[28]

Meanwhile, back in Norfolk, Robert's father had got married again, to Margaret Hewitt. He had also been made a baronet as part of Charles's attempt to broaden his power base, but Oxnead had become a beleaguered island of Royalists in a hostile sea of Puritans: the county was represented in Parliament by two Royalists and ten Puritans.[29] Sir William's calm and peaceable disposition was severely tested as his natural allies were being imprisoned or executed and he was being made to train a local militia. In 1642 he left Norfolk for London in an attempt to avoid becoming ever more deeply embroiled in increasingly ugly local politics. He felt forced to return the following year when his second wife's father had been killed and her brother taken prisoner at the battle of Edgehill fighting alongside King Charles. Battles were swinging the balance of power in Cromwell's favour, and Cromwell attained a position from which he could command Sir William to muster his local Norfolk militia.

Sir William's sympathies were decidedly Royalist, and if he was forced to pick a side, he would have chosen to support Charles's Cavaliers, not Cromwell's Roundheads. However, unlike the ancestral Judge William who relished – and profited from – conflict, this William did not want to pick sides so he promptly fled the country. He stayed in Rotterdam, just over the North Sea, with other Royalists, allegedly 'doing ill offices against the Parliament' and ignoring repeated orders to return.[30] Punishment followed swiftly and, for Sir William's disobedience, the Paston estates were sequestered, their rents were impounded and Robert's stepmother, Margaret, was compelled to hand over £1,100-worth of silver plate to be melted down to pay Roundheads' wages. Sir William returned in 1644, immediately going to London to negotiate the release of his estates. He was successful, but only after paying a fine of £1,376 8s. 4d., based on an estimate of his annual worth at over £5,500.[31] His fine was three times greater than the fines paid by any other Norfolk 'delinquent'.[32] To put these figures in perspective, twenty years later it was calculated that English people spent an average of £6 13s. 4d. per year, so Sir William's fine was two hundred times the average person's annual expenditure. His annual worth was about eighty times the average person's lifetime worth of £69.[33]

The fine, the loss of a year's rents and the melting down of silver plate were financial body blows and, adding insult to injury, Cromwell's regime made Sir William return to his public duties. As Robert entered his teens in the early 1640s, his idyllic 1630s childhood was well and truly behind him. Things were not turning out as he had expected, and the disorienting events that swirled around his family would have seriously shaken all his assumptions about life and his place in the world.

The 1630s had seen a rich blossoming of creativity as England enjoyed a decade of exceptionally lively exchange with artists in continental Europe, and Robert was old enough to experience its abrupt ending. Writing in the 1640s and looking back at the 1630s, the Earl of Clarendon described it as a golden decade in which 'the like peace and plenty and universal tranquillity was never enjoyed by any nation'. He claimed that, for the decade before the Civil War, England was 'the wonder and envy of all the parts of Christendom'.[34] And Clarendon was not a lone voice. Similar views of the 1630s were expressed by Sir William's friend Sir Hamon l'Estrange and many others.[35] This was not just Royalist propaganda, in the modern sense of the word. After all, Clarendon had been openly critical of Charles for not having a Parliament and was fully aware that the king's policy of peace was as much pragmatic as ideological; the king simply did not have enough money to join the Thirty Years' War that tore apart continental Europe and left eight million dead. Clarendon's rosy interpretation of the 1630s was profoundly influenced by biblical and classical models – he interpreted the events of the previous decade in the light of the events he had read about at school.[36] Clarendon's view of the 1630s was coloured by Virgil's first-century BC account of the changing seasons and farmers' inveterate habit of only recognizing good times when they are gone. Robert lived his teens and most of his twenties through the 'Cavalier winter' while hostile Roundheads enjoyed their ascendency.[37]

Yet Clarendon, and Virgil's farmers, should not be thought of as indulging in nostalgia, because nostalgia is not what it used to be. Like propaganda, its meaning has changed. Modern nostalgia is a backward-looking reaction against the dominant idea of progress. On the other hand, traditional nostalgia was an aspiration towards our origins in a biblical Eden or a classical Golden Age. Robert knew his Bible and his classics and, like Clarendon, he too would have seen parallels between current events and past events, even mythical ones. Indeed, instilling such a perspective was one of the aims of an education at Westminster. Today, art and politics are still linked, although domestic and international affairs are filtered no longer through Virgil's *Georgics* but through the much simpler stories available at the movies and on TV and the Internet. Fictions still transform reality.[38]

When Robert returned to Oxnead on his school holidays he would have enjoyed the numerous visitors and his father's tales of Rome, Florence, Venice, Jerusalem and Cairo.[39] Sir William's Grand Tour was a great fund of stories. He had met famous painters, including Guido Reni, and was accompanied at times by Nicholas Stone's two sons. These traveller's tales were no doubt compared with those of his contemporary William Lithgow, who had described how a crocodile that had eaten 46 people was eventually shot.[40] One of the portraits of Robert's father even has a man pursued by a crocodile in its background, and a 1687 inventory listed two stuffed crocodiles in the great hall.[41] But while home was still entertaining, it had become isolated and surrounded by constant threat. Heavy clouds lay on the horizon.

In 1646, aged around fifteen, Robert went to Trinity College, Cambridge, another oasis of relative calm. In the absence of immediate threats, Cambridge was like Oxford, about which the university's Secretary had said a few years earlier, 'we are like those who, resting in a calm haven, behold the ship-wreck of others.'[42] Trinity provided a cloistered environment within a town that was already quite well protected from the tensions that swirled around Westminster and Oxnead. Two years earlier, Cambridge had been purged of political undesirables – the town's MP had been Oliver Cromwell – so by the time Robert arrived, the university was more or less left to its own devices. It may seem strange now that the Royalists Pastons should have sent their son to a Puritan stronghold, but Robert was the fourteenth Paston to attend Cambridge, so the enduring family tradition was obviously more important than the passing political climate.[43] The earliest Paston was recorded in Cambridge in 1435 – it was the first John who would in time become Fastolf's friend – when intellectual connections between Norwich and Cambridge had been firmly established for over a century.

Cambridge was full of boys in their mid-to-late teens and was surrounded by swamp-like Fens so was not the healthiest of places. Malaria was widespread and the use of opium, which helped relieve its symptoms, was rife. Robert may have been introduced to opium in Cambridge, and a recipe written in his own hand in later life shows that he knew how to convert raw opium into palatable laudanum.[44] Robert's Cambridge could have been quite a dreamy place, but he had to abide by the university statutes, so he could not keep a dog or a ferret, a hawk or a songbird, for example. In most other respects he would have enjoyed considerable freedom, and his time was made even easier by being accompanied by other students from Westminster, including John Dryden.[45]

At the same time that Robert studied the classics, Trinity College was fast becoming a centre for natural philosophy, or the 'new science', in part because it had been Francis Bacon's college. While Robert was there, the town may have been insulated from much of the Cavalier winter's violence, but the university was extraordinarily well connected to the rest of Europe and, increasingly, beyond Europe. Novel ideas were flooding in and the noisy political upheavals across the country were quietly being accompanied by intellectual upheavals in the universities. The term 'new science' suggests the emergence of a new, uniform and coherent way of looking at the world, but actually it was a very broad church.

The new sciences were essentially mathematical, but *Mathematical Magick* by John Wilkins, who was briefly to become Master of Trinity, suggests how widely mathematics was understood. It included, for example, the mechanics needed for automata, submarines and flying machines.[46] Wilkins's understanding of mathematics was in the tradition of Dr John Dee's magical arts, which included perspective, architecture, navigation, astrology and music. According to Cornelius Agrippa, it also included dancing, swordplay and the stage-players' art.[47] Mathematics allowed a 'strange participation between things supernatural, immortal, intellectual, simple and indivisible: and things natural, moral, sensible, compounded and divisible'.[48] It was said that 'by imitating this [mathematical] harmony on stringed [musical] instruments or in song, [people] have gained for themselves a return to [the heavenly] region.'[49] Music gave souls composure,[50] and, following other prominent Pastons, Robert became immersed in sensuous, therapeutic and contemplative music. It provided welcome respite from the alienating threats that had enveloped his world. When Sir William was at Cambridge, music had been taught by Robert Ramsey. He died the year before Robert Paston was admitted, but one of his pieces features in the painted songbook held by the girl in the *Paston Treasure*.[51]

The context in which Robert learned music was a continuation of the masques that Charles had staged before the Cavalier winter set in. While the masques' extravagant elements of display were missing from Cambridge, their intellectual framework – Platonism – was still very much present. Spanning the time Robert was in Cambridge, a like-minded group of philosophers assembled in the university. They included Henry More and Ralph Cudworth, and they followed Marsilio Ficino's conception of *philosopia perennis*, or 'perennial philosophy'. The group had significant followers, including Mary Astell and Anne Conway, whose work was in turn respected by the German polymath Gottfried Wilhelm Leibniz. The 'Cambridge Platonists' were convinced that faith and reason were entirely compatible and that they provided complementary approaches to understanding the world. They used reason to argue for the existence of God and had faith that the new sciences were relevant to morality and ethics.[52] They were the first philosophers to write in English, as opposed to Latin, and there is every reason to believe that the spirit of their teaching coloured Robert's general outlook in later life.

However, the Platonist world-view that thrived at Robert's Cambridge was despised across most of the Puritan-dominated country. For example, William Prynne, a London barrister, wrote a blistering attack on Charles's Platonic metaphysical masques. His book's index contained the rather contentious entry: 'Women-Actors, notorious whores'.[53] This was taken as a not-so-veiled insult aimed at Queen Henrietta Maria, who, like her husband, Charles, had appeared on stage. Prynne was arrested and found guilty of high treason. He was fined £5,000, 'stigmatiz'd in the pillorie', had his ears cut off – although, according to John Aubrey, only the upper parts – was imprisoned and then banished.[54] This might seem like rather harsh treatment of a theatre critic, but Royalists and Puritans alike saw the offending index entry for what it really was – a call to revolution.[55]

Details of Robert's education are sparse, but he emerged from Westminster and Cambridge an idealistic Royalist. This made England in the 1640s an extremely uncomfortable place to live. So, at the age of seventeen he went to France, where he apparently became 'skilled in the Lingua' and 'received many Remarks of Favour' from Louis xiv.[56] Escape to France was his first independent action as an adult and it showed that, like his father, he actively sought to avoid conflict. However, unlike his crocodile-encountering father, he was not very adventurous and it was not long before he was back in England. On his return, he made his Royalist affiliations crystal clear by sending money to the exiled Charles, young pretender to the throne, 'fearing his sovereign might want'.[57] Robert may have come back home, but England had changed radically for all sectors of society. For example, cutting off the ears of William Prynne, a gentleman, had upset significant numbers of the gentry. And, in turn, the gentry upset significant numbers of ordinary people in East Anglia by draining the swampy Fens, creating farmland but destroying livelihoods and displacing thousands.

Whole sets of assumptions about life and society had been called into question, if not yet completely uprooted. Robert had grown up thinking of England as a single coherent body. This was an idea that managed to express wholeness, on the one hand, and differentiation, on the other. It accommodated the fact that different members played different roles – feet were made for walking, hands for holding – but all were equally necessary in a complete person. (The image lives on in the description of organizations where 'the right hand does not know what the left hand is doing.') Robert retained the traditional view that the king was the 'head' of the 'body politic', co-ordinating its disparate members. But others had different ideas, and the philosophy of cosmic harmony was in retreat as Thomas Hobbes's philosophy of self-interest found an increasing number of vociferous champions. The traditionalists and Hobbes's followers both drew equally on symbolism, but the old image of an integral body politic was replaced by the image of disparate bodies in motion. Likewise, ideas of harmonious constitution were replaced by anarchy of movement, natural authority was replaced by brute power and organic growth by mechanical construction.

Robert would have seen these ideas as deeply insidious threats to the whole way of life that his childhood had led him to expect.

As a young adult, he focused the blame for these swirling malevolent forces on the person of Oliver Cromwell, the recurring name he associated with the troubles that had torn apart his childhood home. Robert took no active role in the Civil War, partly because of his dislike of conflict but also for the same reason he did little sport at school – he was seriously overweight. However, military participation would have made little difference, as Cromwell was becoming ever more powerful.

Hostilities only ceased when Charles surrendered in 1646, but they resumed in 1648, culminating in Charles's recapture and his trial for treason. He refused to co-operate throughout the trial, frustrating all – on both sides – who hoped for compromise. He was cast as a tyrant, like the biblical Man of Blood who had polluted the land (Numbers 35:33).[58] Charles himself seemed set on an equally biblical mission and took the dramatic high road.[59] Earlier, he had been the sole person from whom court masques emanated and – in a hierarchical audience – the sole person upon whom their single-point perspective conceits converged. The experience helped teach him how to act as if he was the most important individual in the realm, whatever the circumstances. With supreme confidence, he claimed he could not be defeated, only martyred, saying, 'If I must suffer a violent death . . . it is but mortality crowned with martyrdom.'[60] His final act involved walking through the Banqueting House, under Rubens's painting of his father in heaven and out of a window on to a temporary scaffold erected in the street. There, in 1649, he met his executioner. Charles was, once again, on a stage and at the centre of attention.

The king made a speech to those assembled around the black-clad scaffold. He started by professing his innocence, pointing out that 'they began these unhappy troubles, not I' and claiming that he was not the 'cause of all this bloodshed'. He then called upon God to forgive his opponents. He justified his actions: 'If I would have given way . . . to the power of the Sword, I needed not to have come here; and therefore I tell you . . . I Am the Martyr of the People.' Finally, he acknowledged his impending execution: 'I go from a corruptible to an incorruptible Crown, where no disturbance can be.' Upon the king's signal, the executioner severed his head with a single blow.[61] The king represented himself as a defender of the people's rights against tyranny in 'a command performance of great courage'.[62] His death was a radically new twist in the much rehearsed royal theatre of death, and the ritual offered many possible interpretations.[63]

For an idealistic Royalist like the eighteen-year-old Robert, the king's execution made Charles a martyr and confirmed Cromwell's status as a monster who needed to be defeated. The execution did not, however, stop the war. Charles's nineteen-year-old son continued the fight but was defeated within two years. He then escaped the country after living on the run as an outlaw for six weeks and famously evading Cromwell's soldiers by hiding in an oak tree. Royalists interpreted this as evidence that the Stuart monarchy enjoyed divine protection.[64]

Having wound the rhetoric up to fever pitch, absolutely nothing could remain neutral, not even the natural world, as shown by veneration of the Royal Oak. A decade earlier, Charles I's glorious masques had been founded on the idea of harmony between heaven and earth. So, a decade later, with bloody discord on earth, everyone naturally expected to see an equal discord in the heavens. In tune with a long tradition, Sir Walter Raleigh had called heaven and earth – the natural world – the 'language of the Almightie ... whose Hieroglyphical Characters are the unnumbered Starres, the Sunne and Moone ... the letters of all those living creatures and plants'.[65] Half a century later, these everyday natural phenomena were increasingly being conscripted into the English battle for hearts and minds. The heavens and the skies resonated with England's troubles.

Robert could not escape these cosmic signs since they seemed to engulf everything. People studied the heavens assiduously, and across England about 400,000 almanacs were sold annually with about one in four households having a copy of these printed weather forecasts, crop planting schedules and tide timetables.[66] In the mid-seventeenth century, about 60 per cent of yeomen, over 40 per cent of trades- and craftspeople, and nearly 20 per cent of husbandmen and labourers were literate.[67] The English have always liked to talk about the weather but the literacy rates of those able to read the weather 'hieroglyphically' – as opposed to those able to read printed almanacs

– are not recorded. They might have been higher. Sir Robert's friend Thomas Browne said, 'he that cannot read A B C may read our nature,' since our faces have 'mystical' characters that reveal our souls.[68] With the cherished old order crumbling, Robert would have constantly scanned the Book of Nature for clues about which way the war would go and how his fortunes might fare. He was like the person today who knows the nursery rhyme 'One for sorrow, two for joy . . .' and who, after glimpsing the first magpie, habitually seeks the second.

Of course, not everyone thought that magpies, the weather or nature carried personalized messages just for them, and Puritans in particular were sceptical. Some thought the sky's activities could be explained mechanically. For example, Lucy Hutchinson – the Puritan who acknowledged the nobility of Charles I's court – was translating Lucretius, the Roman philosopher who said thunder and lightning were the result of clashing clouds and compared them to the sound and sparks of struck flints.[69] She was busy translating in the 1650s, but by 1675 seems to have had a change of heart and condemned her unpublished manuscript as the product of a misspent youth.[70] Her change of heart may have been in response to the many biblical precedents, such as the star at Christ's birth, the blackness at his death and the blood-red suns that will herald the Apocalypse.

The published evidence suggests that those who studied the weather were most interested in bad weather, which was overwhelmingly interpreted as God's punishment.[71] Good weather was not interpreted as God's reward. Yet the seventeenth century had seen a massive explosion of cheap printed pamphlets and the surviving evidence may simply be an early example of the media distortion we all now recognize. After all, today's news is sensationally biased towards doom and gloom. Yet, in the seventeenth century, the apparent bias may actually have reflected the real situation since modern climate science notes that the period suffered an increased frequency of El Niño events and a decline in sunspot activity that led to consistently bad weather.[72]

The Book of Nature rarely provided simple answers, and the way nature conveyed messages through the weather can be compared to the meaning of something much simpler, like a glass of water.

One person might declare it half-empty, while another declares it half-full. Meanwhile, the glass just is what it is and supports both readings. Its support, however, is not arbitrary or uncritical – the glass is neither completely empty nor completely full. The Book of Nature differed from written texts because it did not explicitly declare anything, allowing more than one possible interpretation, providing guidance while not prescribing. Indeed, the many possible different interpretations of Nature were seen as one of the Book's strengths, and Shakespeare was amongst those who revelled in its multiple readings. For example, in *As You Like It*, Duke Senior found good in the Forest of Arden, Jacques found evil, Corin the shepherd saw neither and Touchstone the fool saw both.[73] Of course, from their own perspectives, they were all right.

The weather had played its part as a backdrop pregnant with meaning in the build-up to, and all the way through, the Civil War. So, for example, when the Thames flooded in 1641, the popular presses responded with two publications, *A Strange Wonder* and *True News from Heaven*. Both interpreted the flood as God's disapproval of recent events, but for one God's wrath was aimed at Parliamentarians and for the other at Royalists.[74] The weather could also predict. Strange weather events could be 'precursors of mischief', bearing in mind, of course, that one person's mischief was another's godsend.[75] Nature had the capacity to foretell, because the patterns it revealed – to those who wished to see them – were eternal. As such, they applied to the future just as much as they did to the present and to the past.

In 1647, three suns appeared over Cheshire and Shropshire and were 'astrologically handled' in William Lilly's *World's Catastrophe*. Armed men were seen in the skies, which 'clearly portended' the Duke of Hambleton's defeat.[76] Multiple suns were seen again over Lancashire, Cumberland and Westmorland and 'stupendous' hailstones, five inches across, fell in Norwich.[77] A ballad of 1648 recounted a day when 'it rained blood' just before the Civil War re-erupted.[78] As might be expected, the number of publications describing such portents increased dramatically in the wake of Charles's execution.[79] *Sinister News from Hereford* recalled a thunderstorm with hailstones as big as eggs, and an earthquake that felled a church steeple and many houses. People and cattle in the fields were killed and 'wonderful apparitions' were seen in the air including an arm, sword in hand, and another holding a bowl of blood. This bizarre weather made the local clerk's pregnant wife fall into labour and deliver triplets who spoke simultaneously. The first said that no one could escape what was appointed, the second asked if there would be enough living to bury the dead, and the third asked if corn alone would satisfy. After their brief utterances, all three died.[80] Such prophecies were great propaganda.[81]

Cromwell declared a Commonwealth of England in 1649, and the Civil War ended in September 1651. Six months later, on Black Monday, a total eclipse of the sun was seen, one of three eclipses in quick succession.[82] Some read this event in political terms, claiming it heralded the ruin of all monarchies. Others interpreted it as a threat to existing governments, hence good news for the exiled Charles II. However, the nearest thing to an official government reaction emphasized the eclipse's predictable nature and restricted its meaning to meditations upon the Day of Judgement.[83] The build-up to the eclipse was accompanied by anxiety and near panic, and streets were deserted. But the event was an anticlimax and nothing followed in its immediate aftermath. For example, no portentous connections were made with it when, three months later, England declared war on the Dutch again.

Through political revolution, England had revolted against God, and, through nature, God was making his displeasure known. Adding to the human cacophony, apparently inanimate things – like clouds and comets – were speaking. Against such a cosmic backdrop, the political fine points argued over in London would have seemed completely irrelevant for the overwhelming majority. It is no wonder the revolution failed. Today, Charles I is widely considered an inept politician; while this may be true, it is also beside the point. It is very clear that, for Charles I, kingship was not the art of politics but was instead the pursuit of conscience. He saw the king's role as the people's conscience.[84] His power as the people's conscience is illustrated in *A Miracle of Miracles Wrought by the Blood of King Charles the First* (1649), which told the story of a Deptford girl with a disfiguring skin condition. A handkerchief that had been dipped in the beheaded king's blood was applied to her skin and she was cured so dramatically that 'many hundreds of people' came to see her from all across the country.[85] And the king's personal sincerity was evident in a book of meditations, *Eikon Basiliké*, much of which he was said to have written when imprisoned and awaiting death. The book was published within days of his execution and was a bestseller. There were 36 editions in the first year alone and it was translated into five languages.[86] It sustained Royalists through their darkest times.

The Cavalier winter had descended in Robert's teens, and by his mid-twenties there were hopeful signs of a coming spring, although, as always, things seemed to get worse before they got better. The Commonwealth of England had collapsed in 1653 and Oliver Cromwell had declared himself Lord Protector, placing the country under martial law. Then, in September 1658, Cromwell suddenly died of natural causes. According to legend, his death was accompanied by storms and many interpreted the gales as a rush of demons taking his soul down to hell.[87] Cromwell's body was embalmed with the top of the skull sawn off, the brains removed and the skull-cap sewn back on. The body was wrapped in cloth and put in a lead-lined 'elegant coffin of the choicest wood', whereupon it 'swelled and bursted, from whence came such filth, that raised such a deadly and noisome stink, that it was found prudent to bury him [in Westminster] immediately, which was done in as private a manner as possible'.[88] An official state funeral intended to bolster the Cromwell dynasty did not take place until over three weeks later, with pomp surpassing that of royal funerals.[89] Evelyn reported that Cromwell's effigy was 'like a king' but that it was the most 'joyfullest funeral that I ever saw'. The start was delayed by disputes between diplomats, then the procession was delayed by a rogue pig and did not reach the Abbey until after dark.[90]

Robert would doubtless have been relieved that the person he blamed for his family's misfortunes was no more. But the Paston family was by now deeply in debt and their troubles did not ease with Cromwell's departure. The following year, to settle a debt of £6,500, Robert's father, Sir William, was forced to transfer his rights to Caister Castle.[91] Sir John Fastolf's magnificent castle – for which the family had fought so hard two hundred years earlier – finally passed out of their hands. And, in his turn, Robert's uncle Thomas fell victim to the old Prior of Bromholme's curse to become a 'Paston fool'. It seemed that the family fortunes were unravelling.

On the national stage, however, the tide was slowly starting to turn. Cromwell's son Richard had taken over the mantle of Lord Protector and the country remained under martial law. However, within the year, Richard Cromwell was forced to abdicate, civil unrest re-erupted and Parliament was dissolved. A new parliament was elected that proved fairly evenly split along religious and political lines. Meanwhile, Robert Paston dutifully struggled on, becoming a Justice of the Peace at the age of 28 and then a Member of Parliament in 1660.

Elsewhere in 1660, an eleven-week-old boy was heard to repeatedly say 'a king'. Another baby boy uttered the king's name at birth, and an infant girl was reported to have repeated 'a king' seven times for three nights running. Speaking through those who were too young to be corrupted, it would have seemed to Royalists that God was calling the monarch back to his proper place.[92] As if in response, Charles II sailed from his exile in the Netherlands and Robert rode down to Dover to welcome him home. The king was tall, slim and handsome, and his battle exploits and outlaw adventures were legendary. The shorter, seriously overweight and rather sheltered Robert would have been overawed by the royal presence.

Charles II arrived in London on his thirtieth birthday, 29 May, which also happened to be Robert's 29th birthday. Amnesties for the overwhelming majority of the Civil War's protagonists were granted and preparations were made for a triumphal coronation on 23 April of the following year. Robert Paston was knighted two days before the coronation on a dismal rainy day. In fact, it rained solidly for ten days before the coronation. In keeping with the connection between heaven and earth, Royalists interpreted this as a divine statement about the end of the Cavalier winter, when the king was in exile and the Roundheads had held sway. The king's coronation lasted two days, during which the weather was uncharacteristically bright and sunny.

Appropriately reflecting the weather, the man-made aspects of Charles II's coronation were also utterly spectacular. Samuel Pepys felt confident that he would never 'see the like again in this world'.[93] The coronation was an excuse for unrivalled pageantry and Charles II processed through the city like a conquering emperor, passing through four triumphal arches. These were intended to draw parallels between seventeenth-century London and imperial Rome, but for 'reason of the shortness of Time', the arches were made from wood, canvas, plaster and paint rather than marble.[94] Their themes were *Monarchy Triumphant*, *Victory at Sea*, *Peace and Concord* and *Plenty*. As Charles II rode through them, his august presence was meant to magically awaken the potential that resided in the images. In addition to harnessing Roman history, biblical parallels were constructed and Charles's return was seen in the light of returning exiles like Joseph, Moses and Joshua. He was even seen as Noah's dove that, 'finding no rest anywhere, was reciv'd again into his own Ark, and brought a peaceable Olive'.[95] His homecoming marked the end of his country's metaphorical 'sea of troubles' and provided the cue for yet another symbolic identity – Neptune. This was a particularly apt mythological figure for an English monarch since the sea had always played a highly charged role in the island realm.

The sea was also taking on new significance as new trade routes were opening up and England's merchants were seeking all possible support for their stake in the burgeoning maritime trade. Henry Bold, the court poet, compared Charles II to Sir Francis Drake circling the world. He also compared him to the sun itself on Easter Sunday, providing symbolic balance for the idea of Charles as the god of water.[96] Charles's identity as a 'Rival Sun' dated from the day of his birth, when 'a Star appearing in defiance of the Sun at Noonday' was witnessed.[97] Of course, such a sign was 'never vouchsafed to any [but] our Saviour'.[98] For Royalists, the execution of Charles I had summoned parallels with Christ's death, so the rival sun that marked Charles II's birth naturally evoked parallels with Christ's birth. Indeed, the official coronation sermon compared Charles II's task of rebuilding the kingdom to a resurrection.[99] Robert had been eighteen years old when he lost his king. He did not regain another until he was 29. Given the extraordinary Royalist rhetoric to which he subscribed, Robert could easily have compared those eleven dark years to the tomb from which Christ arose or the belly of the whale from which Jonah escaped.

As soon as the processions stopped, the rain started again. Most Royalists interpreted the new rains as heaven's tears of joy but Dryden went further, suggesting that, like sacred oil, they were anointing the king.[100] Yet, given that downpours of rain both preceded and followed the processions, the two days of sunshine seemed to echo the parting of the Red Sea that allowed the Israelites' escape from Egypt. The king had just sat down for dinner in Westminster Hall when

> it fell a Thundering, Lightening, and Raining, with the great-
> est Force, Vehemence, and Noise, that was ever known at
> that season . . . to imitate the Fire and Noise of the Cannon
> . . . exactly kept time with that loud Musick . . . the Thunder
> and Lightening still intermitting between each firing of the
> Cannons, as if they had waited.[101]

Even before his coronation, Charles ii had felt sufficiently secure to ceremoniously mark the day of his father's execution. The day of a martyr's death marks their birth into fully sanctified life, so, embracing that symbolism, Charles ii sought a sacrifice for his father, the martyred king. The obvious sacrificial victim would have been Oliver Cromwell but he was already dead. That did not stop Charles. In late January 1661, Cromwell's embalmed body was taken from its grave in Westminster. On the morning of 30 January, it was hung in chains from Tyburn gallows, with its shrouded face directed towards Whitehall. Of course, being shrouded, Cromwell's corpse was unrecognizable so in the late afternoon it was taken down and decapitated. The body, along with those of two other regicides, was thrown into a public grave and the severed head was held aloft for all to see, graphically underlining the monarchy's restoration.

Cromwell's head was then impaled on a stake over Westminster Hall, where, ten years later, a visitor to London wrote: 'One can't view [it] without blanching.'[102] After about another ten years, the pole holding the head snapped in a violent storm and was sent crashing to the ground. The worm-eaten head eventually found its way to the

Russell family, Cromwell's relations through marriage. They surreptitiously took locks of hair (and maybe an ear) as personal souvenirs and, in 1775, sought authentication and valuation from experts. By 1799 it was an attraction in a museum of curiosities in Old Bond Street, although it did not stay long because the room's rent outstripped the takings.[103] The French Revolution's industrial-scale decapitations had evidently devalued severed heads. Cromwell's head was eventually buried at a secret location somewhere in his old college, Sidney Sussex, Cambridge. Some said the body was near Holborn, others said it had been taken to Naseby and yet others said it was sunk in the Thames. Body parts were also said to be in Newburgh Priory, North Yorkshire.[104] Severing Cromwell's head was intended as retribution – a symbolic act that would complete the cycle initiated by Charles I's execution. Yet the posthumous adventures of Cromwell's head suggest that it had a relic-like life of its own. While handkerchiefs dipped in Charles I's spilt blood had healing properties, Cromwell's head – as a piece of the interregnal body politic – kept alive the idea of a republic.

Surprising effort has been put into trying to identify bits of Cromwell's body because as soon as the corpse was disinterred, potent rumours had started to circulate.[105] It was whispered that, suspecting ritual humiliation, Cromwell's supporters had pre-emptively switched bodies in the Abbey's graves. Samuel Pepys, for example, had read that the impaled head over Westminster Hall might even be that of one of England's ancient kings, who were also interned in the Abbey.[106] Uncertainty about the head and other body parts created an uncanny Cromwell, a corpse whose fragments seemed to multiply and spread, sinisterly, across the realm. Charles II's ritual humiliation of his foe inadvertently helped Cromwell to haunt Royalists down the centuries.[107]

In the end, no one really knows whose body provided the props for all this high theatre. No one really knows what happened to the mortal remains of the man whom some had called 'Antichrist'.[108]

Robert Paston, 1st Earl of Yarmouth, c. 1680, mezzotint
by Edward Lutterell, 29.7 Ÿ 23.2 cm; the print has been cut to the oval,
and the frame added in pen and wash.

three

Going Home

Robert and Rebecca Paſton – the Reſtoration – the moon's 'ſtrange spottedness' –
infant mortality – music – the Plague – the Fire – London – shot by highwaymen
– welcome to Norwich – turning the hourglass – colleƈting colours – preparing
canvas – drawing – painting

The year after Charles I's execution, the nineteen-year-old
Robert married Rebecca Clayton. By the time Charles
II was crowned, just over ten years later, the couple had a daughter
and three sons. Their children were Margaret, aged eight, another
William, aged about six, another Robert, aged around four or five,
and a Jasper who was between one and three years of age (some
records have been lost). The Paston letters are best known for the
family's fifteenth-century correspondence, but they kept writing, and
seventeenth-century letters show Robert to have been a very loving
husband and father. His own father may have been a distant figure,
but he was very engaged with his children.

Sir Robert wanted the best for his family, and as an unashamed
Royalist he greeted Charles II's coronation with unbounded enthusiasm. Yet almost immediately, there were signs that while the monarchy
had been restored, the new monarch was quite different from the old
one. For example, over a decade of conflict, Royalists had been sustained
by the old king's book of meditations, *Eikon Basiliké*. However, upon
the Restoration, almost overnight, people stopped reading it. Rumours
spread that it had not even been written by the king. Within months of
his coronation, Charles II had met a minor cleric called John Gauden
who declared he had written it, supporting his claim with impressive
witnesses. A great controversy erupted, much to Royalists' embarrassment and their opponents' glee – was the Royalist gospel a forgery? The
truth was suppressed very effectively for many decades but it turns out
that both sides were right – Gauden had indeed written the book, but
his work closely followed manuscripts written by Charles I.[1]

61

After so much bloodshed, heated arguments and a prolonged cover-up about an apparently trivial question like the authorship of a book were signs that Charles II had learned – and, unlike his father, valued – the dark arts of politics. He had quietly decided that Machiavelli might be a trustier guide than Plato. Unlike his father, he was not going to be the nation's conscience. To help heal the wounds of religious strife, conscience had been turned into a private affair and dismissed from public discourse.[2] As part of the new political order, it was decreed that Charles II's – and Sir Robert's – birthday should be celebrated forever as a national day of thanksgiving to mark the Restoration. Another decree marked Charles I's execution as a day of fasting. Thousands of Royalist sermons were preached annually on these feast-and-fast days until they were abolished nearly two hundred years later.[3] Yet, despite all the sermons, the Puritan perspective prevailed. And proof that Puritans had indeed won the day lies in the simple fact that we now find it almost impossible to understand exactly how the white magic of Neoplatonic masques and symbolic paintings could ever have been such important instruments of statecraft.

The demise of *Eikon Basiliké* marked a profound sea-change. Grand correspondences between the cosmos and the body politic were being quietly demoted to the status of mere poetic metaphors, and Charles II's coronation was destined to be the swansong for the politics of cosmic harmony. English kings had met violent deaths before, but the eleven-year gap was unprecedented and, as an institution, the monarchy had changed radically. Although the monarchy was said to have been restored, actually it was reinvented and Charles II's character did little to ease popular acceptance of a king with divine rights. His six weeks on the run from Cromwell's troops had given him a taste for life beyond the confines of courtly decorum and he evidently liked the freedom that outlaws could enjoy. Charles II was not Charles I: he kept many mistresses and fathered many illegitimate children, and his court has been described as a 'cross between a brothel and a bear garden'.[4] The mystic ideas that his father took so seriously – such as union between the royal body and the nation's body – were parodied mercilessly. While his father's bodily associations were metaphysical and divine, Charles II's bodily associations were sexual and political. A contemporary poem claimed: 'His scepter and his p[ric]k are of a length, And she may sway the one who plays with t'other.'[5] A potency that had come from above was swapped for one that came from below.

Few saw the king as a divine representative on earth. In fact, the symbolism could be completely reversed, and with a country now ruled as if 'by chance', it made 'God at best an idle looker-on, [like] A lazy monarch lolling on his throne'.[6] But it was not just the monarch's role that lost its sacred associations; even everyday phenomena like the weather started to be stripped of significance. For example, Pepys thought the widespread mystical readings of the coronation's spectacular thunderstorm were 'a foolery'.[7] Mystic explanations in popular literature had peaked between 1640 and 1660 and were starting to decline, and political theatre had been utterly transformed since Charles I's Banqueting House masques.[8] In the aftermath of the Civil War and with the proliferation of printed pamphlets and coffee-house debates, politics and aesthetics came to be measured by the popularity of whatever images were projected.[9] Politicians started to perform for the crowd. This was the dawning of the age of expediency.

Nonetheless, the overwhelming majority of people were desperate to believe that the Restoration was indeed a divine sign marking the end of a decade of chaos. The old harmonist world-view supported such a hope, and luckily for that majority its secure roots proved extraordinarily enduring. It survived repeated assaults and thrived most strongly amongst Anglicans and Royalists like Sir Robert.[10] It also had very deep popular support, so even a humble tenant farmer from rural Shropshire could interpret solar eclipses in Aries and Libra in terms of the body politic. Farmer Gough interpreted the first eclipse as marking 'the ruin of a kingdom' (following Messalla, a first-century BC Roman politician) and the second as marking 'the death of great men' (following Proclus, a fifth-century BC Greek philosopher).[11]

As the seventeenth century progressed, social boundaries sharpened and the distance between rural and city folk, and between elite and popular culture, widened. Amongst the urban elite, monsters and prodigies lost their powers – what was once 'horrible' or 'terrible' became just 'strange' or 'marvellous'.[12] John Aubrey, who was just five years older than Sir Robert, recalled 'country-people' who took care not to offend fairies and who put bread and cream out for them at night.[13] But such customs were waning and Britain, which was once 'brim-full of fairy folk', was becoming less and less enchanted.[14] However, the idea that the heavens guided all things on earth – and the closely allied idea that art had Prospero-like magical powers – was not completely destroyed. And its survival was all the more surprising because it was being attacked in a pincer movement: under assault from political self-interest and expediency on one side, and scientific speculations and discoveries on the other. Science was even daring to question the perfection of the heavens themselves. As Sir Robert's friend, neighbour and family doctor, Thomas Browne, said, 'While we look for [perfection] in the heavens, we find they are but like the earth; durable in their main bodies, alterable in their parts . . . perspectives begin to tell tales.'[15]

'Perspectives' were telescopes, and one of the tales they told came from Thomas Harriot, a mathematician, navigation expert and one of the Earl of Northumberland's 'three magi'.[16] In 1609 he made detailed drawings of the moon's 'strange spottedness', the blemishes on its surface that turned out to be craters. The discovery seriously undermined the idea that the heavens were immutable crystalline spheres. Instead, they seemed to contain vast rocks pockmarked by violent collisions, which was 'the strangest piece of news'.[17] (Incidentally, Galileo got the credit the following year, in part because he was a trained artist, able to interpret the dark shapes as shadows caused by the moon's rough surface. Harriot was a poet with no training in the visual arts and had not mastered chiaroscuro.[18] Both would have been influenced by Plutarch's classical descriptions of the moon's surface.[19]) Within decades, the moon turned from being a heavenly body into – according to an early work of science fiction – another New World, explored by a Spaniard and populated by people who communicated through wordless music.[20] A few decades later the very successful but now almost forgotten female playwright Aphra Behn wrote a satirical play about court politics on the moon, as observed by a voyeuristic earthbound scientist with a grotesquely long telescope.[21]

Sir Robert's formative years had prepared him for a beautiful, gentle and magical world; now that was slowly but surely vanishing, as if in the gathering gloom of twilight. New scientific and political realities were only slowly taking shape around him, but their distant, half-formed presence loomed like vague, and ominously dark, shadows. At the same time, shadows crept into his private life. In the year of Charles II's coronation, Robert and Rebecca had a fourth son, John, but he died within weeks. The following year a fifth son, Edmund, was born and also died. Although a high rate of infant mortality was accepted as normal, these deaths were tragic for a man who doted on his children. Within a year or two another son, Thomas, was born, followed a couple of years later by a daughter, Mary. (A sign of Sir Robert's love for his children was his reaction to Mary's death, around the age of ten. She died in London and he was so grief-stricken that he had her heart cut out, transported to Oxnead and deposited in the family chapel.) Another daughter, Katherine, died before reaching her first birthday. Around 1667, Sir Robert and Rebecca's last child was born, a daughter called Elizabeth. Six children survived to adulthood.

The Paston family divided their time between London and Norfolk. For them, the journey from London to Oxnead would have been like stepping back in time. Oxnead was an Elizabethan manor in the orbit of Norwich, which retained many of its magnificent medieval buildings, including scores of churches, a cathedral, a castle and city walls.[22] Rebecca preferred London while Sir Robert preferred Oxnead and they were often apart, but the 'Letter Office', established some thirty years earlier, made staying in touch easy.[23] Sir Robert's letters to his wife usually opened with 'My dearest heart' and closed with 'I am your most affectionate husband and servant', 'I am yours forever', 'he who loves you above the world' or 'yours to the last'.[24]

In London Charles II had reopened the theatres after the Puritan shutdown and even became the first monarch to attend a public theatre. England's first ever commercial concert was performed in 1672 and the novel idea that people might want to pay to listen to music caught on. London concerts could involve up to fifty musicians, including foreign players, and others moonlighting from the court since their salaries could be up to five years in arrears. The king liked French music, with a beat.[25] While his father had commissioned grand metaphysical masques, he preferred the latest toe-tapping tunes.

Sir Robert would have taken the king's taste in music as yet another ominous sign. After all, he knew Plato had said changes in music were harbingers of 'major political and social changes'.[26] Sir Robert's taste was more conservative and he preferred the old English polyphonic style of consort music. His tastes were more in tune with the previous court of Charles I and he understood music not only as an art, but as a science. It had been a large part of his schooling in Westminster, where children had at least two hours a week with the choirmaster and where the headmaster continued to play the organ even after the Puritans had banned them.[27] That Puritan ban, incidentally, would have shown Robert the truth of Plato's connection between music and politics. As Shakespeare had said:

> The man that hath no music in himself,
> Nor is not mov'd with concord of sweet sounds,
> Is fit for treasons, stratagems and spoils . . .
> Let no such man be trusted.[28]

Gentlemen played music in private and Oxnead, at the heart of the family, was the ideal place for consort music. Playing together meant that Sir Robert and his children learned to keep in time and in tune with each other. It involved constant negotiation and compromise because, of course, each was potentially able to play out of time and out of tune. By playing together, the family was rewarded with repeated journeys that progressed from chaos to coherence, from discord to concord. According to Henry Peacham – one-time Master of Wymondham School, Norfolk – music made 'the sweetest Harmony' from discords and it had great moral value because it helped seek out 'that which is good and honest'.[29] Repeated play audibly reconciled things that started at variance with each other, a transformation that

Plato defined as an expression of love.[30] Different family members played different instruments and the family structure was reflected in the instruments themselves, since viols came in a family of different sizes. People even identified with instruments – we still say we can be 'in tune' with events and that they can pull at our 'heart strings' – and instruments, in turn, could embody people.[31] For example, Shakespeare's plays contain many references to the parts of people and parts of instruments, and the viol featured in the *Paston Treasure* has a human head.[32]

With or without carved heads, musical instruments even spoke to each other. Peacham noted that when two lutes were laid side by side and a string on one was plucked, 'the other, untouched, shall answer it' thanks to the almost magical property of 'sympathy'.[33] Similar connections between players and their instruments were part of the science of music. At the Royal Society, Robert Hooke suggested that the way the human ear worked was analogous to the resonance between instruments' strings, so the enjoyment of music itself involved sympathy between instruments and people. Sir Kenelm Digby went still further. He suggested that memories were recalled by similar sympathetic resonances between structures in the mind.[34]

However, the science of music went far beyond the sympathy expressed between instruments, ears and memories. While at Cambridge, Sir Robert's thinking about music would have been shaped by Boethius, the sixth-century philosopher, who considered singing and instrumental performance to be music's least important aspects. More important was the inner harmony of the body and soul, while the most important aspect concerned the harmony of the entire universe. Music united physics, mathematics and theology.[35] The whole universe was a 'mystery' that lay in music's 'profound mathematic' so that, according to Johannes Kepler, the German natural philosopher and astronomer, people 'might play the everlastingness of all created time in some short part of an hour'.[36]

Music was philosophy in practice. Its speculative side gave leisured gentlemen like Sir Robert much to contemplate and its meanings were neatly packaged up in an experience that was at once rigorously disciplined and beautifully sensuous.[37] Towards the beginning of the seventeenth century, musical scales helped Kepler understand the planets' orbits, and towards the end they helped Newton understand the spectrum's colours. In fact, 'the musical string served as a model of the heavens in both a scientific and allegorical sense.'[38] It also had personal, political and divine overtones.[39] The Latin for string was *chorda* and the Latin for heart was *cordis*. The words 'concord' and 'discord' are derived from the relationship of hearts, not strings, but punning allowed 'instruments of state' to be represented as 'string' instruments. This pun allowed another, because a 'string instrument' was *fides* and 'trust' was also *fides*. The string instruments in the *Paston Treasure* imply love, trust and concord. Sir Robert's friend Thomas Browne called music a 'hieroglyphical and shadowed lesson of the whole world'.[40]

Yet for all the puns connecting strings with the heart and with trust, the truth was that they were actually 'the guts of dead creatures, a token of [man's] crueltie'.[41] Sir Robert knew that music had been forcibly evicted from the court and city and had been lucky to find refuge in the homes of country gentry, in stark contrast to the generous radiation of painting from Charles i's optimistic 1630s court. Decades earlier, painting had reached Oxnead through an outpouring of love, but music had followed, retreating there through fear, and he could sense it. For example, court composer William Lawes's music recoiled 'from political stress into a private world of introspection' and made you feel as if you could hear the 'bottom dropping out of the world'.[42]

Much as Sir Robert may have loved retreating into the brief consolation of consort music with his family, he had little choice but to face the wider world. He loved music but had aligned himself with the court so had to play the game of politics, with rules set by the king. However, the rules kept changing. Charles ii had few resources at his disposal and needed to tack through rival competing interests. While they were not particularly noble, let alone regal, attributes, he became a master of ducking and diving. For him, the stakes were high and he played his cards close to his chest, keeping everybody guessing.

The king's political honeymoon had been very short-lived and within a couple of years there were new taxes and growing discontent.

The mood was summed up in a saying – 'The Bishops get all, the Courtiers spend all, the Citizens pay for all, the King neglects all, and the Divills take all' – and an impression of incompetence gathered around the king and his government.[43] Whereas Charles I's court had been famed for its 'temperate, chaste and serious' nature, Charles II's court was known for its 'revelling, drinking and whoring'.[44] Like many of their ancestors, the Pastons divided up their responsibilities, and since Rebecca preferred London she undertook much of the court politics, negotiating her way through a fog of disinformation spread by scheming courtiers.

Meanwhile, both inside and outside the court, a centuries-old and much-feared danger returned to threaten everyone. London was hit by the plague, a terrifying invisible and completely indiscriminate killer. Its progress was tracked with trepidation. In April 1665 Pepys mentioned 'great talk of a comet' and 'great fears of the sickness'. In May he mentioned discussions about the plague in coffee houses, in June he was counting the number of doors down Drury Lane daubed with red crosses and by the end of the month he was recording the weekly death toll. (There were 267 plague victims out of a total of 684 burials, including the casualties of bombardment by the Dutch fleet.) The second week of July saw 725 dead, the following week 1,089, then 1,843, then 2,010, then 2,817.[45] And the plague was not restricted to London. A distant relative wrote to tell Sir Robert that Great Yarmouth had seen sixteen plague deaths in the first week of June and thirty in the second week.[46]

Plague struck when Sir Robert and Rebecca were in their early thirties, often split between London and Norfolk. They were desperate for news of each other's well-being and dependent on letters that took three days to arrive. The plague was to be avoided at all costs and there were many ways to try and evade its grip. For example, the University of Cambridge simply closed down, allowing Newton to flee to deepest Lincolnshire. Yet if you stayed in an infected town, you had to take elaborate precautions, which, amongst other things, often included the wearing of amulets, medical devices like charms, usually worn on necklaces or bracelets. Different amulets acted on different diseases and they were very common throughout the seventeenth century. (The painter Rubens was given four amulets by a would-be patron.[47])

Robert Boyle, the self-styled 'sceptical chemist', said dismissing the action of amulets might have been acceptable in the past, but after William Harvey's discoveries about the circulation of blood, there was no longer any reason to doubt their effectiveness.[48] Some, like *zenexton*, were said to prevent catching the plague.[49] The ingredients of one version included arsenic, orpiment, silver, pearls, coral, oriental sapphire and dittany roots mixed with a young girl's first menstrual blood and eighteen dried, pulverized toads.[50] The ingredients were mixed into a paste, cut into small cakes and placed in capsules that could be attached to jewellery or clothing. Many plague remedies included toads, which typically had to be procured during the correct phase of the moon, one recipe suggesting they should be suspended for three days during a waning moon in July.[51] Powdered silver, pearl, coral and sapphire obviously made these medicines very expensive, so physicians also had cheaper versions that used mercury, vitriol, salt and verdigris packed into a hazelnut or cooked into a plaster and cast into small coins to be wrapped in red silk.[52]

Scores of other prosaic and exotic recipes existed and Sir Robert wrote several of his own. One was based on *rosa solis*, a cordial made from the carnivorous sundew plant, with added sage, celandine, rosemary, rue, wormwood, mugwort, pimpernel, scabious, peony and numerous other herbs. Another was a malmsey, a sweet fortified wine with added rue, ginger, nutmeg and pepper.[53] His eldest daughter, Margaret, also made medicines, and in a notebook written years later she recalled how her father's plague-protecting powder kept the family safe while bodies of the dead were piled up within sight of their house in Lincoln's Inn.[54]

The confusing variety of remedies was matched by a confusing variety of explanations about how they worked. For example, some said toads were effective against plague because their skin corresponded to the swellings, lesions, spots and sores on plague victims' bodies. Also, toads' diet of worms corresponded to the worms found in plague victims.[55] Others said that toads' innate fear of humans imprinted itself on the cause of plague and made it too fear humans, thus scaring the disease away.[56] Many of these explanations drew on traditional medical ideas, such as sympathy between the ingredients and the body or the agent of disease. Others drew on ideas of occult forces such as magnetism, with the amulets supposedly able to suck disease out of the body: an amulet's covering of red silk could turn blue, for example, to show when the pestilence had been extracted.[57] Newly fashionable corpuscular theories came up with even more explanations, some suggesting that the agents of diseases were very small particles with shapes that corresponded to the shapes of pores in the body. One London apothecary regretted that, if they in fact existed, they were too small to see even using the best microscopes.[58] The particles entered the body, circulated and settled in particular locations where they altered the texture of organs, disturbing their proper function.

There was no agreement about how these toad-based – or any other – medicines worked, but there was a general agreement that they did indeed work, that plague could be treated. Yet, actually, of course, they did not always work, a problem that greatly worried physicians. And sometimes they could do more harm than good because many amulets were made from highly poisonous ingredients. Boyle, for example, recalled the unfortunate case of a man who, wearing an arsenic-based amulet and overheated by a strenuous tennis game, was killed by its fumes.[59] If there was no agreement about the disease or its cure, there was also no agreement about what caused it. Putrefied air, swarms of rats and goods imported from the eastern Mediterranean were all blamed, as were witches, emanations from the stars and acts of God.[60]

Given the fear and confusion that surrounded the plague, it is not surprising that people differed in their responses. Some saw plague as a miracle – different from others in its expression of God's wrath rather than his mercy, but nonetheless a divine phenomenon that asked for a spiritual response. Others saw it as a 'miasma', an all too earthly phenomenon the transmission of which needed to be controlled. These two very different points of view produced two very different reactions. The afflicted needed either neighbourly support or strict segregation. These responses were obviously irreconcilable and the conflict went to law. After much wrangling, individuals or communities afflicted by plague were eventually defined as infected parts of the body politic, and the legal concept of immunity – as in 'immunity from prosecution' – was used to question the status of individuals' or communities' rights. Were they special or should they be curtailed?

The arguments were won by those who said plague was earthly and transmitted.[61] People's rights were curtailed and quarantine was enforced, often with great violence, to prevent contagion. The death that came to those in quarantine may have been due to disease, to starvation or to a combination of disease and malnutrition. Such legally sanctioned violence against a part in the name of the whole became an accepted part of modern politics. The legal concept of immunity became medical, while the medical ideas of contagion entered politics, as in today's fears about 'radicalization'.[62]

The way in which the plague was handled politically, along with a growing number of other social phenomena, was with laws and obligations and contracts. This was a brand-new way of governing – a way based on negotiating agreements – and it drew much of its force from the new mercantile ways of doing business. No longer were rules established on old principles like the aristocratic codes of honour that had been instilled into Sir Robert at his father's house, at Westminster School and at Trinity College. His customary hospitality and generosity could not be extended to the afflicted for fear of prosecution. It was also possible that fleeing London for Oxnead could put his loved ones at risk. Sir Robert found himself caught in unwinnable situations as the world around him seemed to spiral into chaos.

If the death rate that Pepys recorded in August had continued, then more than two-thirds of Londoners would have been dead within a year. But, as the dog days drew to a close and the nights lengthened, the invisible waves of death slowly receded. It has been estimated that the 1665 plague cost the lives of about one in four Londoners.[63] The few of Sir Robert's letters that survive from this time suggest that he did not want to worry his wife with details – he mainly reported his progress with the court's interminable political machinations. In June of the following year, however, he told Rebecca that 'the sickness is decreased' and that there were only 'eight [deaths] of the plague'.[64] No one knows why it abated, just as no one knew why it came in the first place, or how to deal with it.

Two months after Sir Robert wrote that reassuring letter, London was hit with yet more drama. At the beginning of September, fire raged for four days and destroyed two-thirds of the medieval city. The emergency response was seriously mismanaged, first, because the Lord Mayor failed to authorize the demolition of properties to make fire breaks and, second, because old Civil War enmities hampered the effective deployment of troops. The flames only stopped spreading when, after three days, the heavens intervened with a change in wind direction. Some blamed the Great Fire on divine retribution. Others blamed it on the Dutch – a few months earlier, Sir Robert had reported the 'bells and bonfires' that celebrated an English victory, whilst a few months later the Dutch humiliated the English, capturing two ships and destroying thirteen more in Chatham Dockyard.[65] Yet others saw the Great Fire as part of a papist plot. Wild xenophobic rumours were fuelled by the conflagration and more may have died in the civil unrest that followed than in the fire itself. The Great Fire made 70,000 people homeless and destroyed the city's commercial infrastructure. Recovery took over five years.[66]

The Pastons emerged from the Great Fire unscathed. In fact, being able to speculate, they even profited from it. The devastation did not touch them, because they lived in aristocratic districts, outside the old city walls. At the end of May, Sir Robert's twelve-year-old son, William, was playing cricket on Richmond Green, so they were comfortably west of the City.[67] They had a series of short-term rents in a succession of smartly furnished houses across London, each occupied for a session of Parliament or the court. One of their homes was in Suffolk Street, just off Pall Mall, one block west of today's National Gallery and then a fashionable street for gentry and ambassadors. Pepys noted that Charles II kept a richly furnished house there for one of his many mistresses, an actress, Miss Davis. This was, he felt, a 'most infinite shame'. Pepys thought Miss Davis was a 'most impertinent slut', and her close neighbour, Rebecca Paston, would probably have agreed.[68] Rebecca soon moved round the corner on to Pall Mall.

Avoiding undesirable neighbours was one thing, but avoiding undesirable people on the street was quite another. In 1671 Sir Robert's close friend Thomas Henshaw warned him about highwaymen operating around Kensington.[69] Three years later, after a pitched battle on Hampstead Heath, five notorious highwaymen were brought to justice. The gang had robbed at least fourteen men and women, killed at least two and were planning 'To trip o're the Ocean, where none should us find'. However, they were delivered to Newgate Prison, where one died from his wounds while the others were tried and hanged within the month. Their confessions were told in a booklet, a pamphlet and a popular ballad (of eleven verses):

> Our Crimes upon Earth hath bereav'd us of hope,
> The thread of our lives is spun out in a Rope;
> We Rob'd Night and Day, Upon the High-way,
> And spent it on Wine and on wenches and play.
> *Chorus*: But to this sweetmeat sour sauce must be had;
> Destruction treads on the heels of the bad.[70]

In August 1675, a year after the famous fracas in Hampstead, Sir Robert's coach was attacked in Kensington, exactly where Henshaw had warned danger lay. His coachman was killed and he received gunshot wounds. Sir John Holland expressed shock because the newspapers did not even bother to mention it – such attacks were evidently all too common.[71] Nonetheless, news of the attack and of Sir Robert's 'mortal' wounds spread quickly and Rebecca received a flood of concerned letters. Slowly, over the weeks, the letters' tone changed as it became clear that his life was no longer in danger.

When he had recovered sufficiently, Sir Robert ventured back to Norwich, accompanied by friends. After two days and ninety miles, he was greeted at Thetford by the pealing of church bells and the mayor and dignitaries who came out to drink his health. One of those in Sir Robert's convoy described the scene to Rebecca, recalling that 'musicians are said to frame the sweetest music out of discords.' Sir Robert himself wrote to Rebecca, back in London, to report that his health had improved since 'the approach to my native soil I presume gives me some vigour,' just as it seemed to have done for his seafaring ancestor, Sir Clement.[72] Leaving Thetford for Norwich, some thirty miles away, they were stopped repeatedly by well-wishers offering cider on the roadside, followed by a three-course lunch of venison, 'fish and fowl in perfection . . . with several sorts of liquors'. News of a waiting welcoming committee in Norwich curtailed the impromptu hospitality and they set off again, their ranks swelling as they neared the city. Within a mile or so, Sir Robert's coach had been joined by six others carrying 'baronets, knights, esquires, gentlemen and clergy, aldermen' and more. In the city, they were greeted by the bells of dozens of churches, forty more clergy and three hundred on horse-back, plus countless citizens on the streets and at doors and windows. Such triumphal processions were usually reserved for individuals of much higher status, so the scale of the spontaneous welcome was a true indication of his wide personal popularity.

The spur-of-the-moment roadside lunch had delayed them and the city's planned welcome was so lavish they could not leave until after sunset. Sir Robert's convoy had to make the last ten miles guided by the moon. To prepare for his homecoming, candles had been lit in every room, so his first hint of Oxnead would have been from about half a mile away when he glimpsed a welcoming glow through the woods. Getting closer, the house would have been underlined by glit-tering reflections on the River Bure and framed by statues illuminated by the moon's cool silver on one side and his home's golden warmth on the other. Dozens of windows blazed their welcome and a letter reporting his return home said that their final approach 'seemed as noonday'.[73]

After a well-earned rest, Sir Robert visited neighbouring Great Yarmouth and was greeted by a reception that rivalled Norwich's. The official pomp and ceremony included gun salutes and an elementally balanced four-course meal with provisions gathered from 'the earth, water and air' interspersed by entertainment from a fire-eater. (As we shall see, such elemental balance was thought essential for maintain-ing good health.) He distributed £10 for the poor and returned home, leaving a town that had expressed itself 'so full of love and honour' that, as Rebecca was told, the heart of a man could not 'desire more'.[74]

Back in Oxnead, Sir Robert was surrounded by well-wishers and safely away from the risk of highwaymen, conflagrations, wars, plague and politics. He had the opportunity to relax and indulge his loves – his children, his music and his family's great collection of treasures. It was his chance to play the 'virtuoso' – a term coined around the time he was born to describe people with wealth and leisure who engaged with diverse activities as proud 'amateurs' and 'dilettantes'. These are now pejorative terms, but the word amateur derives from *amour*, or love, while dilettante shares its root with the word 'delight'. Virtuosi were passionate, with romantic sensibilities, and were interested in things for their own sake, not their potential utility.[75] Sir Robert certainly enjoyed playing music and he may also have found the chance to practise some other arts. The only product of his leisurely repose in Oxnead that survives today is the *Paston Treasure*, the large still-life painting that turned up one day in our conservation studio.

As Sir Robert's neighbour Thomas Browne said, 'there is no antidote to the opium of time.'[76] But you can choose whether to chase or dodge its consequences or, instead, to just ride its rhythms. The experiences of time in Oxnead and in London were very different, and back home time was not pressing. Compared with London, Oxnead was almost timeless – it was surrounded by gentle agrarian cycles that offered refuge from the city's relentless change. In the first Clement Paston's time, Norfolk had been the richest part of England, but by Sir Robert's time, the county was in a steady decline. As far as the rest of the nation was concerned, what happened there mattered less and less. Time moved very slowly in the old house, the roots of which penetrated deep into the past. Even the furniture was different in Oxnead. Unlike the smart, up-to-date decor in the Pastons' London houses, Oxnead's heirlooms evoked the family's ancestors, with a long, rich past nourishing the present.[77]

We do not know exactly when the *Paston Treasure* was painted, but it may have been just after Sir Robert's father died in 1663. The painting might even have been initially commissioned by Sir William, but, if so, by the time the painter arrived in Oxnead, Sir William was on his deathbed and responsibility for overseeing the painting's creation passed to his son.[78] If that was indeed the case, then our scientific examination of the painting provided no evidence of any delays or pauses in its execution or any change in methods of construction. The process of making anything has its own time frame. From our knowledge of Oxnead and our observations in the conservation studio, it seems that the painting was made in one continuous campaign, by one painter following the guidance of one person who may or may not have accommodated others' wishes. Since Sir Robert evidently enjoyed Oxnead's slow, predictable country rhythms, we can imagine that he might also have appreciated the slow, predictable rhythms of making the painting.

The *Paston Treasure* depicts one crafted object that Sir Robert might even have made himself. Most items in the painting – like the mounted shell cups – are the products of extraordinary skill, but one item appears quite crude in comparison and might seem out of place, unless it had personal significance. The hourglass above the globe is rather rudimentary compared to the engraved nautilus shell cup it stands behind. The glass was undoubtedly blown by a professional, but the wooden frame could easily have been made by an amateur or dilettante virtuoso. Certainly, the vogue for aristocratic wood- and ivory-turning had grown as the relevance of mechanical arts to military and political practice became recognized from the fifteenth century onwards.[79] Lathes were fashionable accessories for Continental nobles and even sovereigns, from the dukes of Saxony in the sixteenth century through to Peter the Great of Russia and Queen Louise of Denmark in the eighteenth century.[80] By the seventeenth century, wood-turners were employed to teach princes and their work ended up in cabinets of curiosity to be appreciated by, amongst others, the Royal Society of London.[81]

Sir Robert's father had been praised for his 'polite judgment' of and 'rare fancy and invention' in 'turnings'.[82] This suggests that Sir William had been a connoisseur of items made on the lathe and might have produced designs for them. Could he or his son have had a lathe and actually made the rather simple wooden frame for the *Paston Treasure*'s hourglass? If so, such handiwork would have significantly contributed to their gentlemanly reputations. After all, it was only by becoming actively involved in the physical process of making something that the craftsperson's 'mental dexterity' could become as clear as their obvious manual dexterity.[83] Sir Robert was obviously interested in craft skills, because the recipe book that contains his plague remedies also contains recipes for making artists' materials.[84]

Sir Robert may not have painted himself, but he certainly engaged a number of painters. For example, one of his letters to Rebecca mentions paying £16 to bring an unnamed painter up from London in order to decorate Oxnead's chapel as 'you approve best'.[85] While his wife obviously took responsibility for that particular commission, Sir Robert must have been deeply engaged in the process of painting the *Paston Treasure*. After all, the unknown painter's image was very idiosyncratic. It is absolutely certain that no artist would have been entrusted with selecting a few treasures from the family's extensive collection, and it is highly unlikely that any competent artist would arrange them on the canvas in such a bizarre manner, ignoring the conventions of single-point perspective. Sir Robert must have taken pleasure in the process of directing the painting, since its odd composition and repeated changes indicate that he did not just let the painter get on with the job. He enjoyed being involved in the creative process. Today, albeit on a rather more modest scale, something of the same pleasure is felt by people who arrange their breakfasts before sharing them on social media.

A number of books about painting were published for virtuosi, including *The Compleat Gentleman*, which was written by Henry Peacham while living in Wymondham, just the other side of Norwich.[86] The way the *Paston Treasure* was painted suggests that Sir Robert did not just instruct an artist from a distance. Its peculiarity suggests that he was closely involved in its execution. It is highly unlikely that precious and fragile shell cups were sent out to a studio, either in Norwich or in London, risking potholes and highwaymen. It is also very unlikely that the items were sketched and the painting later assembled from a collection of drawings. One of the main reasons for painting things like silver and mother-of-pearl was the opportunities they provided to show off the skills of rendering unique surfaces.[87] All in all, it is much more likely that – just like the person who decorated the chapel – a painter was found and brought up to Oxnead.

The speculative art market was brand new so artists were usually not the sole author of most paintings. Most often, they followed instructions from their patron. It is quite improbable, for example, that any European painter would routinely add men pursued by crocodiles to portraits, so the crocodile in Sir William's portrait would have been the patron's suggestion. A few decades after the *Paston Treasure* was painted, the Earl of Shaftesbury explicitly treated pictures as collaborations. In his case, evidence of artistic collaboration can be found in his specification of a painting's setting and attributes, in personal letters and in a published treatise.[88] The identity of the *Paston Treasure*'s painter is not known in large part because so much of the painting is due to Sir Robert.

Sir Robert may not have held the paintbrush, but he certainly directed the whole operation. In fact, the painter may eventually have regretted coming to Oxnead, given how much influence Sir Robert wielded over his work. As a result, no other painting looks quite like the *Paston Treasure*. It is one of a kind.

The unknown artist's technique suggests that they were probably trained in Holland, and they might well have brought the necessary materials with them when they came to Oxnead since there were seasonal fairs for artists' materials in the Low Countries. There were also specialist shops in London, and the earliest surviving advertisement for a supplier of artists' materials in London is dated 1675, mentioning the 'Sign of the Globe' (a map-maker's shop on the Strand) and the 'Sign of the Pestle and Mortar' (an apothecary in Long Acre).[89] The painter who decorated Oxnead's chapel under Rebecca's supervision was given £6 by Sir Robert to buy materials and equipment in London.[90] Closer to home, just over fifty miles away, the Suffolk painter Mary Beale was supplied with pigments by her husband, who also supplied other artists – including top society painter Sir Peter Lely – from 1660 and through the 1670s.[91] There were also artists' suppliers in Norwich, but you did not even need to go shopping to get good colours.

One local, and completely free, pigment would have been chalk. The whole of Norfolk rested upon it and Norwich was riddled with medieval tunnels dug through it. If you wanted to buy chalk, it would have been so cheap that there would have been no point bringing it from anywhere else.[92] The painter also used two black pigments that were local and very cheap if not completely free. Bone black was traditionally made from chicken bones rescued from the dog and charred in the fire after dinner.[93] Bone black was mainly used as a pigment, but black paints could also be made from charcoal, which was commonly used as fuel and usually manufactured locally.[94] The bone black and charcoal in the *Paston Treasure* almost certainly came from birds and trees on Sir Robert's estates. East Anglia also had rich red and yellow earths that could be dug up, ground and processed into paint. But East Anglia did not have all of the other mineral pigments found in the still-life's paint. These include azurite, a blue which was probably imported from Germany, and another, more exclusive blue, ultramarine, which certainly came from Afghanistan.

In fact, the painting's materials and tools could have come from any number of outlets while some of them would already have been at Oxnead. One inventory listed two stones 'to grind colour' and a muller, and Sir Robert complained in a letter that a servant had failed to wash a grinding stone properly and had contaminated a batch of powdered marble with traces of lead white.[95] He seemed to have a very hands-on knowledge of the materials that went into his painting.

Once you had all the materials and tools, the next thing you needed to make such a big (246 × 165 cm) picture was a very large piece of cloth. You would expect it to be easy to find large pieces of cloth around Oxnead since Norwich was the centre of the English textile trade. For example, the village of Worstead was less than five miles from Oxnead – it had been settled by refugee Flemish weavers and gave its name to worsted cloth. However, most Norfolk cloth was made from wool, and the painting's canvas was linen, probably imported from across the North Sea. Linen was woven from threads that were spun – by armies of women – from fibres that were beaten from the long stalks of flax plants. However, Sir Robert wanted his painting to be bigger than the widths easily available in Norfolk. So the very first task was to sew two pieces of canvas together. In the finished picture the seam runs vertically through the lobster and parrot.

One of the deeply satisfying things about making a painting – especially for someone escaping the chaotic trials and tribulations of post-Civil War London – would have been the orderly growth. Once the idea, the artist and the materials were in place, what followed would be the gradual unfolding of a vision. For Sir Robert, engaging in the whole process would have been a bit like being a player in a game of chess. He would have settled down at the beginning of the game with a warm feeling of anticipation. On the one hand, he knew exactly what was going to happen – he knew the rules of chess. On the other hand, he had absolutely no idea what would unfold – he would have had to wait till the end to discover the outcome.

The rules of painting had to be followed in order for Sir Robert's vision to emerge from twenty small bags of dry pigments, a few bottles of oil and turpentine and one large seamed canvas. Making the painting involved assembling and then preparing the support, defining the design, gradually working up each part, then finally unifying the whole with finishing touches and eventually a varnish. Each stage in the process had its own rules and no stage could be rushed, because each subsequent stage had to build upon earlier ones. Slowly building up the picture was indeed like a game of chess in that each move was both enabled and constrained by all the previous moves. For Sir Robert, whose life outside Oxnead was buffeted by the unpredictability of highwaymen, conflagrations, plague and wars, it would have been a very welcome respite. There was a comforting inevitability about the flow and rhythm of activities that the process imposed upon both artist and patron.

To prepare the canvas, four very sturdy pieces of wood were assembled into a rectangle bigger than the painting's intended final size. Two of the beams were over eight feet long, the other two were nearly six feet and their corners were reinforced with sturdy braces. This heavy-duty 'strainer' was laid on the floor and the canvas was stretched over it and attached, either by nailing or threading with strong string. The canvas was then soaked with rabbit-skin glue dissolved in warm water. (This 'size' might not have been literally made with rabbits' skins, but from scraps of leather or parchment or from hooves and horns from the knackers' yard.) The wet, warm size would soak into the threads and make the canvas shrink. The strainer needed to be very strong indeed because the shrinkage of such a large piece of canvas would build up significant tension. Each of the wooden beams had to be about two inches thick and six inches wide in order to be able to withstand the force. The canvas also had to be nailed or strung quite closely to prevent it ripping. In fact, we know that the attachments were about every two or three inches, because X-rays show how the tension is, even now, still locked into the canvas. The weave around the edges of the painting became distorted as the once-straight threads were pulled into a scalloping rhythm of waves that crest every two or three inches.

The tension removed much of the distortion introduced by the weaving process and forced the warp and weft threads to flatten out. This preparatory stage made the canvas easier to paint on and made the finished painting more able to withstand changes of humidity.[96] Once dry, the canvas probably had the largest of its 'slubs' removed with a sharp knife or by rubbing with a pumice stone. Slubs are those thick threads that are valued today as evidence of natural fibres and are an important part of linen's 'signature'. However, their presence in the *Paston Treasure* could have caused bumps in areas of paint that may have been intended to be smooth. Depending on how the canvas reacted to the rabbit-skin glue, it might have been re-stretched on the strainer and more size applied. It would again be left to dry. All this would have taken a week or so, depending on the weather, and would have smelt quite unpleasant. It was probably done in an outhouse.

The dry, taut, sized – and no longer smelly – canvas would then be moved into the room that was to become the painter's temporary Oxnead studio. At this point it might have been transferred to the smaller, lighter strainer that would eventually support the painting in its frame. Moving the canvas and strainer would take three or more people – at least two strong men to lift it, plus someone to open doors and guide it cautiously through a house fit to receive a king. Once in place, it was secured more or less upright on a makeshift easel and the entire front of the canvas was coated with a layer of 'ground' or 'priming'. This was a cheap paint made from a thick mixture of lead white and chalk in linseed oil, the traditional Dutch way of preparing a canvas. The painter may have prepared the canvas, but since there were many painters working in Norwich, these initial tasks might have been done by a local specialist. In 1668 the author of *The Excellency of Pen and Pencil* wrote that few London painters 'prime [canvases] themselves, but [most] buy it ready done'.[97]

Whoever did it, the paste-like ground paint was applied with a knife with a slightly curved blade about eight inches long. In the *Paston Treasure* the knife's traces are evident as free, sweeping, broad streaks in the X-ray, which also shows that the person who applied the ground was not too concerned about its appearance. The knife pressed the thick paint into the recesses between threads and made the canvas even stiffer. This ground layer was allowed to dry, which would have taken a few days, and then painted over with a uniform pink-beige-coloured priming. The pigments in this linseed oil priming layer included lead white, chalk, charcoal and red and yellow earths. All these stages would also have been quite smelly, but oil and turpentine, with their traces of aromatic essential oils, smell much nicer than collagen-based animal glue.

Sir Robert would have specified the painting's final dimensions and assigned rooms for the work, and may only have taken a passing interest in these early stages. However, once the pink-beige priming was dry, again only a few days later, he would have needed to be very closely involved indeed. This is because the next stage defined the painting's composition, which – because it is so different from every other Dutch seventeenth-century still-life – was obviously designed by Sir Robert. Each painter had slightly different ways of transferring designs on to canvas. Some would roughly block out areas of colour for each item to be depicted; others would carefully trace their outlines on to the priming layer. If the items were not in the studio, then their colours and outlines could be copied from a sketch-book, but, of course, everything in the *Paston Treasure* was available right there in Oxnead. Sometimes the whole ensemble of objects would be sketched out on paper to see how they related to each other, which may have been the case for this very complex painting. But, if so, such preparatory drawings have not survived. The more precious items were almost certainly kept in a treasury and brought out one at a time when needed. The Paston's strongroom may have been a thirty-foot brick-built cube with a vaulted roof, buried deep below one of the lawns at Oxnead. It is now only accessible via a manhole and perilous shute.[98]

When the painting was being treated in our studio, we took advantage of its many small damages to investigate the way this particular painter may have transferred the design. Conservation studios are guided by ethical standards, and – after consultation with the owners – it was deemed acceptable to take tiny samples from the edges of some historic damages. Those samples were mounted in plastic and polished to reveal sequences of layers of paint. At the bottom of the samples were traces of the white ground layer, followed by the pink-beige priming. After that, each layer was different, depending on the paint passage from which it was taken. These microscopic samples showed how the painter built up the colours for each depicted item. But they did not show whether the painter had drawn an outline around each item.

With such a complicated composition, it was very hard to imagine how the painter could have proceeded without some kind of carefully drawn outlines. Traces of outlines are sometimes seen using a technique called infrared radiography so we tried it but, once again, found no sign. We also tried another technique, called macro X-ray fluorescence (macro-XRF), but the preparatory drawing – if there was one – still eluded us. We concluded that the painter probably drew his outlines in chalk. These would have been visible at the time, but would have been smudged by the act of painting, effectively erasing them as work proceeded.

The final effect was usually achieved in just two or three layers of paint on top of the ground and priming. The build-up of paint for each passage was quite simple, but it varied for every single paint passage. There are four bunches of grapes in the painting, for example, and each is executed with a different mixture of pigments and with different sequences of layers. Just one paint passage can illustrate the general process. The lobster was outlined along with everything else. Then it was painted with flat, opaque reds – red lead and vermilion in a minimal amount of oil – which were left to dry for a week or so. The lobster then had its shaded areas reinforced with layers of transparent reds – cochineal in richer mixtures of oil – and was again left to dry, this time probably for a week or two. Finally, it was finished with a few highlighted details in lead white in oil, some of which were glazed again after they too had been allowed to dry. The lobster probably took around an hour or so to paint, but in several sessions spread over a month or so.

Each depicted object has neatly defined edges, so any small overlaps can give clues about the order in which the things were painted. It turns out that one layer of each of the objects was painted at a time, moving around the composition to avoid smudging wet paint. This is an efficient way of working since the artist did not have to wait for paint to dry – while the underlayers of one passage were drying, they could work on other paint passages. The small overlaps show that Sir Robert's precious shell cups were finished first, and then the fruit, flowers and instruments were finished to fill in the gaps between them. As a result, each time Sir Robert checked on progress in the studio he would have seen different parts of the composition at different stages of completion. For example, first the lobster was just a chalk outline, then the line was filled in and became a uniform bright red patch, a week or so later it could have its volume modelled with shadows, then later still its texture been could have defined with gleaming reflections.

The artist may have worked on different passages that needed similar mixes of paint at the same time. For example, the vine leaves, the servant's green tunic, the green chair upon which the girl – probably Sir Robert's daughter Margaret – sits, as well as the dark green box upon which the hourglass stands might all have been gradually built up over several weeks with spurts of activity on the same few days. This would have meant that the artist did not need to wash his brushes so often, thus losing time and materials. However, some paint passages – like the areas of flesh for the servant and for Margaret – were painted with a different technique. These were done 'wet-in-wet', taking advantage of the fact that the oil took several days to dry so different paints could be blended with each other on the canvas rather than just being painted over already dry layers. The whole process was quite formulaic. At any one time, a paint passage and its neighbours would have different levels of completion.

Yet, even though the picture emerged from bare outlines and flat patches in a colour-by-numbers fashion, it still needed enormous skill and also involved some rather enigmatic decisions. For example, while all the greens were painted with the same pigment, the blues were not. The whole painting could have used just one blue pigment, but the macro-XRF elemental mapping revealed several different, and expensive, blues. There was no obvious rhyme or reason to the use of blues – azurite, indigo, smalt and ultramarine – but the golds were different too, and their use showed a discernable pattern. The mounts for the shell cups were all painted with orpiment, but the servant's clasps and chain, as well as the tablecloth's fringe and the clock-face, were not. The final visual effects were very similar, but the chosen pigments were very different. The higher-status central objects were depicted with orpiment, which was a quite special and rather archaic material, while lower-status peripheral objects were depicted with relatively prosaic yellow earths.[99]

Watching the painting take shape would have been like seeing different themes jostle together as they emerged, coming into focus in seemingly odd fits and starts. The full logic of construction is lost on us as we cannot know exactly what was happening around the studio. There was a creative tension between the chess-like precision of the craft and the messy world in which it was practised. For a month or so, Sir Robert would have seen quite an abstract, almost psychedelic, patchwork growing. Watching it slowly emerge would have been the visual equivalent of hearing an orchestra warming up – rehearsing, prefiguring and hinting at fragmentary themes that would, in time, meld into a coherent composition. Well, of course, this fairly typical painting process usually resulted in a coherent composition.[100] The *Paston Treasure*'s disconcertingly incoherent, cluttered and jumbled appearance is due to Sir Robert's guidance, not to the painter's technique. Sir Robert's reasons for wanting such an odd-looking image will be considered in the final chapter.

The work took shape methodically – from outlines to patches to forms to textures – continually leap-frogging from one part of the canvas to another, week after week, each stage building on the previous stages. Everything seemed planned but the plan was not inflexible. For example, the parrot seems to have been an afterthought (its foot overlaps the music book's completed score). Oxnead had an aviary so perhaps it was Margaret's pet and she suggested including it. The very last passages to be finished were background elements – like the walls, tablecloth and red curtain. They had been roughly blocked in early in the process but were modelled last, with shadows and highlights, to fill in the gaps between all the completed objects. These finishing touches are quite hastily executed, although from a normal viewing distance you could never tell. They effectively tied the objects together and brought the painting to a satisfying conclusion.

Sir Robert also knew exactly how he wanted the painting to be presented when finished, and he had a frame made to echo the style of the mounts for some of his shell cups. Several of these had 'auricular', or ear-shaped, bases and the picture frame was carved with similar ear- or shell-like ornamentation, with masks and marine forms emerging from sensuous rippling lines. Making the frame probably took place in parallel with the painting. The frame was a very personal choice as the auricular style was already going out of fashion, but it would have allowed the painting to blend into Oxnead's old and eclectic decor. The whole job – preparing, painting and framing – would probably have taken between two and three months and the paint layers would have been allowed to settle before varnishing, maybe six months to a year later. The original varnish, now long gone, may even have been one of Sir Robert's own concoctions since one of his notebooks contains a recipe for picture varnish.[101]

Sir Robert would have been very closely engaged with the painter throughout the whole process. The original design was his and not the painter's. In fact, Sir Robert had several different ideas about the picture as it was being painted – where we now see a wall-clock, there was once a large silver platter and then an exotically dressed woman. These changes are now buried under the visible paint and they only showed up during examination of the painting with microscopic samples, X-rays and XRF mapping. If the painting had indeed been made in the wake of Sir William's death, then these changes may reflect jostling amongst the family as his assets were divided. Adding the parrot was a quite minor change but those other changes, to use a sporting analogy, moved the goalposts very significantly, not once but twice. They show that the painting process responded to what was happening in Oxnead. They are physical evidence of detailed conversations held by Sir Robert and the painter, which were a two-way affair. Sir Robert learned from the painter, gaining insights into the qualities and processing of materials, just as he may have done if he had turned the wood for the hourglass.[102] As his recipe books show, Sir Robert was deeply interested in the ways that materials behaved, and his few months with the *Paston Treasure* as it evolved in Oxnead were a rare – and very privileged – opportunity to witness a handful of diverse materials being manipulated with consummate skill into a satisfying whole.

Most of Sir Robert's activities required frantic juggling in response to momentous events that lay completely outside his control and demanded his immediate attention. His projects in the wider world were regularly thwarted and were punctuated only by the brief solace of sweet music and fine dining at home. Making the painting was a very different experience.

The *Paston Treasure* was constructed in accordance with a sound technical tradition that stretched back at least five centuries, and its painter would no doubt have dedicated a decade or more to becoming completely immersed in that tradition. It took over three centuries to acquire the wealth needed to create the *Paston Treasure* and the objects it depicts were gathered over three generations. The whole painting took about three months to make, not counting the time needed to weave the canvas, spin the thread, grow the flax, or prepare any of its other ingredients. Each of the depicted objects took shape on the canvas over the course of a few days or weeks, and while nothing could be rushed, everything in the picture took shape in timescales that Sir Robert could influence. He orchestrated the subject-matter, the necessary materials and the painter's skills. The painting grew, slowly and surely, from an initial idea that adapted to opportunities and events in Oxnead, through to a finished product, one step at a time. All issues could be resolved at a leisurely pace and the painter could easily accommodate even the patron's later radical changes of mind. The whole painting, and each of its parts, had a well-choreographed beginning, middle and end. Unlike most other aspects of his life, Sir Robert was in control of every single detail – juggling contributions from his family and the painter – as the *Paston Treasure* came together before his very own eyes. Far from London's bustle, the unknown painter's skilled hands were like those of a calm midwife who expertly delivered Sir Robert's vision into the world.

'To compare small with great things': a page from Robert Farley's
1638 emblem-book *Lychnocausia*.

four

The Gathering

Still-life paintings, collections – theatrical curtains – parrots – pets – slaves –
black skin – cochineal insects – Andean silver – Spanish silver – blue-and-white
porcelain – Chinese silver – snail shells – ostrich eggs – herrings – the globe –
Polynesian navigation – knowledge exchange

Since Sir Robert seemed to show so much interest in how the
Paston Treasure was painted we can only hope he delighted in
the finished product. As an Englishman, he was unusual in wanting a
still-life painting. Just over the North Sea, the Dutch seemed obsessed
with them, and in the 1660s about one in six Dutch pictures was a
still-life,[1] including *pronk* or *pronk-vanitas* pictures. *Pronk* was Dutch
for 'show-off', and still-life paintings were popular because their exotica could reflect pride in long-distance trade and assert status in the
newly mercantile country. In a culture that was uncomfortable with
too much material wealth, this 'show-off' aspect was tempered with a
vanitas aspect, to which we will turn in the last chapter.

Few English patrons commissioned still-life paintings, because
they were at the very bottom of the hierarchy of images – portraiture,
history, mythological and religious paintings all had much higher
status. Modern commentators have been divided over the still-life's
value. Some see them as simple records of commodities, while others
see them as vehicles of meanings, which may have been readily accessible or purposefully hidden. There have also been arguments about
whether any of these meanings were religious, scientific or stylistic.[2] I
will assume they were all these things. The *Paston Treasure* is certainly
not constrained by a single theme – it is very eclectic and a 'powerful antidote' to the idea of 'a single standard of taste'.[3] Above all, the
painting shows Sir Robert to have been a highly original free-thinker.
Perhaps, for him, some of its value lay in the things it depicted. He
could have chosen to show absolutely anything from his collection,
which inventories suggest included over six hundred objects. As it is,

the *Paston Treasure* is a portrait of a tiny fraction – a mini-cabinet of curiosities that is always open. However, the things it displays are not necessarily the most expensive, so it raises the questions of why he might have chosen these particular objects and how he valued his collection. Sir Robert left no clues, but there are clues about how things were valued in a contemporary's quite similar collection.

To escape problems caused by his father's bankruptcy, William Courten (alias Charleton, 1642–1702) spent 25 years touring the Continent collecting art and curiosities.[4] In 1686 this 'modest and obliging' man's collection was worth about £8,000, even after giving much away; his stuffed crocodile, for example, ended up in the Royal Society.[5] Courten made catalogues that show how he thought about his collection, and accurate paintings of natural specimens were amongst the highest value items. For example, a small painting of snakes and lizards cost £75 whereas a full-length portrait by top society painter Sir Peter Lely was only £50.[6] He also had Old Master drawings and paintings, arranged by artist's name, medium, genre or subject and quality. It is clear that 'quality' was not the same as monetary value, since he owned a Dürer that cost £2 but one of his 'best' was a Rembrandt that cost 1*d*.[7] Like Sir Robert, he evidently appreciated how artists made their images, yet this may have been unusual and some art lovers just focused on what paintings depicted. For example, Sir Henry Wotton said that things in pictures 'stood not upon [canvas or panel] but as if they were acting upon a stage'.[8]

With nearly one-quarter of the *Paston Treasure* taken up by a large red curtain, it is as if its crowded tabletop was indeed a stage upon which all the objects could play their parts. Curtains can be 'drawn' – meaning both opened and closed – to conceal or reveal, cover or discover, and nowhere is revelation or discovery more concentrated than between the curtain's rise and fall over a theatrical stage. Actors make personal journeys in order to reach their place on the stage, and once there they play out other journeys. We too go to the theatre or the cinema to make journeys, to be transported out of our everyday lives and into whatever is conjured when the curtain rises. A play can simply be a conscious diversion – like Courten's escape from financial problems – but it can also transform the way we see the everyday world to which we return when the curtain falls. According to Wotton and many other contemporary viewers, paintings such as the *Paston Treasure* would have been just such a theatrical ordering of the world. Sir Robert and his friends could enter into the picture and enjoy the play enacted by its many parts. Some may even have emerged transformed by the spectacle.

We too can share some of Sir Robert's stories. For example, since many of the objects made long journeys to reach his stage-like tabletop they have travellers' tales to tell. Some of their journeys and stories were shrouded in mystery; others were known in dizzying detail or straddled fact and fable. Some of those stories featured momentous events that changed Sir Robert and his world, and still shape our world today.

Even the theatrically lifted curtain could play its part, because – assuming the *pronk* picture was a way for Sir Robert to show off – it suggested his familiarity with the classics. A rich draped curtain, together with a bird about to eat some grapes, might allude to one of the oldest jokes in the history of art, a joke that certainly featured in other seventeenth-century still-life paintings.[9] According to Pliny the Elder, the ancient Greek artist Zeuxis painted grapes so realistically that when he lifted the curtain from the easel to reveal his painting, birds flew down to try and peck at them. Not to be outdone, another artist, Parrhasios, set up what seemed to be another curtain-covered painting on an easel. Zeuxis went to lift the curtain to reveal the painting only to discover that the curtain *was* the painting. While Zeuxis had fooled the birds, Parrhasios had fooled Zeuxis.[10] Pliny did not say what kind of bird was deceived by Zeuxis' grapes, but the *Paston Treasure*'s bird was a parrot. It might have signified 'memory' since parrots were renowned for remembering and repeating phrases. Finding such associations was part of the appeal of these paintings. But the parrot was more than just an allusion to an obscure joke or a reference to memory.

The *Paston Treasure*'s parrot (whose bright red tail has now faded) came from Equatorial West Africa and says something about the global reach of Sir Robert's collection. It was apparently free to roam Oxnead, and since it was depicted walking over Margaret's music book, it also says something about people's relationships with animals. Exotic animals were nothing new in England. One hundred years before the first Clement Paston rode his horse to market, Henry III had an elephant, and one hundred years before the *Paston Treasure* was painted, parrots flocked into the country from the Americas. These earlier American parrots brought with them something quite intangible, without which Sir Robert's African parrot would never have got in the picture. American parrots helped change the way Europeans related to animals. Before parrots arrived in Europe, domesticated birds were mainly associated with hunting or husbandry, the business of high-class males or low-class females, respectively. Of course, close emotional bonds could develop between men and their hawks and between women and their chicks, but the animals were primarily there to serve a purpose. The idea that animals could simply offer companionship dawned only quite slowly as hunting dogs morphed into lap dogs (including Cavalier King Charles Spaniels), but the idea of animal companionship was reinforced with exotic creatures like parrots.

Back in the Americas, parrots had very different relationships with humans. There, shaman-like *nagualli* believed they could dissolve the boundaries of human identity to become god-like or animal-like, and be endowed with their powers. In this fluid shape-shifting culture, parrots, amongst other creatures, were adopted, tamed, used in religious ritual and eventually given as gifts to Europeans. On being transported across the Atlantic, the birds may have lost some of their spiritual significance, but the indigenous American magic rubbed off on Europeans and parrots retained their role as human companions. (Of course, European witches had their 'familiars' – including black cats – but parrots were animal companions that did not invite persecution.) The modern concept of the non-utilitarian 'pet' owes much to Native Americans' profoundly spiritual relationships with animals.[11] The *Paston Treasure*'s record of playful engagement with a parrot, and a monkey, is evidence of a subtle softening in the way Europeans interacted with animals.

Along with the parrot, the painting shows another African whose presence indicates that, at the same time Europeans' engagement with some of their fellow creatures softened, their engagement with others hardened. No black servant is recorded in any surviving documents, but the young man must be considered part of Sir Robert's exotic collection since more or less contemporary Dutch sources record the monetary value of servants and slaves. Depending on market conditions, they could cost between forty and one hundred pieces-of-eight, more if well trained. Through the 1660s, the Dutch traded the most slaves; by the 1690s the Portuguese became the major suppliers and the English came to dominate in the early eighteenth century.[12] However, the English Navigation Act of 1677 did rule that Africans could be classed as commercial goods.[13]

In seventeenth-century England boys like the Paston servant were treated as 'trophies, toys and pets'.[14] Europeans had been collecting exotic humans for about a century before the *Paston Treasure* was painted, and in the 1570s 'this new prey' had included Eskimos.[15] The young man in the painting certainly looks like a trophy, and as such his position bears some relation to the position of early modern children and wives. However, in two important respects, children and wives had more options open to them. First, to escape their subjugated status, children could become adults and wives could become widows. (Women, of course, could also avoid marriage altogether by entering a nunnery.) Second, the official age- and gender-based hierarchies were tempered by an unofficial system that was summarized by Richard Busby, Robert's old headmaster at Westminster. He accounted for his remarkable ability to weather numerous political storms by observing: 'The fathers govern the nation and the mothers govern the fathers, but the *boys* govern the mothers, and *I* govern the boys.'[16] (It seems that girls had to find their own way.) There were no such obvious systems or routes to help Africans mitigate or escape their lowly position in the hierarchy.[17]

The servant in the *Paston Treasure* obviously enjoyed high status as an exotic specimen and, alongside Margaret, as a reminder of human diversity. He was, after all, included in the picture without any hint of shame or embarrassment. His clothes are a mix of Roman and Renaissance styles, loosely based on masque costumes. The striped sash around his waist is a callimanco, a type of fine worsted, given a glossy sheen by mixing wool and silk, hot-pressing and buffing with wax. These fancy fabrics were made in Norwich, mainly for export. The boy is far-flung exotica, but he is clad in local exotica.[18]

It is in the nature of images, with their absence of words, to enable multiple interpretations. Just like the parrot, the servant appears in the picture as if by magic, with no explanation. His journey to Oxnead is left unspoken, and since his name does not survive in the Paston records, we cannot assume anything. He might have survived the barbarous journey from Africa.[19] Yet, equally, that journey may have been buried quite deeply in his ancestral past because, by the beginning of the seventeenth century, there was already an established 'black European identity', with Africans constituting just under half a per cent of London's settled population in 1600.[20] Indeed, Shakespeare's Othello – who was the model of nobility – was described as being 'of here and everywhere'.[21]

Being in England in the 1660s, this particular servant straddled a major change in European attitudes towards Africans. In the wake of Europe's exploitation of the Americas, Africans changed in the European imagination from being human curiosities to becoming human resources. Through the seventeenth century, debates about slavery shifted their focus from morality to expediency, and, rather awkwardly, it became increasingly clear that the concept of slavery contradicted all the assumptions of the newly emerging capitalism. Either slaves had to stop being commodities or they had to stop being people. In the interests of Europe's stake in global trade, the latter solution was adopted and a new variant on racism emerged.[22] The Latin term 'slave' was racial (from Slav), but the first texts that are racist, in modern terms, only appeared around the time the *Paston Treasure* was painted.[23] One of them was Dutch (1660) and another French (1684).[24] Although racism soon became ingrained in European culture, Sir Robert's Oxnead was not racist in any modern sense of the word.[25] Perhaps surprisingly, the servant's presence in the painting is actually a sign of the brave new world of science that was being conjured up in Europe.

The servant's rich dark skin was a source of mystery.[26] There were two main theories of blackness. A climatic theory connected black skin to the region closest to the sun. Shakespeare's Prince of Morocco, for example, explained his complexion as 'The shadowed livery of the burnish'ed sun, To whom I am a neighbour and near bred.'[27] This was mythologized as a side effect of Phaeton's ill-advised trip in his father's sun chariot, to which Ben Jonson alluded by claiming, 'before [Phaeton's] heedless flames were hurled about the globe, the Ethiops were as fair' as Europeans.[28] An alternative, biblical theory asserted that Ham, one of Noah's three sons, either defied or derided his father and was 'smitten in the skin'.[29] Both theories implied that mankind was originally white and that blackness was acquired, associated with death in one case and disinheritance in the other. Both also suggest that blackness was the result of a son transgressing a father's rule. In the eyes of Europeans – descendants of Japheth, Noah's honoured eldest son – this put Africans, descendants of the disgraced younger brother Ham, into a position of servitude. The Pastons' possibly fictitious ancestor Wulstan shows just how important family was to people's sense of identity and to others' acceptance of that identity. People could relate to the story of Noah's family drama and it helped define racial identities. Globally, it helped justify European incursions into Africa, and locally it justified the servant's place in Oxnead.

Thomas Browne wrote about black skin in 1646, possibly before the boy in the painting was even born. He devoted two chapters to black skin in his *Pseudodoxia epidemica* (a book that took issue with 'vulgar errors'). He considered Africans' colour along with questions like why grass is green and why northern foxes are white. He dismissed the idea that blackness was a punishment, observing: 'Moors are not excluded from beauty . . . but hold a common share . . . with all mankind.'[30] This was because he saw all peoples as one, saying, 'There is all *Africa* and her prodigies in us.'[31] In the *Paston Treasure*, the servant's presence was a topical twist on the traditional celebration of natural variety and difference. As Shakespeare's Miranda exclaimed in *The Tempest* upon meeting strangers, 'How beauteous mankind is, O brave new world, That has such people in't.'[32]

People and living creatures rarely feature in still-life paintings or play only minor roles in them. Very unusually, four of them grace the *Paston Treasure* – the servant, the girl, a parrot and a monkey.

Much more often, still-lifes feature human skulls and dead creatures, of which there are plenty in this painting. The cooked lobster and stag's antlers are obvious, as are the shells of long-dead molluscs. However, paradoxically, the overwhelming majority of dead animals in this painting cannot be seen. Today, their presence is revealed only by chemical analysis, yet Sir Robert knew all about them without recourse to any scientific equipment.

The rich red curtain was dyed with the juice of thousands of dead insects. In earlier centuries, they would probably have been imported from around the Mediterranean (if the dye was kermes) or from a swathe of northeastern Europe, from Sweden to the Ukraine (if it was cochineal). Other red-dye-producing insects came from the Middle East and Central Asia (Armenian red), or from India and Southeast Asia (lac). All these insects had all been continuously imported into England in bulk for over five hundred years.[33] Indeed, the Pastons' prosperity – as well as that of the city of Norwich and county of Norfolk – rested in part on these insects because the region's wealth depended on the textile trade and its close links with the European dyeing centres in the Low Countries, just across the North Sea. Red was the most expensive colour and some red clothes could be worth their weight in gold. The countless insects that dyed Sir Robert's very expensive red curtain were probably from Mexico or Peru, the New World cousins of the northeastern European cochineal insects. Through the sixteenth and seventeenth centuries they were the second most valuable commodity to be traded across the Atlantic.

Hundreds of tons of dried insects crossed the Atlantic every year as pea-sized 'grains'. The juices extracted from them were 'fixed' to fabric with a colourless mordant, the preferred one being alum, which was made by roasting a particular type of rock. Many thousands of tons of sulphur-rich shales – like the rocks exploited today in fracking – were cooked at a constant temperature for many months on end. If the rocks were not hot enough the chemical reaction that made alum would not happen, and if they got too hot the alum would be destroyed by other reactions. After cooking, the alum was extracted from the burnt rock with water.[34] Pliny described the process in the first century AD and it continued more or less unchanged for well over a thousand years.[35] Christendom imported most of its alum from the sphere of Islam until the mid-fifteenth century, when religious conflict complicated trade. Providentially, the appropriate rocks were then identified in Italy, giving the papacy an effective European monopoly on alum until the mid-sixteenth century. Then religious conflict again complicated trade and northern Protestants started looking for their own sources. The alum used to fix cochineal to the fabric of Sir Robert's red curtain may have come from Yorkshire.[36]

New World cochineal and possibly Yorkshire alum were not only in Sir Robert's red clothes and Oxnead's red curtains – they were also in the *Paston Treasure* itself. As Sir Robert knew, painters obtained their transparent red pigments from waste cloth, recycling it from offcuts in the manufacture of clothes and from worn-out garments.[37] Red cloth was dissolved in caustic solutions and the colour – still fixed to its mordant – was collected, dried and added to the painter's palette to be mixed with oil. So the red matter in the *Paston Treasure*'s painted red curtain could very well have been recycled from a real red curtain.

If dried cochineal insects were the Atlantic's second most valuable item of trade, the most valuable was silver. There is no silver in the painting itself but there was a lot in the ornate mounts of the painting's shell cups. Silver had been extracted industrially in England and across Europe for millennia. Germany and Hungary had particularly prolific sources, but even they tended to be depleted within decades, so European precious metal mining involved rapid cycles of boom and bust. The shell cups' ornate mounts also contained gold, and since European sources were even smaller, for over five hundred years much of that gold had come from an apparently inexhaustible source in Wangara in West Africa, also the source of some New World slaves. Historically, this gold had been obtained in a mysterious system of 'silent trading' where neither party met the other but both left goods of equal value on the sand under cover of night. If either party thought the goods were not of equal value, then they could adjust their offering the next night, and exchange happened only when both parties were satisfied.[38] In the early sixteenth century the metal was mainly shipped by the Portuguese via the Gold Coast, but by the end of the century, the main sources had switched to Mexico and South America – both of which are purposely shown in the *Paston Treasure* on the edge of Sir Robert's globe.

Sir Robert may not have known exactly how silver and gold were valued in the New World, but, as will become clear, had he found out he would not have been too surprised. In the Americas gold was understood to be the sweat of the sun while silver was the tears of the moon. Male gold and female silver were also associated with the origins of the Andean ruling dynasty.[39] Silver and gold had such cosmological and social significance that indigenous American base-metal objects were enriched with them even when their colour was not visible. (This contrasts strongly with Sir Robert's shell cup mounts, which had extraordinarily thin veneers of gold over silver.) Andean metalworking was very sophisticated and was perfectly capable of refining silver and gold, but for ideological reasons metalworkers chose to integrate rather than separate their metals. In a world where everything – including parrots – was animated with divine and transferrable forces, silver and gold were 'divine' metals that 'gave life' to objects made from lesser metals.[40] This technical aspect of enriched metal alloys faithfully reflected the structure of the society that made them. Just as silver and gold permeated Andean alloys, so nobility suffused the whole body politic.

Indigenous Andean metalwork fulfilled diverse roles – from the symbolic to the utilitarian – in a hierarchical culture where, while all were not equal, all were equally important. All labour in Andean society was undertaken in a rota that included a significant amount of public service. The origins of this public service labour seem to have been religious, but the system, known as *mit'a*, was adapted by the Inca for imperial purposes that included agricultural and military service as well as infrastructure projects. These collective tasks were interspersed with private tasks in recurring rhythms that reflected the changing seasons and the motions of the heavens. They were, for example, tied to changes in the constellation Pleiades, or Seven Sisters, which helped predict El Niño and plan crop planting.[41] Such strange customs – whether accurately recounted or impossibly garbled

– formed the basis for the travellers' tales for which Oxnead had become famous.

The arrival of the Spanish changed everything in the New World. Spaniards were attracted to silver and gold for reasons that were superficially similar to the reasons they were already significant across the Americas – they were bright and shiny.[42] In the European tradition the two 'noble', or rustless, metals were also associated with the two brightest heavenly bodies – gold with the masculine sun and silver with the feminine moon. This is why Sir Robert could have appreciated the Andean value system. Gold and silver were scarce and were not particularly good for making most tools or utensils but drew their enormous cultural significance from the Neoplatonic metaphysics of light, the very same philosophy that informed Charles I's single-point perspective masques. In Europe gold and silver developed their economic importance on the back of a pre-existing symbolic importance, as material manifestations of light. After all, the ever-shining metals embodied the light of God's creative command 'Let there be light' and Christ as 'the light of the world' (Genesis 1:3 and John 8:12).

Based on their perhaps surprisingly similar indigenous metaphysics, the Native Americans greeted the Spanish in their bright, shining armour as almost supernatural beings. Indeed, it was said that the Aztecs foretold the Spanish arrival by reading portents in the sky similar to those that guided Royalists and Parliamentarians through the English Civil War.[43] However, the initial common ground between the Native Americans and their visitors evaporated very quickly indeed. The Native Americans appreciated other shiny materials, like European glass beads, and the Spanish appreciated the luminous nature of birds' feathers, but their main interest in gold and silver was as materials rather than as sources of light. The Aztecs described the Spanish as seizing gold like monkeys and stuffing themselves with it like pigs.[44] It is therefore perhaps appropriate that Panamanians dispatched some captured Spaniards by pouring molten gold down their throats.[45] Sadly, the rapid military and social decline that the Native Americans suffered seemed entirely consistent with their mythology. As their life-giving metals were stolen by the rapacious Spanish, their own culture's life force ebbed away. The metals moved out of the New World and some found their way to the workshops of Europe's silver- and goldsmiths. Their exquisite work can be seen in the mounts of the shell cups that generations of Pastons had bought from the Netherlands to grace the tables of Oxnead and, in turn, the *Paston Treasure*.

The richest source of silver in the Andes was a mountain that the Spanish called Cerra Rico – literally, 'rich hill'. It spawned Potosí, a town with a population similar to that of London, its scale due to ruthless Spanish exploitation of the existing *mit'a* system.[46] For 125 years the Spanish forced the male population into the mines for one in every seven years, transforming an enduring co-operative social structure into an intolerable burden.[47] Whereas the Inca had seen silver as the tears of the moon, the Spanish just saw it as a profitable commodity. Different attitudes towards silver perverted a flexible method of reciprocal work into something that resembled a sacrificial tribute, like the seven Athenian youths and maidens sent every seventh year to feed the Minotaur. The Incas called Cerra Rico the 'man-eating mountain'.[48]

By the time the *Paston Treasure* was painted, there was more waged than forced labour in the Spanish colonial silver mines for the simple reason that disease had taken its toll and the appropriate skills were hard to find. The metals were refined using a combination of indigenous, European and probably West African methods, since some slaves had been taken from regions associated with the old metalworking traditions of Wangara and the Gold Coast.[49] The availability of slaves shaped the way metals were processed, and in turn the scale of mining shaped the processing of slaves – human life and technology were inextricably interwoven.[50]

Most Europeans knew about the trade in American silver over the Atlantic, through Europe and ultimately to China. However, an approximately equal amount went from the Americas over the Pacific, via Manila, to China. And given the huge volume of traffic it should come as little surprise that collecting was a two-way process. By the eighteenth century, English silverware could be found in royal collections across Polynesia.[51] But Europeans were not silver's prime movers

– they were more like bit players struggling to become middlemen in a pre-existing traffic.[52] Dutch ships outnumbered English ships in the East, but all the European ships put together were outnumbered ten to one by Chinese junks of similar size.[53] The driving force for global trade was definitely in the East, although that East was not nearly as alien as many Eurocentric histories have suggested.[54]

Since most New World precious metals came from regions conquered by the Spanish, back in Europe, Spain initially reaped most of the benefit. Yet it rapidly turned into a case of too much of a good thing and, paradoxically, Spain's silver was in large part responsible for its downfall relative to other European economies.[55] Spain had grown on the back of satisfying China's demands with American silver and China's appetite caused inflation, the first ever global economic phenomenon. As profits dwindled, so did Spain. For example, just a few years before the *Paston Treasure* was painted in Oxnead, Diego Velázquez painted *Las Meninas* in Madrid for King Philip IV. The painting evokes the Spanish court's riches, but when Velázquez – the court painter – died in 1660 he had not been paid for seventeen years. The richly dressed Infanta Margarita had tantrums over food shortages and refused to eat a putrid capon because 'it stank like dead dogs'.[56] Amazingly, by the mid-seventeenth century, Spain had practically no silver. However, sudden enrichment did not inevitably result in deep impoverishment. At the same time, Japan was also supplying China with silver but it avoided Spain's fate. Rather than using its wealth to wage war beyond its borders, Japan consolidated internally and won autonomy.[57]

Something was bound to flow back to the countries that enabled China's consumption of silver. On their return journeys, European ships carried, amongst other things, blue-and-white porcelain for which Europeans had in turn developed an insatiable appetite. The *Paston Treasure* features one such imported Wan Li bowl, but although it started its journey in China, blue-and-white utensils did not originate there. Their journeys were much more circuitous. Some eight hundred years earlier, pure white translucent Chinese ceramics had been exported as far as Persia and Egypt where, like jewels, they were endowed with magical properties. Early modern Europeans also saw porcelain as a magical material.[58] Middle Eastern potters had tried to imitate it but failed, managing only to cover their brown earthenware with an opaque white glaze made from tin oxide. However, this new white pottery was still a major advance and it duly spread west, as majolica in southern Europe and as Talavera in the Americas. In 1576, a century before the *Paston Treasure* was painted, an Italian seeking haven from religious turmoil in Antwerp introduced white tin oxide glaze to the potteries in Norwich. By the seventeenth century, tin oxide earthenware had found its way to British settlements in New England.[59]

Of course, as they were developing these tin oxide glazes, the Middle Eastern potters had their own craft traditions to draw upon. They had access to a unique glaze made from cobalt oxide which, 3,000 years earlier, the ancient Mesopotamians had used to tint their glassware a rich, deep blue. So, around the twelfth century, Persian potters started to glaze their new tin oxide white ceramics with blue cobalt oxide. At the same time, back in China, potters were playing variations on the theme of translucent white ceramics and modified their processes slightly to make what we now call porcelain.[60] These two technical innovations took place quite independently, a quarter of a world away from each other. Then, in the thirteenth century, Genghis Khan swept across Asia, uniting the lands between Persia and China. Thanks to the great Mongol Peace, the two pottery traditions fused together. Middle Eastern and Chinese craftsmen entered into a remarkable collaboration initiated by Muslim merchants based in Quanzhou.[61]

The Muslim merchants knew there were problems with the Persian blue-and-white ceramics (the patterns could blur as the blue cobalt oxide diffused into the white tin oxide background). They also knew Chinese porcelain had an ideal surface for decoration and was strong enough to be made into the big basins and platters favoured in the Middle East. The merchants obtained samples of the cobalt oxide – it was sold as a medicine in Basra's pharmacies – and took Middle Eastern silverwork and carpets as sources for appropriate designs. (Middle Eastern decoration played with geometric design, symmetry and rich elaboration of surfaces, while Chinese decoration was more organic, asymmetric and with a dynamic sense of space.) They gave the patterns and the cobalt oxide to Chinese potters and blue-and-white porcelain was created in an aesthetic, technological and commercial enterprise that spanned the best part of 5,000 miles. Blue-and-white porcelain was a spectacular technical advance, but it did not originate in any one culture and was not an imitation by any one culture. The innovation required two strong and distinct cultures – one provided a key ingredient, the aesthetics and a potential market, while the other provided the base materials, skills and manufacturing infrastructure. They were brought together by imaginative and opportunistic traders. By the time the first Clement Paston rode his horse to market, the Chinese pottery centre, Jingdezhen, had become the largest industrial complex on earth.

Jingdezhen produced enormous amounts of porcelain, but you cannot eat or wear it and it is not very convenient for building houses or paying taxes. The sheer scale of Jingdezhen's output stretched existing mechanisms of exchange to breaking point. The Chinese authorities went to extraordinary lengths to try and accommodate the economic imbalances caused by porcelain's global popularity. In the seventeenth century, to integrate the vast ceramics workforce, they introduced a new tax system with a uniform silver-based currency. It was China's fiscal response to the rest of the world's appetite for blue-and-white porcelain – their own market preferred simpler ceramics – that fuelled their appetite for silver.[62]

Blue-and-white porcelain may have started with a steady stream from China to the Middle East, but other cultures were caught in the turbulence stirred up by the trade. For example, the ceramic traditions of Southeast Asia's archipelago were completely decimated by the flood of porcelain that flowed through their waters. There, the material – utterly different from the local earthenware – was deemed to be of divine origin and it took on enormous cosmological, political and spiritual significance.[63] Closer to home, Norfolk tin oxide glazes were also submerged by the tidal wave of superior Chinese imports.

As in the Middle East, Europe tried to imitate porcelain, first in the south and later in the north. European monarchies and aristocrats vied with each other but its secret was not cracked until forty years after the *Paston Treasure* was painted. An alchemist called Johan Friedrich Böttger had been forcibly put to work on the problem by Augustus of Saxony in a Dresden dungeon. The embittered Böttger hung a sign over his laboratory entrance that said, 'God the creator has made a potter out of an alchemist.' Nonetheless, he stuck to his task and, after seven years, finally made porcelain in 1708. A year later, Augustus opened the Royal Saxon Porcelain Manufactory in Meissen. China's millennial monopoly on 'white gold' had been broken.[64]

But, for Sir Robert, porcelain was still a hotly debated mystery as its materials and methods were both unknown.[65] In the thirteenth century, Marco Polo had said its raw materials were exposed to the elements for forty years and that 'when a man makes a mound of this earth he does so for his children.'[66] Thomas Browne summarized contemporary reports by observing that 'authors agree not'.[67] Porcelain had come to Oxnead from the other side of the world and it embodied a strange but very fashionable fusion of the exotic, the natural and the artificial.[68]

In terms of colour, strength, surface texture and translucency, porcelain seemed to mimic shells and mother-of-pearl. A century earlier, some Portuguese authorities had even said porcelain was made from ground-up oyster shells.[69] Oyster shells often feature in seventeenth-century still-life paintings, and although the *Paston Treasure* does not show any, it does depict shells from nine of oysters' cousins plus numerous pieces of mother-of-pearl. Several shells came from the Indian and Pacific Oceans and they would doubtless have accompanied porcelain in ships returning from China. The *Paston Treasure's* shells and mother-of-pearl are all in the form of precious vessels, like the Wan Li bowl. As such, Sir Robert's exotic shell cups are neither natural nor artificial but are instead another fusion of natural and artificial. Yet even as natural objects, simple snail shells and seashells were also something of a mystery. Significant effort was devoted to understanding how porcelain was made and, perhaps surprisingly, significant effort was also devoted to discovering the genesis of shells.

Shells were obviously made by snails, lowly members of the animal kingdom which also feature in numerous still-life paintings.

Sir Robert's education at Westminster and Trinity made him see the animal realm as a stairway that ascended from lower forms of life (like snails) through more advanced creatures (like parrots and monkeys) up to the summit, which was occupied by human beings. In theory, at the very bottom of the cosmic stairway – below all animals, vegetables and minerals – was the Aristotelian *hyle* or primordial 'matter'. At the very top of the stairway – above humankind and the ranks of angels – was the Aristotelian *morph*, or 'form'. In practice, though, everything was a mixture of matter and form, with lower life composed of more matter and higher life composed of more form. Snails, which slithered over damp land or lived under the sea, were mainly matter. Like their cousins, slugs, snails were soft-bodied, bloodless and relatively 'un-formed'.

Snails were cold and slimy, like mud. Sometimes they seemed animated – if only at a definitive 'snail's pace' – and when hibernating they seemed dead. As well as being physically slippery, they were also intellectually slippery because they were difficult to classify. And, as if to underline their seemingly primitive nature, they seemed capable of spontaneous generation, apparently being coagulated out of the moist earth by the warm sun. It was said that snails were fertilized by dew and so could symbolize the Virgin's immaculate conception.[70] When the *Paston Treasure* was being painted, the secrets of snails' sexuality had yet to be exposed to all and sundry; however, now the cat is out of the bag and we know they are hermaphrodites. They do not necessarily need partners in order to breed, so for observers like Sir Robert, snails' eggs just seemed to appear spontaneously and miniature snails simply emerged from the earth. This gave them an anomalous position in the hierarchy of creation. They seemed to skip the vegetable stage, going straight from the mineral realm to the animal realm. It was as if there was a mysteriously hidden stage somewhere between the mineral and vegetable realms – what might be called a 'naturally alchemical' zone – capable of engendering life.[71] As we shall see in the next chapter, Sir Robert was interested in all things alchemical and this may have influenced how he selected items for depiction in the *Paston Treasure*.

The hard mineral shells made by soft organic snails were obviously lifeless 'matter', yet they displayed very obvious 'forms' with a multitude of different shapes, colours and textures. Indeed, it was precisely because lower life like snails themselves possessed relatively little inherent form that their shells had such a wide variety of different forms. (To use alchemical terms, their diversity indicated that Aristotelian matter was 'volatile' if not 'fixed' by Aristotelian form.) The enormous variety of forms embodied in shells was therefore worthy of contemplation, which is why there were so many in paintings. By the time Sir Robert arranged his treasures on the table, shell collecting already had a very long history – it was considered part of 'busy leisure' and shell collections were evidence of time well spent.[72] Charles i's gardener, John Tradescant the Elder, had been a keen collector and his shells contributed to the core of Oxford's Ashmolean Museum.[73] Shells were recognized as little 'machines of the mind', objects that mobilized desirable mental processes.[74]

As objects for meditation, shells were often given as gifts. Jan Brueghel the Elder, for example, gave them to his benefactor, the Archbishop of Milan, and in his *Allegory of the Four Elements* (1606) they represented water.[75] Apart from their obvious marine origins, they were also associated with water through Venus, who was born in a shell and who reinforced their erotic overtones. Shells were also symbols of maritime travel, and – especially bivalves, like those on the silver livery jug held by the *Paston Treasure*'s servant – became pilgrims' tokens.

One of shells' most obvious features is a rough, weathered outer surface combined with a smooth, polished inner surface. As natural structures, they seemed to resonate with the cosmic architecture of Inigo Jones's Banqueting House, where the inside and outside complemented each other. Of course, the process of building houses and shells was very different. The hard shells mysteriously emerged from soft bodies, just as the organic bodies themselves mysteriously emerged from mineral mud. In a world that seemed to play with inversion – mineral becoming animal in order to become mineral again – the idea of inversion was an organizing principle. For example, it was a commonplace that the 'low reflected the high' and, in the words of royal physician Theodore de Mayerne, 'the smallest shows forth the greatest.'[76] As a masque had said, 'Outsides have insides,

shells have kernels [or snails] in them and under . . . everything, lies
a moral.'[77]

Lowly garden snail shells and exotic Eastern seashells had very
lofty associations indeed. They were central characters in the Book
of Nature and some even seemed to have letters literally written on
their surfaces.[78] Actually, in the *Paston Treasure*, the only shell with
legible signs is from an Indian star tortoise, not a snail. (It is to the
right of the globe, half-hidden by lute strings.) Its surface mark-
ings echo the hemisphere of the firmament, in keeping with snail
shell whorls, which echo the orbits of the planets. Yet shells did
not need letters written on them in order to have meaning. In 1614
Sir Walter Raleigh had described the whole world as composed of
'heiroglyphical characters' and in 1643 Thomas Browne said such
signs were not 'composed of Letters, but . . . forms, constitutions,
parts and operations, which aptly joyned together, make one word
that doth express their natures'.[79] Indeed, shells' variations on cones,
spirals and vortices were all meaningful.[80] Gentlemen like Sir Robert
saw them as material reflections of a rotating universe, and peri-
winkles were even described as being made on a cosmic lathe by the
divine turner's 'handsome hand'.[81]

Shells were also compared with the earth and they contributed
to the idea that the world was dynamic, ever-changing and unimaginably old.[82] The occurrence of seashells on mountain tops was proof
that what had once been low became high. This – like the emergence
of snails from mineral mud, and mineral shells from snails – was a
sign that the world was a realm of inversions.[83] Nature, it seemed,
was full of jokes, and part of Sir Robert's pleasure in contemplating
such enigmatic objects with friends was to see how they might help
one unravel and recombine the many twisting threads that made up
life's rich tapestry.

The way two fundamental threads – Aristotelian form and
matter – were woven in shells was particularly intriguing. Just as
music made mathematics audible, so the growth of shells made mathematics visible. Spiralling happened because the part of the shell
furthest from its centre grew fastest. Lengthening resulted from the
shell growing along an axis extending from the centre. The combined

growths made a helix and as it grew, it expanded. But those growths were just like the bass line in music, and were elaborated upon by more complex polyphonic rhythms. Pigments could be produced as the shell grew and if produced continuously, then spiral or radial lines were made. If pigment production was discontinuous, then patches and patterns were 'painted' that could even look like written characters.[84] Likewise, the amount of matter produced could change as growth proceeded, making ribs, ridges, bumps or spines. In the *Paston Treasure* the engraved shell on an eagle's talon is painted to make its genesis particularly obvious. All shells express complex relationships between time and space. Their shapes are frozen music, multiple rhythms played out and superimposed upon each other in a visible, architectural harmony. Sir Robert and his friends could appreciate some of the shell's intertwining rhythms while others were, and remain, a mystery known only to the 'divine turner'.

Seeing shells as if they were turned on a cosmic lathe encouraged parallels to be drawn between natural and man-made structures like gear wheels and clocks.[85] It also prompted contemplation of the differences between natural things that seemed to 'grow' from their own internal designs and artificial things that were 'made' to designs imposed externally by craftspeople. Of course, neither type of design, or 'form', was completely 'fixed' in practice. For example, snails that usually make shells spiralling in one direction can sometimes make shells that spiral the opposite way.[86] Just as Sir Robert had seen with the genesis of the *Paston Treasure*, exactly how something develops depends upon what is going on around it. And everything changes, because, once grown, the shell's form can be transformed – engraved and mounted by a craftsperson or crushed by waves and turned into a mountain top by mysterious forces. Given these interests in 'growth' and 'manufacture', natural wonders were transformed into crafted hybrid wonders.

In addition to the whole-shell cups, the *Paston Treasure* shows an Indo-Portuguese Gujarati mother-of-pearl construction. (It is just to the left of the Indian star tortoise shell, half-hidden by the globe.) The shell panels may have covered, or their shape may have alluded to, an ostrich egg, the collecting of which also had a long history. They were grave goods in ancient Egypt and hung in Greek temples.[87] They hung in mosques and Sufi saints' tombs, and were inscribed to be presented to holy sites.[88] They hung on chains with lamps in the Eastern Church as a reminder of the need for concentration and devotion.[89] Their significance came from the *Physiologus* (a popular medieval collection of moralized animal tales that had its roots in a second-century text), which said that ostriches hatched their eggs 'through the power of the mother's [concentrated and devoted] gaze'.[90] By the thirteenth century that tradition had spread to the Western Church where the eggs signified that people would return to God upon recollecting him. Eggs became associated with Easter from the fifteenth century, probably owing to Crusader and trading links with the Islamic world since painting eggs was an established Easter custom in Coptic Egypt.[91] With ostrich eggs, a 'mutually intelligible symbolic order' radiated out from religiously plural Middle East to Christian Europe, Muslim Africa and beyond. (No such historic links connect the Old and New World mythologies of silver and gold. They were either linked in prehistory or developed independently.) In Europe ostrich eggs then migrated out of the Church and one – carved with Charles I's coat of arms – formed part of Tradescant's 'closet of rarieties'.[92] And they have continued to fascinate. For over thirty years, art historians argued about whether or not the egg shown hanging in Piero della Francesca's *Virgin and Child* was an ostrich's.[93] Even if it was not, it still alluded to concentration, devotion and rebirth, thanks to the life-giving power of the ostrich's gaze. Sir Robert had ostrich eggs in his collection and the *Paston Treasure*'s X-ray shows that, in an earlier version of the painting, one may have hung in front of the column, above the servant's head.

The gilt silver mounts for such natural curiosities reflected their histories and their age-old medicinal uses, combining nature and art, joining God's and craftsmen's designs.[94] To drink from a mother-of-pearl or nautilus cup – in the full knowledge of its genesis – was to place upon one's lips a wonder of *cosmopoesis*. It was to drink from the universe as poetry. Of course, what the universe gives us to drink as our lives unfold can be sweet. And it could be all the sweeter for being poured from a green turban shell, such as that by the servant's head.[95]

But it can also be bitter. In fact, the creatures that lived in some of the most beautiful shells were highly venomous, and numerous collectors were killed by the snail that made a highly esteemed shell called, perhaps appropriately in a Protestant country, the Pope's Crown.[96]

Some of the items that Sir Robert chose to include in his painting were reminders of the bitter things he had to swallow. The hourglass, the clay pipe and the gutting candle, with its glowing wick and plume of soot, are traditional symbols of transience and loss. Their hints at loss are reinforced by musical instruments which have bows threaded through the stings, a visible sign that the performance was over. These features are common to many still-life paintings and the more affluent the scene, the more it seems poised on the brink of chaos.[97] Sir Robert's pleasure contemplating the *Paston Treasure* was all too often interrupted by the demands of the outside world.

Sir Robert had civic duties to fulfil. Charles II's court in London was a constantly moving target but life was also changing in Norfolk. The more or less predictable rhythms of a rural economy were threatened by changes in the wider world as global trade opened new markets and threatened old ones. Over Sir Robert's lifetime, about a third of a million people – mostly men between fifteen and twenty-four – left Britain for the New World.[98] He had to try and provide stability. Norwich's main trade was in textiles and was co-ordinated with the Low Country's dyeing industry, so it was not made any easier by repeated wars with the Dutch.

Great Yarmouth's main trade was catching and smoking herrings. Vast shoals of these fish lived in the North Sea but they were hard to catch even in the absence of Dutch warships. The herrings' movements were difficult to predict and they were hunted by following subtle clues in the Book of Nature. For example, detached fish-scales floated on the sea's surface in the shoal's wake, glittering like snow, and when the sun was in the right position, its light was reflected off the moving shoal, pulsating in the sky. When spotted, fleets of fishermen set off in the direction indicated by the flickering cloud-base and then followed the glittering trail. However, they could not necessarily just head straight for the signs. In order to catch the shoal safely, they had to navigate around another type of shoal, the North Sea's treacherous shifting shallows. Their livelihoods depended on catching one shoal and their lives depended on avoiding the other. Tracking the first type took hours, but tracking the second took decades and generations. For over a thousand years, experienced sailors had known where they were in the North Sea by 'sounding', repeatedly dropping weighted lines and retrieving tiny samples of the seabed. From the depth and nature of the seabed – its types of shingle, sand, mud and weed – they picked their way safely across a hidden, and dangerously undulating, only just submarine landscape.[99]

A book that sang the praises of herrings and herring fishermen called Great Yarmouth the 'principall metropolis of the redde fish'.[100] Its author, Thomas Nashe, compared the smoking of herrings to alchemy, likening their skins to the Golden Fleece and comparing them to the beautiful Helen, boasting that they drew more ships to Yarmouth than she drew to Troy. There was, however, a serious side to his jokes and method in his madness.

Nashe knew all about the contemplation of shells. He knew that 'small things we may express by great, and great by small, though the greatness of the red herring be not small.'[101] He also chose to praise red herrings because they were hybrids – part natural and part artificial, just like Sir Robert's shell cups – and they challenged the way the world was understood. Natural things, like fish or shells, were thought about in terms of Aristotelian form and matter whereas artificial things were thought about in terms of craft knowledge. Smoked herrings and shell cups needed both types of understanding. Nashe also chose to write about catching and smoking herrings because authors had usually ignored such activities. The usual description of places was called 'chorography' and featured geographic features and great families, and such chorographies complemented 'chronicles', the description of times based on wars and royal acts.[102] Recording commercial activities had no such pedigree. Nashe's satire was in tune with the changing times, since some decades earlier a German physician had written about mining and some decades later London's Royal Society would instigate the writing of a 'History of Trades'.[103] His local homily also resonated with what was happening with colonization of the New World. After all, a vast tract of South America was given a name that completely ignored its geographical features, its great families, its wars and royal acts. It was called 'Argentina', recognizing its main commodity – argent, or silver.

Sir Robert may not have ventured far afield himself, but he was something of an armchair traveller, outward looking and drawn to the mysteries of the unknown. The *Paston Treasure* shows one of the tools that helped him escape the burdens of London, Norwich and Great Yarmouth – a globe. It was made by Pieter van der Keere, who emigrated from Flanders to England and then to Amsterdam, where he worked for about forty years until 1630. It bears the Amsterdam and Dutch Admiralty coats of arms and van der Keere evidently hoped it would find its place onboard every ship of the Dutch East India Company. Although this particular design was intended for professional mariners, it also had a ready market as 'educational furniture' for gentry like the Pastons. Sir Robert's father, Sir William, had been in Amsterdam in 1643 and could have bought it at Janssonius's shop, since Janssonius re-edited the globe until at least 1645.[104] In fact, Sir William bought two globes there, because they were made in pairs and all terrestrial globes were accompanied by sister celestial globes.[105] Two globes are mentioned in an Oxnead inventory.

Maps were critical business tools for expansionist cultures, although to us Sir Robert's globe does not look particularly accurate – the west coast of North America is delightfully vague. Inaccuracies in maps could be a matter of life or death for sailors, and European knowledge of the Pacific lagged far behind local knowledge. For example, by the time Sir Robert's globe was made, the whole Pacific had already been navigated for over a thousand years. Ten thousand years before the ancient Greeks were making short hops between visible islands in the Aegean, Pleistocene sailors were undertaking epic journeys to islands hidden way over the Pacific's horizon.[106]

A century after Sir Robert, it was acknowledged that Polynesians' knowledge of the stars was 'far greater than would be easily believed by a European astronomer'.[107] Polynesians tracked 39 stars, plus the planets, along groups of seaways connected by shared rising or setting stars.[108] They also found islands using signs even more subtle than those that guided Great Yarmouth's fishermen towards herrings.

They harnessed the well-known superficial marine phosphorescence and a mysterious deep-sea phosphorescence that disappeared when approaching shoals, reefs or islands.[109] Nothing was written down and the numerous seaways – along with the means of compensating for currents, drifting or tacking – were memorized in ritual chants.[110] Long journeys required sailing through the day, with sunrise and sunset determining east and west, and noon determining north and south. On calm days, around noon, the way the sun's rays were refracted into the sea subtly indicated the direction of land. The sea's surface also held clues with long swells, shorter waves and 'knots' where swells and waves from different directions met, as well as patterns made by swells' interactions with islands beyond the horizon or with invisible submarine shoals and reefs.[111] The way these clues were used can be compared to the way the world looks from a moving train. The canoe was imagined to be static, the stars were like slow-moving mountains in the background, and the passing islands and swell knots were like fast-moving trees nearer the railway lines, all slipping backwards as the journey progressed.[112]

Compared to keen Polynesian eyes and enigmatic ways of sharing the significance of almost occult phenomena, the Europeans' magnetic needle may seem like a blunt instrument. Yet the needle enabled Europeans to develop a completely new way of engaging with the world – the only relevance your current position held was its relationship with your goal. Generations had become dependent on the needle and blind to the special qualities of the places they passed through – not noticing the clues that helped Polynesians find their way – because their eyes were fixed on some point in the distant future. Europeans saw the needle's constancy as the sign of an occult phenomenon and, despite everyday appearances, they had an unshakeable faith in the world's circularity. So, with heroic courage in their convictions and a compass to keep them westward, after months in the – to them trackless – ocean, landfall somewhere on the vast Americas was inevitable if death did not intervene. Again, with good fortune, sailing west from the Americas they were bound to reach China and, ultimately, home again. (Of course, indigenous Americans were called Indians because Europeans were initially aiming for India.) Actually, European sailors – or 'tars', as they were called in the English Navy – had the same skills as Polynesians. But their traditional sign-reading was being sidelined as a low-status form of knowledge while the gentlemen's or officers' instruments, charts, mathematics and needle became the accessories of a newly asserted high-status knowledge.[113]

Some form of reliable navigation, whether high or low status, was important because, as the canvas and plaster ceremonial arches of Charles II's coronation acknowledged, Europe's view of the world had become tightly linked to trade. In the 1660s it had been proposed that 'Money begets trade and trade begets money.'[114] However, contrary to the concept of *pronk*, not all collectors displayed luxury goods to show off their wealth. After all, unlike Sir Robert, most people did not actually own the things depicted in their paintings. A single tulip could cost the same as a house, and the owners of flower paintings did not necessarily own the flowers they depicted. (Identical tulips can be found across numerous paintings, each copied from a study in a pattern book.) In any case, once things were treasured enough to be worth painting, they might no longer be in economic circulation and their price could be completely irrelevant. Even when in circulation, price might still be irrelevant because they could have been gifts. For example, a flower collector in Zeeland contacted a flower breeder in Holland through a network of friends and sent requests for particular flowers along with gift boxes full of lemons, pomegranates, chestnuts, wine and other delicacies. Only occasionally did their correspondence mention money, and then only very apologetically, as if anything other than the mutual exchange of gifts would be insulting.[115] Above subsistence levels, one person's luxury might be another person's necessity and, whether originally purchased or given, once in the picture they are just there to be shared with the viewer.[116]

The most successful 1660s traders made lots of money as individuals, but despite appearances the whole activity quickly proved economically unsustainable.[117] Luckily, the exchange of goods – and presentation of images like the *Paston Treasure* – offered much more than just opportunities to make money. Collections of riches were important links between the worlds of commerce and natural history, so instead of just demonstrating wealth, some collectors used art and curiosities to demonstrate and share knowledge.[118] It may well be that knowledge could lead to wealth through informed decision-making but, nevertheless, knowledge was valued for its own sake.[119] Everything about the *Paston Treasure* suggests that Sir Robert offered its contents in a spirit of generosity as a place 'where friendship was celebrated'.[120] They were a social focus, like a chess game, tennis match or play in the theatre. It has been said they were 'intended as a bastion against time and trouble, an attempt to salvage a sense of stability and civility in a period of social and cultural disintegration'.[121] Such collections played an important role in the emotional recovery from Civil War. They were one manifestation of the pleasure to be found in, and the healing power of, engagement with nature.

Sir Robert was all too painfully aware of 'social and cultural disintegration' and knew that some of the pain was due to England's precarious place in a new global market. The *Paston Treasure* was painted as European exploration was waning and Europe was starting to define itself by its relationship with the rest of the world, especially a New World constructed from Iberian ideas of conquest and northern ideas of commerce.[122] Sir Robert and his friends had much to digest and the painting provided a forum for discussions about the new world order.

Today, globalization is all about the flow of money, and for us the contribution made by distant lands is mainly reflected in the (cheaper) cost of commodities, not in their (richer) content. For us, modern branded items are not enhanced by being assembled in some foreign land but may even be tarnished by local working practices. On the other hand, for Sir Robert the social value of his global possessions was precisely the fact that they represented contributions from strangely different cultures. He and his friends could luxuriate in the fabulous richness brought by globalization in a world that could still be the stuff of fables. They would have relished tales of silver that wept with the moon, of shells that echoed not just the sound of the sea but the structure of the cosmos, and of navigators who sat still while the world and the heavens slipped passed their canoes. The value Sir Robert placed on his possessions was very closely linked with the mystery or difficulty of their acquisition, qualities associated with great distances across the globe and great distances into his ancestors' past.

The *Paston Treasure* celebrated those journeys and is not a work of self-aggrandizement. After all, Sir Robert chose not to include himself or his home in the painting. With a flick of his finger he could have spun the globe to show Europe, England and Oxnead, but instead he made it show China, the Pacific and Americas. The globe's positioning suggests he wanted to acknowledge the origin of his riches, and that impression is reinforced by a poem celebrating the collection, which said Oxnead provided

> [w]hatever lies beneath the constellation of the bear, whatever is hidden in the lap of the goddess Thetis, or is concealed in the ample gulf of the sea; or whatever the sun's radiant eye looks upon, with the perpetual fever of the burning dog-star, among the foaming rivulets of the waters, or whatever the careful Indian or keen Ethiopian seek under the waves.[123]

The collection's ultimate value was as a magnet that attracted visitors, each of whom had different interests and saw different things. Even the tiny part of the collection represented in the *Paston Treasure* was the source of endless stories. People – both his many visitors and the 'careful Indian or keen Ethiopian' who lay behind the objects on display – always see things differently. Thanks to Jesuits like Matteo Ricci and Athanasius Kircher, Sir Robert was even exposed to, and had opportunities to learn from, the way things were seen in China's almost unimaginably advanced civilization.[124] As his life unfolded, it became clear that the 'careful Indian', 'keen Ethiopian' and Chinese ways of seeing things were very different from the perspective inexorably taking over European minds.

Sir Robert had grown up through the Civil War and suffered the destructive side of different points of view. But here at home, learning from his visitors and exploring the products of distant cultures, he could enjoy the positive side of seeing things differently. After all, seeing things from another's vantage point is the only way you can see your own blind spots. And, thanks to the extraordinary technology of oil painting, Sir Robert even managed to share some of his global collection with us 350 years later. In the tradition of his ancestors, he created an heirloom, a physical artefact that embodied the past and was capable of enriching the future.

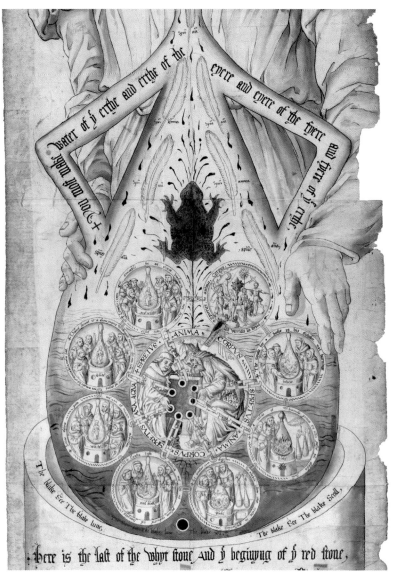

Double pelican flask detail from an untitled 16th-century 'Ripley Scroll',
a format associated with the alchemist George Ripley (*c.* 1415–1490).

five

Red and White Elixirs

The book from the well – Hermes, merchants, thieves and the crafts – the Royal Society – gunpowder, saltpetre and bird droppings – *aurum potabile* – iron-eating oStriches – making colours – the royal art – secrets – corporations – the volatile, the fixed and salt – *Atalanta Fugiens* – failure

Sir Robert's father died in 1663. They had not been particularly close. But perhaps that should not come as a surprise since, after his mother died, his father had abandoned him to go travelling and then sent him off to Westminster, two and a half days away. Nonetheless, Sir Robert was very much made in his father's mould. He had been born with a silver spoon in his mouth, but he paid a price by having to slot into predestined roles and dutifully follow a calling not of his asking.

On Sir William's death, though, Sir Robert evidently felt the need to assert himself, to make his own mark on the world and not just follow in his father's footsteps. He had travelled, but only to France, not anywhere exotic like Egypt or the Holy Land like his father. He had collected luxury goods and art, but the heart of the collection remained his father's. He had maintained his father's place in politics, but despite his best efforts, disillusion and frustration had set in. Even the pleasure he got from involvement in the *Paston Treasure*'s creation may have been due to a commission initiated by his father. In order to establish himself as something other than just another link in the family chain, he needed to find and wholeheartedly commit to a vocation he could call his own.

Six weeks after his father's death, Sir Robert received exciting news from Clayton, his brother-in-law. Clayton's letter mentioned a 'book of secrets' that he had bought from a Benedictine monk in Florence. He understood that it had been found hidden at the bottom of a well, sealed in a lead box and covered by a marble slab. The book had a key, three silver clasps and three gold clasps and was called *Phoenix*

Hermetica, or 'Hermes Reborn'.[1] Sir Robert's well-stocked library already had many books of secrets, including, of course, the bestseller written by his ancestor Sir John.[2] However, Clayton's mysterious book was particularly intriguing. Its title was a give-away and Sir Robert hardly needed an education from Westminster or Cambridge to recognize the call of the Greek god Hermes. He chose to respond to that call.

Overseeing the *Paston Treasure* and sharing the family's riches was stimulating but it cost Sir Robert little effort – vicarious creativity and bountiful hospitality were too easy. It was all too easy. The collection's many exotic objects came ready with their histories, the painter came with their skills and visitors came with their insights. He just received them all, comfortable in his familiar home. Emerging from the darkness of Civil War, change was in the air and Sir Robert wanted a challenge, an active and personal voyage of discovery. For that, he needed a guide. He chose Hermes.

Hermes was the god of travellers and merchants. The things in Sir Robert's collection had travelled great distances and passed through the hands of many merchants, so they came to him under Hermes' protection. Hermes was also the god of thieves, and considering the way European merchants conducted their business with the rest of the world, this might seem quite appropriate. However, whereas European merchants often used force, Hermetic theft involved cunning, stealth and trickery. Hermes might be called an 'opportunist', a word that shares its root with 'porter' and 'portal'. As a porter he carried things through portals – as a merchant he might knock on the front door, but as a thief he would quite happily try the back door. As well as being associated with trade and theft, Hermes was also the god of messengers, travellers who carried information as opposed to goods. Of course, one and the same person could be both a messenger and a merchant, like those who carried knowledge of local design practices from the Middle East to China and then returned carrying blue-and-white porcelain.

Hermes was also the god of music and craft. He was credited with inventing musical instruments and was said to have discovered the art of making fire, which was essential to metalworking and most arts, crafts and sciences.[3] His influence could be seen in much of Sir

Robert's picture. Hermetic trade was only a means to an end. For Sir Robert, the shell cups were silent messengers, carrying knowledge of distant lands and strange skills. Anything from afar had the touch of Hermes, bringing with it a slightly disorienting and magical effect. After all, shells are made the same way the world over, but a garden snail shell is hardly worth a second glance while a foreign nautilus shell is a fascinating thing of beauty.[4]

Imported artefacts simultaneously manifested three of Hermes' roles – they were crafted, they were traded and they had travelled. Today, the phenomenon of museum loans to international blockbuster exhibitions continues this Hermetic tradition of 'silent messengers' in the interests of modern 'cultural diplomacy'. Craftspeople themselves could also be messengers and play diplomatic roles. For example, Rubens, the Flemish artist who painted the Banqueting House ceiling, acted as a diplomat negotiating peace missions between Spain, France, the Netherlands and England. Indeed, as part of those diplomatic efforts, he gave Charles I his *Minerva Protects Pax from Mars*.[5] Sir Robert's only political act of national significance had been to propose a war fund to fight the Dutch, yet at the same time he was perfectly happy to entertain a diplomatic Dutch painter in his home while making the *Paston Treasure*.

Even if craftspeople or artists did not physically travel, they were still Hermetic messengers. They transported disembodied ideas down from the invisible realms of pure Aristotelian form into the visible realm of mixed Aristotelian form and matter. After all, it was a painter who transformed Sir Robert's vision into a thing of oil and canvas, and the same was true of musicians, who transformed imagined inaudible harmonies into played, audible harmonies. Travellers, merchants, thieves, messengers, musicians and craftspeople all needed Hermes' protection because they all moved between realms and crossed boundaries. In fact, the name 'Hermes' came from the Greek for 'stone heap', and such heaps marked the crossroads and borders that were the traditional points of commerce between strangers.[6] Boundaries – like rivers, mountain ranges or the sea – can be seen as the limit of one's world. But they can also be seen as ways of contacting another's world. The nature of a boundary is simply a matter of perspective.

Hermes was able to cross borders into strange realms because he had cunning and stealth and was the personification of trickery.[7] He called many different people to follow many different paths. Sir Robert was interested in the path that, by the seventeenth century, had become most closely associated with Hermes. For a number of years he had been mixing with people who were pursuing 'natural knowledge'. (They included Henshaw, the man who had warned him about Kensington's highwaymen.) Sir Robert's interest in the natural world made him join the Royal Society, a loose collection of mainly London-based natural historians, or natural or experimental philosophers. Many of these historians or philosophers were actually theologians; however, the activities they promoted would become known as science so, for the sake of brevity, I shall call them 'scientists'. The year his father died and he first saw the *Phoenix Hermetica* he was elected as a Fellow, a role in which he was meant to help fund the organization's activities.

The Royal Society had been founded three years earlier, one month before the slave-trading Company of Royal Adventurers into Africa was founded. The two groups had overlapping membership – although Sir Robert himself had no connection with the Royal Adventurers – and they co-operated closely.[8] Traders provided information for the 'scientists', who in turn provided intellectual legitimacy for traders, thus reinforcing the Hermetic link between merchants and messengers. The inquisitive and the acquisitive were deeply entangled. The *Paston Treasure*'s African servant therefore represents more than just human diversity; he also represents a connection between two Hermetic paths and the blood that was spilt to fertilize the 'new science'.

The Royal Society wanted Sir Robert's money but he wanted more active involvement. He had identified science as an area in which he could try and prove himself as more than just another link in the Paston chain. In particular, he was attracted to alchemy. This was another way of reading the Book of Nature, but rather than observing clouds or stars over which one had no control, it involved observing changes in materials that one could actively manipulate. He embarked upon a very daunting task with a very specific goal

– the ultimate alchemical adventure, the search for the Philosopher's Stone. The Philosopher's Stone is now dismissed as the stuff of fantasy, but in the seventeenth century it was taken very seriously indeed. In fact, Sir Robert had started his adventure before his father's death and had already been described as 'a great Chymist' at the tender age of 24.[9] Appropriately for the quintessential Hermetic activity, alchemy attracted followers for many different reasons – it could be a means of exploring one's self, a selfless exploration of nature, or simply a money-making operation. Given the financial difficulties that had dogged the family since the Civil War, Sir Robert probably had mixed motives.

Sir Robert's response to Hermes' call did not involve growing a long beard and becoming a hermit, because, at the time, alchemy underpinned business and supported European involvement in global trade. In the final analysis, the presence of exotic shell cups in Norfolk was the result of superior firepower, which depended upon gunpowder (which in turn, again thanks to Hermes, had come from China some four hundred years earlier[10]). Over those years – and even before – Europe had been the most persistently belligerent region on earth so Europeans had devoted much ingenuity to developing weaponry and honing warfare. Like blue-and-white porcelain, martial firepower was the result of mixing attributes from two cultures – China's technology and Europe's belligerence. Consequently, when Europeans eventually spread beyond their own shores, they possessed a distinct military advantage.[11] Europeans rationalized their hostility by blaming the heavens, and a contemporary said those who dwelt in the globe's northwest quadrant 'were governed by Aries, Leo, Sagittarius and the rule of Jupiter'. They were therefore 'independent-minded, liberty-loving, bellicose, pugnacious and industrious'.[12]

When Sir Robert was a boy, his school had ordered twenty pounds of musket shot to defend itself against Puritans. Yet that musket shot would have been useless without twenty pounds of gunpowder, which was a mix of saltpetre, charcoal and sulphur.[13] Charcoal and sulphur were easy to come by, but saltpetre or 'spirit of the earth' was much harder to find. England imported it from as far as Russia and North Africa, and earlier Henry VIII and Elizabeth I had hired

German expertise in attempts to boost their domestic stocks.[14] The Royal Society's secretary had asked the governor of the then British slave colony of Jamaica whether it produced saltpetre.[15]

By the seventeenth century, England had become self-sufficient in saltpetre but between 1640 and 1660 naval demand increased four-fold. It fuelled the Civil War and after the Restoration Charles II needed five hundred tons a year to fight the Dutch.[16] You could not have gunpowder without saltpetre and saltpetre was made by alchemy. So, when Charles II returned from exile, he brought with him an alchemist together with laboratory equipment in the equiva-lent of a diplomatic bag, exempt from import duties and barred from searching.[17] Of course, today's diplomats are more concerned with weapons-grade uranium than with weapons-grade saltpetre. However, saltpetre's – or potassium nitrate's – chemistry lives on in the devastat-ing fertilizer bombs favoured by those who eschew hi-tech explosives.

Shakespeare said 'villainous' saltpetre was torn from 'the bowels of the harmless earth'.[18] Conjuring up an image of the earth's bowels was entirely appropriate since saltpetre seemed to occur where three things coincided – earth, dung and urine.[19] In the 1620s there were grand plans to harvest the dung and urine of London workhouses in order to mix with earth and make saltpetre. The plans never took off, but searchers routinely took advantage of men's habit of reliev-ing themselves against walls and the fact that walls were often made with mixtures of earth and dung. So, people dug around walls' foundations to process the urine-soaked, dung-enriched earth and sometimes buildings collapsed, a hazard of which Sir Robert would have been aware. (When he was four, Norwich town hall and gaol were seriously damaged by overzealous saltpetremen.) Dovecotes or pigeon-houses were particularly favoured in the search for saltpetre, and a large one in the young Christopher Wren's garden was acci-dentally destroyed by excessive extraction of saltpetre-rich earths. The spectacular collapse of this twenty-foot building may have caught the imagination of the five-year-old future architect. In theory, those who mined saltpetre were meant to 'replenish and make up' the ground they searched.[20] However, the interests of state security clashed with individuals' rights, and in this new world of mercantile negotiation the rights of the individual usually suffered, as they had done with plague regulations. In practice, saltpetremen wreaked havoc and they provoked widespread civil disobedience. Until quite recently, historians have focused on issues related to state security, so we now celebrate warriors, generals and military strategists and have forgotten the saltpetremen. However, it is humbling to recall that for centuries many of the grand theatres of war we celebrate were actually built upon a foundation of pigeon droppings.

One of those interested in the rarefied alchemical theory of saltpetre extraction, as opposed to its squalid practice, was Sir Robert's friend Henshaw. He even wrote about gunpowder, or to be more precise, he plagiarized a German treatise.[21] In letters to Sir Robert, Henshaw wrote about a new source of Indian saltpetre that was, perhaps surprisingly, gathered from 'barren desert . . . where there are no pigeon-houses'.[22] He was very interested in 'dove-house earth' and thought there was treasure hidden in 'a dunghill' that could be discovered by 'a wise man . . . when a fool cannot find it in gold'. Earlier, he had written to Sir Robert about a 'universal sperm' that could be extracted from the ever-potent earth and he evoked the experience of 'every refiner of saltpetre' to argue its importance. Henshaw was deeply interested in the material he interchangeably called 'pidgeonshite' and 'surreverence'.[23]

Earlier in the century, the word 'surreverence' had meant 'extreme reverence'. How could such a sublime idea turn to excrement? The two meanings hint at radically different ways of looking at the Hermetic art of alchemy. Hermes protected those who explored strange uncharted territories, and pigeon shit, with its surprising properties, was a precious, if shadowy, landmark in the dark, trackless wastes that Sir Robert was intent upon crossing. Even now, trying to follow him across such mysterious territory, we risk getting hideously lost. The ever-shifting wilderness he was exploring dipped into the Aristotelian matter that underlay all minerals, supported all vegetables and even spontaneously generated slugs, snails and lobsters. It was the fluid foundation upon which the stairway to heaven rested and it seethed with potential, pregnant with possibilities. It was so fluid that those who traversed it did not leave tracks or footprints, they simply made ripples.[24] With such territory, it is worth stepping back and taking heed of the very real danger of not being able to see the wood for the trees.

From a respectable distance, some twentieth-century scholars saw alchemy as a dry, proto-chemical scientific activity. Others saw it as an obscure mystical pursuit. The two camps rarely communicated, like weary troops on battle lines drawn up in the nineteenth-century war between science and religion. But more recently, it has been recognized that there were many overlapping alchemies, spread across a spectrum from proto-science to pure spirituality.[25] At one end of the spectrum, acquisitive career alchemists tried to improve their patrons' military capabilities. At the other, contemplative vocational alchemists would have appreciated the paradoxical fact that in saltpetre the wishes of the body politic were enforced by the products of bodily waste. For well over half a millennium, that which delivered death was extracted from the earth to which we are all destined to return. The transformation of pigeon shit to war dead, by way of saltpetre, was poetic. And exactly the same cosmic symmetry or poetic justice suggested that the 'universal sperm' or 'spirit of the earth' extracted from a dunghill could save as well as take life. For example, Henshaw thought that Sir Robert's experiments with pigeon shit might yield 'the richest and noblest medicine in the world' next to the Philosopher's Stone.[26] For Sir Robert, the hidden qualities of pigeon shit were signposts that pointed towards his ultimate goal – the Philosopher's Stone.

In 1669 Sir Robert wrote to Thomas Browne claiming to be 'on the brink of a menstruum to dissolve metals'.[27] Such alchemical operations were crucial stepping stones on the way to his goal but they also had medical, as well as military, applications. Five years later he wrote that he had made a solution of 'gold as sweet almost as sugar'.[28] He was making *aurum potabile*, a traditional panacea. Obviously, dissolving metals, tasting and then self-medicating was risky. Chronic heavy-metal poisoning and a variety of dreadfully painful deaths were just some of the dangers that awaited the unwary Hermetic traveller.

Browne, Sir Robert's physician, was not sure that such medicines were worth the risk. In print, he speculated about *aurum potabile* in several contexts, including, maybe unexpectedly, in a text about

1. Paston.   4. Somerton.   7. Hengraue.   10. Gerbridge.
2. Peche.   5. Walcot.   8. Watsham.   11. Peyvir.
3. Leeche.   6. Berrye.   9. Hetherset.   12. Mawtby.

The Paston family crest, with supporting ostrich holding a horseshoe; from the herald Francis Sandford's *Genealogy of Robert Paston, Lord Yarmouth* (1674).

Anon., *Paston Treasure, c.* 1664, oil on canvas, 165 × 246 cm.

Anon., *Paston Treasure*, X-radiograph assembly.

Digital reconstruction of the *Paston Treasure*, initial version, with silver platter and correction of faded pigments.

Digital reconstruction of the *Paston Treasure*, second version, with unknown woman and correction of faded pigments.

Digital reconstruction of the *Paston Treasure*, final version, with antlers and clock and correction of faded pigments.

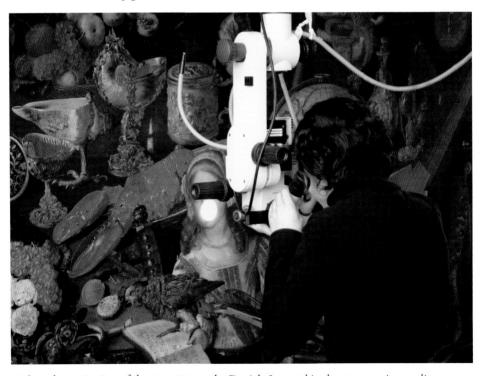

Technical examination of the *Paston Treasure* by Daniela Leonard in the conservation studio.

The *Paston Treasure* before removal of old varnish and overpaint, photographed in 1999.

The *Paston Treasure* after removal of varnish and overpaint (white areas correspond to areas of putty filling losses in original paint).

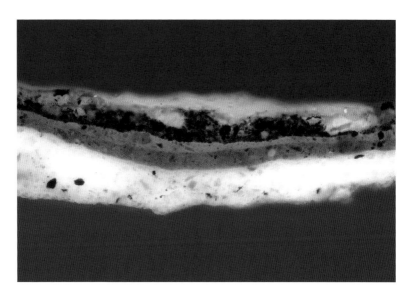

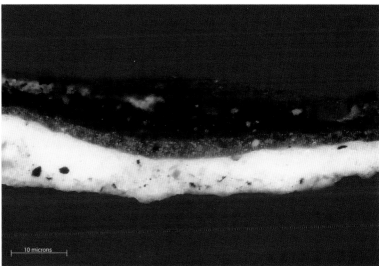

Cross-section of paint through woman and platter (delaminated from ground layer). *Top*, as seen under ultraviolet light; *bottom*, as seen in visible light. The lower layer corresponds to the silver platter (lead white, charcoal and smalt), second and third layers to the dress (vermilion followed by red lake glazes), fourth layer to the visible clock (charcoal) and fifth layer to the lute string (lead white) followed by varnish.

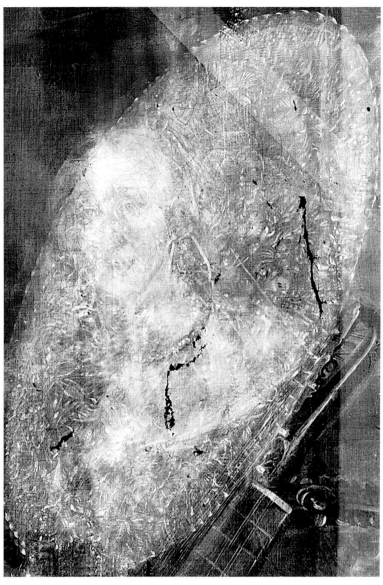
X-radiograph detail of the hidden woman and silver platter.

Macro-XRF of the woman and platter showing the distribution of mercury (Hg, red), copper (Cu, green) and cobalt (Co, blue). Black areas show either an absence of the three featured elements or their masking by subsequent X-ray-absorbent layers.

Macro-XRF detail showing the distribution of mercury (Hg, red), copper (Cu, green) and cobalt (Co, blue). Mercury (as vermilion) is in the parrot's tail, the lobster and candle flame and their now-lost reflections. Copper is in the parrot's body and globe's coastlines (as azurite), in the foliage and its now-lost mirror image (as a glaze) and in the gutting candle smoke (as a drier). Cobalt (in the form of smalt) is in the porcelain blue, the girl's eyes and in the roses and shells (as an optical whitener).

Anon., *Paston Treasure*, detail of the Pieter van den Keere globe.

Anon., *Paston Treasure*, detail of the score for Robert Ramsey's song.

Anon., *Paston Treasure*, detail of the 'Surrey' enamel cup that survives in the collection of Norwich Castle Museum and Art Gallery, Norwich.

Anon., *Paston Treasure*, detail showing the other surviving nautilus shell cups. The gilt mount of the one on the left is now fitted to a new shell and is on display in the Rijksmuseum, Amsterdam. The complete shell cup on the right is now in the Stedelijk Museum het Prinsenhof, Delft.

The River Bure flowing past the point at which its bank was once graced by Oxnead's terrace garden.

'sparrow-camels' or ostriches. Ancient tradition suggested that not only could ostriches hatch eggs with the power of their gaze, they could also digest iron. Browne acknowledged that ostriches could indeed eat iron but he queried whether or not the iron was actually digested. He speculated that the iron might play other roles, like the stones eaten by birds and grass eaten by dogs. To try and clarify the issue he experimented, comparing the fate of iron eaten by ostriches with the fate of other metals swallowed by humans – for example, silver was affected by stomach acids and went black.[29] He knew that gold passed through the body without losing any weight or density and concluded that none remained in the body. However, he did not discount the possibility that gold may have some magnetic or electrical properties – like lodestone or amber – with therapeutic value, a 'special cordial of great efficacy'. He suggested that a 'criticall trial' of *aurum potabile* should be made 'by public enjoinment' to finally resolve the issue.[30] It may seem strange that claims about iron-eating ostriches were deemed worthy of serious investigation by a busy and highly respected doctor. However, Sir Robert would have been more interested than most because, coincidentally, his family's crest featured an ostrich holding a horseshoe in its beak.

Iron-eating ostriches throw light on the nature of the journey on which Sir Robert had embarked. His expedition of discovery had no obvious path, for the simple reason that there were so many paths. Each one – no matter how apparently unpromising – might prove to be the right one. Sir Robert was navigating a labyrinthine landscape, not knowing where his chosen path might take him. Round the next corner might be a dead end, vertiginous drop, expansive vista or awesome revelation. Along the way, new paths kept presenting themselves and Sir Robert had to choose whether to explore or ignore each one. The further he travelled, of course, the harder they would have been to ignore. The quest could become obsessive because, if he stopped, he would never have known whether he had stopped just inches from his goal. Under the circumstances, Sir Robert would not have dismissed seemingly tall tales, like the one about the ostrich in his family's crest. They all deserved serious attention. And it turns out that iron-eating ostriches might even have been slightly garbled accounts of a perfectly functional piece of craftsman's lore with potential value for his alchemical research.

For Pliny, the idea that ostriches could eat iron was shorthand for their apparently indiscriminate appetites.[31] Yet there is more to it. In the eighth-century Norse *Thidrek's Saga* it is recorded that Wayland, the legendary smith, once made a sword that failed to satisfy his exacting standards. Perhaps surprisingly, his immediate response was to starve his chickens for three days. He then filed the sword into a fine powder, mixed it with chicken feed and gave it to his very hungry birds. He waited a day or so, collected all their droppings and extracted the iron to make another sword. But this too was substandard so he starved the chickens again, filed it down and fed it to them. This time, however, the droppings provided the metal for a third sword, Mimung, which proved fit for a hero.[32] Strange though it may seem, the chemistry of Wayland's apparently bizarre process is entirely logical. Filing and digestion would have increased the iron's carbon content and decreased its phosphorus content (egg-laying birds need lots of phosphorus in their diets). Starving the chickens would increase the strength of their stomach acids and the iron would also absorb nitrogen from urea in the bird droppings. Together, the changes in carbon, phosphorus and nitrogen content made the steel harder and stronger. The effect was verified in a modern experiment – or 'criticall trial', to use Browne's term – that fed iron filings to a single duck instead of a clutch of chickens. So, what looked like a dead end – an iron-eating ostrich – was actually an advance in the processing of steel. And Wayland may not have been alone, because a medieval Arabic source claimed that the blade of an iron sword that passed through an ostrich would become unbreakable.[33] In fact, Wayland's method pre-dates the modern industrial Gilchrist-Thomas steel-making process by over one and a half millennia.[34] If there was some vague recollection that, in the dim and distant past, the materials for superior weapons could be extracted from chicken shit, then perhaps the search for gunpowder's mystery ingredient in pigeon shit becomes more understandable.

Thomas Browne was interested in iron-eating ostriches because alchemy helped him make medicines. He and his friend Sir Robert could both buy verdigris from the same shop, one intending to make *zenexton*, the other to make paint. In the seventeenth century the Latin word *pigmentum* did not distinguish between drugs and artists' colours. An early eighteenth-century cabinet of materials that survives in Queen's College, Cambridge, shows the breadth of a chemist's interests in colours and medicines.[35] London's Royal Society was interested in the wide and seemingly ever-expanding variety of artists' colours.[36] The earliest volumes of its innovative publication, the *Philosophical Transactions*, included recipes for pigments like lead white and insect dyes like kermes and cochineal, as well as alum and methods of fixing dyes to cloth, plus mixtures of colours. Its Fellows also wrote about the ingredients for some synthetic colours, such as 'quicksilver', or mercury, and 'brimstone', or sulphur, both of which were needed to make bright red vermilion.[37] Sir Robert himself wrote recipes for the synthesis of pigments. One of them – for mosaic gold – was copied from John Evelyn, who had in turn copied it from Jerome Lanier, Charles I's picture restorer.[38]

Some in the Royal Society were interested in recipes for colours because then, as now, fashion was big business. Others were interested because the processes that made dyes and pigments were particularly clear – if relatively short – pathways through the apparently trackless wilderness of Aristotelian matter. Pigment recipes represented reliable routes through the labyrinthine possibilities of material behaviour. They were predictable examples of change in an unpredictable world. For example, artists knew that, after a month under horse manure, coils of copper turned green, giving you verdigris, while coils of lead turned white.[39]

Pigment recipes were also collected by physicians who – through concepts like sympathy and analogy – used them to consider how changes might occur in their patients, and about how people moved from states of sickness to health.[40] Some of them, like de Mayerne, the king's physician, were in delicate diplomatic positions and could use pigment recipes to think about how changes took place in the body politic. Numerous physicians, alchemists and artists all lived within walking distance of each other around the Strand, Covent Garden and St Martin's, London. Professional observations and 'tricks of the trade' were doubtless swapped in coffee shops, providing light relief to interminable discussions about the progress of plague or Anglo-Dutch wars.

Sir Robert's alchemical interests were inextricably entwined with the 'tricks of the trade' and journeys associated with painting materials. Artists' materials have always travelled. The ancient Greek silver-producing region of Mount Pangaeum was known as the 'haunt of Hermes' and the silver from Mount Laurium as the 'gift of Hermes'.[41] And, once artists' materials arrived in their studios, they were transformed by cunning or 'crafty' tricks that had an air of Hermetic magic. Before pigments could be manipulated by sleights of hand into images of fruits and flowers, servants and girls, parrots and monkeys or shell cups, some of them had to be made.

In his search for the Philosopher's Stone, Sir Robert could have picked up clues from the way the *Paston Treasure*'s painter prepared his materials. About twenty different pigments have been identified in the *Paston Treasure*. Of these, only about a quarter were unambiguously natural colours, another quarter were so highly processed that they might almost be considered synthetic, and about half were unambiguously synthetic. Many of the processes that made these pigments could have been undertaken by an alchemist and some artists' manuals actually described some of them as 'alchemical'.[42] Of course, artists themselves could also be alchemists.

One artist-alchemist was the Dutch painter and printmaker Hendrik Goltzius, whose apprentice, Cornelius Drebbel, had duties that included preparing red lake pigments. One day, he made a red from cochineal that did not use the usual alum extracted from slow-cooked shale but instead used tin oxide, the potters' imitation-porcelain white glaze. The result was a truly excellent red. Some time later, Drebbel moved to England and worked as an alchemist for Henry, Prince of Wales, who installed him in Eltham Castle. Drebbel also spent time in Prague, was employed by the English Navy and was famous for many inventions, including a submarine that was demonstrated in the Thames. However, his best-known invention was a perpetual motion machine. He was fair-haired, handsome and gentle-mannered but sadly acquired a reputation as a charlatan and ended his life in relative poverty, running a London pub. Drebbel died when Robert Paston was just a toddler. He had the wrong social background to be a virtuoso, but he was a typical alchemist, dabbling in many projects, some successful, others less so.[43] The red cochineal-and-tin-oxide dye was by far his most successful discovery and it was used in textiles and paintings right up to the twentieth century.[44]

Cornelius Drebbel's alchemical contribution to artists' materials was the direct result of his habitual Hermetic boundary crossing. He travelled from the Low Countries to England, to Prague and back to England, gaining the patronage of princes. He traded with the military, like the saltpetre alchemists, and he tricked with a fraudulent perpetual motion machine, like Ben Jonson's alchemist Dr Subtle, who fooled Sir Epicure Mammon. Such boundary-crossing travelling, trading and trickery could be very productive, and the combination of cochineal and tin oxide was the fruit of crossing the boundary between the worlds of ceramics and textiles. Tin oxide reds came to be used by painters because other Hermetic artists had already crossed the boundary between textiles and pigments. After all, the red stuff in the *Paston Treasure*'s painted red curtain had been extracted from red cloth.[45]

Tin oxide started as a ceramic glaze, became a textile dye and then ended up in paint, and it was not the only bit of Hermetic boundary crossing that contributed to Sir Robert's *Paston Treasure*. Cobalt oxide – the ancient Mesopotamian glazier's blue that crossed over to Basra's medieval potters and then to China's blue-and-white porcelain – also made its way to Venetian glaziers. It then started to be used by manuscript illuminators who took the blue glass and, rather than melt it, ground it up as a powder and mixed it with egg to make paint. From there, it crossed over to easel painters' studios and found itself in canvas paintings, this time mixed with linseed oil.[46] The potters' glaze became the painters' 'smalt'.[47] Just as the *Paston Treasure*'s painted curtains and Oxnead's real curtains both owed their red to the same insects, the painted and real porcelain bowl both owed their blue to the same mineral.

New sources for making smalt were discovered in Europe in the sixteenth century and these minerals also contained arsenic, an extremely poisonous material with alchemical significance in its own right. Arsenic could also be extracted from the mineral orpiment, which had many alchemical uses, including the purification of gold. Orpiment was itself a golden colour and its name comes from *aurum*, or gold, pigment.[48] Appropriately enough, in the *Paston Treasure* orpiment was used to paint the shell-cup mounts' gold while their highlights were painted with a pigment called 'lead tin yellow'. This pale yellow was entirely synthetic. It was made by taking the definitive 'base' metal, lead, and subjecting it to trial by fire in the company of tin and other materials that were together alchemically transformative.[49] It was a convincing golden colour made from lead – not quite the gold made from lead that alchemists sought with the Philosopher's Stone, but nonetheless a profound transformation and one upon which Sir Robert could meditate.[50]

There were many overlaps between the synthesis of pigments and the search for the Philosopher's Stone but the closest connection was with vermilion. The pigment and Stone shared the same colour and ingredients. Well, actually, the Stone was made from (upper case) Sulphur and Mercury, whereas vermilion was made from (lower case) sulphur and mercury. The pigment's ingredients were the 'vulgar' analogues of Sulphur and Mercury, which were the philosophical principles of 'fixed' Aristotelian form and 'volatile' Aristotelian matter.[51] The Philosopher's Stone was the elixir of life, and it might be significant that vermilion features most prominently in the *Paston Treasure*'s lobster, a 'lowly' life form that, like snails, was thought to be a product of spontaneous generation. Whether or not the choice of pigment was intended to reflect the lobster's origins in some 'naturally alchemical' zone somewhere between the mineral and vegetable realms, the pigment may itself have had unusual origins.

Artists' manuals commonly acknowledged that vermilion was made by alchemy. But artists were usually trying to make a simple colour, and if this particular pigment had any thing to do with Sir Robert it may have had a more complex genesis. The possibility is suggested because the colour has faded so spectacularly on the *Paston Treasure*. Vermilion is known to be unstable, but it is rarely as bad as we see on Sir Robert's painting. Could his vermilion have been contaminated with traces of other alchemical materials and continued to transform dramatically after being placed in the painting?

The mysterious alchemical landscape Sir Robert was trying to traverse had an extremely important third dimension that required profound shifts of navigation from one level to the next. The rules of one level might even completely contradict the rules of another level. (Were not the Banqueting House's interior and exterior opposite? Did not the small reveal the great and the great, small?) In addition to assisting with the manufacture of gunpowder, medicines and paints, alchemy offered mystical and suprarational ways of understanding the world. This spiritual dimension had very widespread appeal all through the uncertainties and anxieties of the Civil War and its aftermath.[52] Royalists and Parliamentarians alike embraced the so-called Royal Art.[53] References to it in contemporary literature shifted away from satire – a typical late medieval response – towards the idea of alchemy as a path of moral transformation, personal purification and spiritual health. Alchemy may have made saltpetre and gunpowder but, much more importantly, it was linked to the apocalyptic destruction of the biblical 'last times' and to the prospect of imminent worldly transformation.[54] After all, global trade and the Royal Society could have been seen as apocalyptic signs themselves because, as the end of time approaches, 'many shall run to and fro, and knowledge shall be increased' (Daniel 12:4). Sir Robert's treasures were the result of merchants running 'to and fro', while his laboratory was a site where knowledge 'increased'. There was deep anxiety that the urge to go further and to know more seemed uncontrollable and insatiable. For example, John Wilkin had estimated that, at 1,000 miles a day, it would take six months to reach the moon and that the 'Pleasure and Profit' it promised was 'inconceivably beyond' the 'Discoveries in America'.[55]

As a politician, Sir Robert had no choice but to struggle with external forces, yet he had chosen to also take on a struggle with internal forces. Whether labyrinthine alchemy would permit or forbid access to hidden treasures depended on the searcher's innermost personal qualities. Sir Robert had not been seduced by the siren song of profits from saltpetre, so he had not fallen at the first hurdle but had successfully negotiated the 'slippery' science's entry level.[56] However, gunpowder chemistry was very simple compared with alchemy's inner levels, interest in which was not at all incompatible with his Anglican beliefs. After all, Thomas Vaughan (brother of Henry, the metaphysical poet), a contemporary alchemist who wrote a history of magic, described himself as a 'resolute Protestant in the best sense of the Church of England'.[57] Alchemists knew the biblical prophecy that Elias would return before the Day of Judgement (Malachi 3:23). Indeed, some thought that Elias Artista had already appeared – they thought the man destined to reveal nature's secrets and unveil Utopia was the sixteenth-century alchemist Paracelsus.[58] The seventeenth-century alchemist Isaac Newton said little explicitly, but he evidently felt a special connection with God and certain that he was destined to reveal an ultimate truth. One of the hints was an anagram of his name that he jotted down in several places. Making 'I' and 'U' interchangeable with 'J' and 'V', he turned 'Isaacus Neuutonus' into 'Jeova sanctus unus', or 'Jehovah, holy one'.[59]

In such a heady environment, the book of secrets from the bottom of a well might potentially hold knowledge that could help build a keenly anticipated Utopia. Sir Robert was pursuing science for a better world, his own contribution to progress. But his idea of progress involved radical personal change and was quite unlike the modern idea of gradual social change. For him, progress meant transforming yourself to accommodate the world in which you found yourself, not trying to bend the world to your will.

This was the mysterious material and spiritual territory Sir Robert was exploring, the personal quest that set him apart from other Paston patriarchs, and he was fully aware that his adventure was very dangerous. Vaughan, for example, died in an explosion at his laboratory in 1666. At the University of Oxford, Dr Robert Plot called his flammable materials 'ignivomous [fire-vomiting] dragons'. He suggested that one should avoid 'these beasts' altogether unless one knew how to handle them 'ingeniously and gently'.[60] Plot's 'dragons' may have been figures of speech, but the image was not as far-fetched as we might think. For example, on his journeys between Oxnead and London, Sir Robert regularly passed near Saffron Walden where a nine-foot-long winged serpent was reported to have repeatedly harassed travellers through the late 1660s.[61]

Toxic and flammable materials were very obvious dangers; others were more obscure, as befitted a science with apocalyptic overtones. For example, it was noticed that Elias Artista was an anagram of *et artis salia*, 'the salt made by human art', another name for the saltpetre that wrought havoc across all nations of the earth.[62] Sir Robert saw connections between different levels in the outside world, between politics and the weather. He also saw connections between that outer world, the macrocosm, and the microcosm, the inner world. As he tacked across uncertain terrain, he knew that he was exposing his soul – as well as his body – to great danger. Alchemy offered access to life-changing forces, but these have always been fiercely guarded, which is why the laboratory's everyday physical dangers could be seen in terms of monstrous supernatural guardians. The path upon which Sir Robert had embarked could prove to be the path of Faust, the man whose quest required selling his soul to the Devil.

Prynne – the man who had his ears cut off for calling Queen Maria a whore – claimed that during the performance of Marlowe's *Tragical History of the Life and Death of Doctor Faustus*, real demons appeared on stage and some of the audience were driven mad. Even less partisan commentators, such as Aubrey, said the performances were so disturbing that the lead actor, Edward Alleyn, felt the need to atone by devoting his later years to charitable acts.[63] Prynne's demons and Alleyn's atonement suggest that Faust's story was taken to heart and could unsettle the mind. While we might think it was merely play-acting, we should remember that Charles I's play-acting was an extremely serious Neoplatonic tool of government that implied very real connections between the theatrical world of ideas and realities outside the theatre. In fact, both the court masques and the public theatre were influenced by the work of Elizabethan magus Dr John Dee, and were peculiarly English variants on the Hermetic tradition.[64] Theatre had deep religious roots and only moved indoors when street pageants were suppressed as the Reformation promoted internal devotion over external ritual. Theatrical stages – including the *Paston Treasure*'s tabletop – were places upon which life's dramas could be enacted.

The theatrical stage was an artificial place where disparate things could be brought together – telescoped in time and space – in order to explore their relationships and interactions. As such, it had much in common with the studio in which the *Paston Treasure* was painted and also with two other artificial environments that were being invented at exactly the same time – the concert hall and the laboratory.[65] The concert hall and laboratory were so closely linked that one Fellow of the Royal Society, Robert Boyle, felt it necessary to distance his activities from those of play-actors or musicians. He claimed that the natural 'works of God' – the subject of his experiments – were 'not like the tricks of jugglers, or the pageants that entertain princes'.[66]

Yet, however much Boyle might try to distance himself from the fun fair, links between the stage and laboratory were very real. A successful London play in the 1670s parodied experiments undertaken at the Royal Society, and the Royal Society's own experiments were thoroughly rehearsed, just like plays. There was a big difference between 'trying' an experiment in private and 'showing', or performing, it in public. They had to be shown in public, since natural 'laws' only attained their legal status upon being witnessed. Private trials were like 'undisciplined animals' and to be properly scientific, phenomena had to be made 'docile'.[67] Only when tamed were drama-filled and life-threatening procedures deemed fit to show, and they were still being performed publicly long after the *Paston Treasure* was painted. For example, Joseph Wright of Derby's 1768 *An Experiment on a Bird in the Air Pump* shows a parrot suffocating in the interests of either science or entertainment. Also, whether or not Boyle liked it, some experiments were just funny and the Royal Society's own patron, Charles II, laughed at their attempts to weigh air.[68] The king called the Royal Society's Fellows 'jugglers' and 'court jesters' and placed bets on the outcome of their experiments.[69] (He may have had an eye for the less than 'docile' experiments that refused to be tamed.) Eventually, however, the jester had the last laugh. It has been said that 'having begun his journey as a humanist in search of courtly patronage, the scientist ended it as a courtier ready to dispense favours.'[70] Boyle had made his laboratory into a very serious theatre of nature, and his rigour paid off. In their own constructed spaces, the scientists' conceits were transforming reality.

Sir Robert was amongst those virtuosi who developed the scientific laboratory as a place dedicated to the study of nature.[71] Like his commissioning of the *Paston Treasure*, it was one of his consolations of being at home, in a controlled place where he could withdraw from the world in order to better understand the world. The new scientific laboratories were highly artificial environments designed to isolate and explore a very small part of the world that lay outside their walls. Like the theatre and like painting, the idea of the new science was, paradoxically, a way to find truth through artifice.

By isolating a minuscule portion of nature within the laboratory, scientists seemed to have turned the tables on nature. They saw that reading the whole Book of Nature outside the laboratory had been fraught with ambiguity, which was why Royalists and Parliamentarians alike could claim the weather spoke exclusively to them. On the other hand, they thought that reading a tiny snippet of the Book of Nature in the artificial space of a closed laboratory allowed nature to speak to them directly and unambiguously.[72] As long as experimental ingredients and conditions did not change, nature always did the same thing. A century after England had been torn apart by different interpretations of scripture, it started to look as if laboratory-constrained nature would provide more a reliable guide to life. After all, you could not always trust what people said, because 'The Devil can cite scripture for his purpose.'[73] Yet you could always trust what things said since, for example, iron always fizzes in acid while, under horse dung, copper always goes green and lead goes white.

Well, in theory they do. In practice, sometimes they do not. Scientists reacted to this inconvenient truth in two ways. They varied experimental conditions and correlated them to outcomes (until experiments were 'docile').[74] Then, in a typically creative Hermetic manner, they moved the goalposts and changed the language. The word 'probable' used to mean 'provable' and still has that meaning today in the context of 'probate', the testimony of a person's proven estate. So, for example, through the Civil War 'probable connections' meant 'demonstrable evidence of connections' between the weather and outcome of battles. But scientists changed the word's meaning to 'having the appearance of truth', with varying levels of likelihood. 'Probability' used to be associated with certainty and acts of God, but the word was downgraded to being associated with the outcome of games of chance.[75]

Other language games proliferated outside the laboratory because post-Reformation and post-Civil War England had become very wary of activities undertaken behind closed doors. Some wished to exploit the laboratory's products and others felt threatened by its dangers. Sir Robert had to protect his work, but at the same time he needed the advice of others exploring the same territory. Robert Boyle navigated openness and secrecy using the 'principle of dispersion', scattering logically connected ideas through different texts.[76] The American alchemist George Starkey claimed to act as a go-between for the imaginary 'Eirenaeus Philalethes'.[77] John Wilkins wrote a whole book about encoding, encrypting and a 'universal' language intended to facilitate exploration and trade. He named it after the Roman version of Hermes: *Mercury, or, The Secret and Swift Messenger: Shewing how a man may with privacy and speed communicate his thoughts to a friend at any distance.*

Sir Robert balanced accessibility and security by writing in a mixture of English, French and Latin.[78] In one of his notebooks he wrote medical recipes in English, but alchemical ones in Latin.[79] He also used codes and ciphers. This was absolutely standard practice and even painters sometimes used codes when writing their pigment recipes. In the same notebook, Sir Robert's recipes for mosaic gold (tin sulphide, also known as Aurum Musicum and Purpurine) refer to the metal mercury by the planet's astrological symbol and to tin as 'Jupiter'.[80] He also used codes and ciphers when referring to politicians, just in case his letters were intercepted.[81] He used what many considered to be secret ciphers quite openly. There is even one in the *Paston Treasure* – it is Margaret's music book.

Musical literacy was relatively rare and, as if to confuse outsiders, there were three different musical notations. The musical score that features in the *Paston Treasure* shows 'staff' notation, which had already been in use for centuries, but there was also 'tablature', which indicated finger positions, and 'solmization' like today's *do re mi fa so la ti*. Since many musicians in England were foreigners and were also fluent in three different 'arcane symbolic systems', some people thought they were spies, skilled in cryptography. After all, did not the people on the moon communicate through music?[82] In fact, some musicians were indeed spies, just like the painters who doubled as diplomats, and Sir Robert's relative Edward could read English, French, Spanish and Italian tablature systems.[83] In tablature letters corresponded to frets and lines corresponded to strings, so music for a seven-stringed viol would have seven lines populated with sequences of letters. The possibilities for alchemical interpretations of such notations are implied in a contemporary illustration of a laboratory. This showed a seven-stringed viol along with seven metals and seven colours, which together corresponded to the seven notes of the musical scale, seven planets and seven steps towards wisdom. Henry More, the Cambridge Platonist and an enthusiastic lute player, also correlated the seven musical notes with the seven vials of wrath (Revelation 15–16).[84] All seven metals were used to make colours for artists and four of them – alchemically transformed – are physically present in the *Paston Treasure*.[85]

Sir Robert corresponded – with varying degrees of openness – with alchemists and virtuosi, but he did not get his hands burned with the dangerous fire-vomiting materials of alchemy. He seems to have been assisted by at least two people. In letters written over the course of a fortnight, Sir Robert asked his wife, Rebecca, to give instructions to William, his laboratory assistant.[86] He was also assisted by Richard Brickenden, who was mentioned in a letter from Henshaw.[87] We might call Brickenden an assistant but his relationship with Sir Robert was actually quite complicated. He wrote to Sir Robert after copying a version of George Ripley's enigmatic alchemical scroll in the University Library, Oxford, so he evidently made intellectual contributions.[88] Like laboratory assistant William, he may also have had practical experience – like the *Paston Treasure*'s painter – which would have told him what particular materials were 'apt and good for'.[89] Everyone knew that birds flew and fish swam, but those who transformed matter

– like alchemists and artists – also knew that even apparently inanimate things like rocks and metals had their own particular dispositions and tendencies (as revealed by their 'signatures').

Sir Robert's relationships with William and Brickenden – as well as with the *Paston Treasure*'s painter and a person who possibly taught wood-turning – were based on professional skills. So they had their roots in age-old professional relationships, like that between the fifteenth-century John III Paston and his farm manager, Richard Calle. However, while Calle helped make food for money, William and Brickenden helped make knowledge for money. Inevitably, the ripples created exploring Aristotelian matter spread, and they had ramifications at every level. The ripples shook established social structures so that Sir Robert's laboratory relationships were being forged in completely uncharted territory.

Never before had the rich employed people to study on their behalf in universities, and at the same time craftspeople were increasingly being recognized for their own expertise. For example, shoemakers could be the heroes of popular plays in London and the seventeenth-century German shoemaker Jakob Böhme was a great mystic philosopher.[90] Together, Sir Robert, William and Brickenden were a brand-new knowledge-based 'company', in the business sense that was emerging in newly mercantile London. Their novel affiliation was a social, political and economic mutation in the body politic and their relationship helped spawn a new type of body – the commercial 'corporation'. The old corporations had been grounded in cities, each with a mayor, judiciary and hierarchy of craft guilds, but these new knowledge-based corporations were not 'fixed' to any particular location. In time, when coupled with new mechanisms for sharing investment and risk, such intellectual affiliations would grow into corporate bodies big enough to ride roughshod over the body politic of whole cities and, eventually, whole nations.

This new, 'volatile' corporate power emerged because relationships based on knowledge exchange cut across the old boundaries that had previously divided society. But, to complicate things, these transgressed boundaries had also provided the frameworks for assessing people's credibility or creditworthiness in society. So it is not surprising that such boundary-crossing corporations opened up new opportunities for tricksters, as in Ben Jonson's *Alchemist*. Relationships amongst experimenters raised troubling questions about whether you could trust someone who gave you information for money. This is something we have now learned to live with, but in the seventeenth century William's, and maybe Brickenden's, words could not be trusted, simply because they were being paid. Sir Robert's word, and Henshaw's word, on the other hand, could be trusted because they were gentlemen who were not paid.[91]

Despite the complicated relationships they spawned, there was something of a mania for building laboratories in the 1660s.[92] Charles II had two, one for his official alchemist, the Frenchman Le Fèvre, and one 'under his closet' where Pepys saw 'a great many chymical glasses and things, but understood none of them'.[93] Robert Boyle called his laboratory 'a kind of Elysium' and 'sacred space', and access to laboratories could be controlled by placing them at the rear of houses.[94] The exact site of Newton's laboratory or 'Spirituall Chamber' at Trinity was discovered by analysing soil samples for heavy metal residues. It turned out to have been right next to the college chapel, just south of the altar.[95] We do not know where Sir Robert built his laboratory, or 'still house', in Oxnead.[96] Alchemists may have engaged in boundary crossing themselves, but they fiercely defended their own boundaries against others. Laboratories were the exclusive domain of gentlemen and their assistants. In the 1680s, when Oxford's Ashmolean Museum first opened to the public, the learned community felt their boundaries had been 'grossly breached'.[97]

Laboratories were complemented by rather more congenial coffee houses, nodes in a vast knowledge-exchange network which has been described as an 'invisible college' or a 'republic of letters'.[98] That network included Sir Robert and Thomas Browne. They corresponded about alchemy, exchanging alchemical recipes, including some written by royal physician de Mayerne. Browne also corresponded with Elias Ashmole, collector, alchemist and founder of the Ashmolean Museum.[99] Browne was close friends with his neighbour and fellow physician Dr Arthur Dee, the son of Dr John Dee, Elizabeth's court magus, many of whose manuscripts he possessed.[100]

Browne had also seen Ripley's alchemical scroll – another version of the one Brickenden copied in Oxford – in John Dee's library.[101] Thanks to printed books and ancient manuscripts, the written word enabled the republic of letters to embrace strangers in distant lands as well as voices – like Hermes' – from beyond the grave.

This invisible college provided Sir Robert with plenty of potential gentleman collaborators. Yet his collaborators were not all men, because, unusually, he included his wife in alchemical discussions, although it must be admitted that his contemporary Vaughan and the famous fourteenth-century Nicolas Flamel also worked closely with their wives. Despite the expense and the danger, it seems that Rebecca did not disapprove of her husband's alchemical activities. And her at least tacit approval is all the more surprising since one of Sir Robert's active collaborators may even have been their daughter Margaret. After she married, Margaret had her own laboratory and – in a book of medical recipes – she recalled making oil of hypericum from St John's Wort flowers with her father.[102] The sweet little girl in the *Paston Treasure* might be the 'sorcerer's apprentice' and the roses she holds may allude to medicinal attar, prepared with her father.[103]

Thomas Henshaw became a close collaborator and a letter described how he selected £5 of glassware for Sir Robert's Oxnead laboratory.[104] Henshaw lived on '£200 or £300 a year', so it is clear why he collaborated with Sir Robert – he simply could not afford to undertake serious alchemical experiments on his own.[105] The same letter mentioned getting another £1 10s. worth of glassware, so the total of £6 10s. was almost the same as the average person's total annual expenditure of £6 13s. 4d.[106] Doubtless other equipment was needed, as well as the materials and money for William's wages. Alchemical experiments could get very expensive.

Making saltpetre, *aurum potabile* and cochineal and tin oxide red were tangible spin-offs from the outer circles of the obscure territory that Sir Robert was exploring. They may have been profitable, but they would have been considered peripheral distractions for the serious alchemist who wished to get to the heart of the maze – to the Philosopher's Stone. In 1668, five years after arrival of the *Phoenix Hermetica*, Henshaw showed Sir Robert one of his most precious recipes. Sir Robert copied it down in the back of a manuscript that had once belonged to the king's physician, de Mayerne.[107] He called the recipe 'Manna' and said it made 'red mercury'.[108] It was a detailed description of how to make the 'red elixir' or Philosopher's Stone. Henshaw had got it from William Oughtred, who, less than a year before he died (aged 88), had boasted that if he had been just a few years younger, he 'doubted not to find the Philosophers' Stone'.[109] The recipe itself bore 'a striking resemblance' to Nicolas Flamel's fourteenth-century *Exposition of the Hieroglyphical Figures*, which had been published in 1612.[110] It was also very similar to a recipe in the *Phoenix Hermetica*.

The first five leaves of Henshaw's manuscript gave the recipe. It ended with the statement, 'There thou hast four ounces of our red elixir which thou mayest multiply to thy lives end. Thank God for it.'[111] The next six leaves reported an earlier, unsuccessful attempt and described laboratory activities in a diary. The first recorded date was a Saturday on the 12th of August and work proceeded when the astrological conditions were right, with planets in particular positions in the heavens. Sir Robert's brother-in-law, Clayton, estimated that the recipe in the *Phoenix Hermetica* would take more than five months from start to finish.[112] From correlating days, dates and planets, it seems that the previous attempt may have started in 1654.

The whole procedure revolved around the union of the 'fixed' and the 'volatile'. The fixed was also known as 'Sulphur' while the volatile was 'Mercury', philosophical analogues of the sulphur and mercury that artists united in vermilion.[113] The union of Sulphur and Mercury made the red elixir which was believed capable of transmuting base metals into gold. Although the workings of alchemical transmutation were unseen, transmutation seemed to be at work in everyday life. After all – for some – bread and wine were regularly transformed into the body and blood of Christ, and – for all – bread and wine were transformations, thanks to the mysteries of baking and brewing. If yeast raised bread and turned sugar into alcohol, then why should not a yeast-like Philosopher's Stone raise the base to nobility, turn lead into gold and thereby end Sir Robert's money troubles?

Alchemical transmutation assumed that metals were not inert. This assumption was reinforced by events in the sixteenth and seventeenth centuries which suggested that metals had mysteriously started to influence the course of human history in more subtle ways than simply inspiring Spanish lust for New World silver and gold. For example, silver and gold appeared to have taken on lives of their own after they were torn from the New World and released into global circulation. When they were in the hands of the Inca, the world economy had been relatively stable. However, as soon as the Inca lost their stewardship of silver, the world suffered the previously unknown effects of inflation. This phenomenon is now so familiar to us that we take it for granted – and even worry at its absence – but inflation was a brand-new experience in the early modern world and some even denied its very possibility. It was an extremely disquieting phenomenon because it suggested that silver did not simply facilitate exchange. Instead, silver seemed to have powers of its own and its behaviour could change people's lives across the globe.[114]

So, Sir Robert's recipe for 'Manna' was playing with extraordinarily potent cosmic forces. It all hinged upon a mysterious salt that mediated between the 'fixed' and the 'volatile'. Clues to the exact identity of that salt lay hidden in the maze and opinions varied. Brickenden gave Sir Robert details of 'a salt for infinite health and riches' that could be extracted from drops of dew gathered in May.[115] But many, including Charles II's alchemist, thought the 'universal salt' was gunpowder's key ingredient – saltpetre. Sir Robert's recipe for making the salt, *Spiritus salis*, was evidently important because he wrote it in Latin.[116] Henshaw evidently held it in great esteem because he signed one of his letters to Sir Robert as 'your faithful old servant, Halophilus'.[117] His *nom de plume* meant 'salt lover'.

The salts were thought to act as magnets that attracted the 'principle of volatility' or 'philosophical Mercury'. In earlier letters, Henshaw mentioned a 'fixed salt of Saturne' but in later experiments other salts, like saltpetre, were also used.[118] The principle of volatility or the philosophical Mercury had to be extracted from something called a 'sublimate'. All the salts, as well as the sublimate, had to be prepared before the process could start, and when ready they were pure white crystals. They were added to water, stirred a few times and then vanished into a completely clear solution. This solution was poured into a round glass flask – sometimes called the Philosopher's Egg – and heated for forty days (the duration of Noah's flood, Jesus' temptation in the desert and quarantine for plague victims). Slowly, as if by magic, things started to appear in the clear, sealed glass egg.

The first version – using the salt of Saturn – would have produced a reflective silver liquid resting at the bottom of a clear liquid filled with visible white crystals, like a reflective pool in a snow-dome.[119] The silver liquid metal was mercury, and the snow-dome crystals may have been either the 'white elixir' or 'Virgin's milk'. The process was described so cryptically that we cannot really be sure of much but, chemically, 'Virgin's milk' was related to the ubiquitous 'alchemical' artists' pigment, lead white.[120]

This white elixir marked the half-way stage of the alchemical journey. Its appearance in the glass would have been met with elation. Sir Robert had started with something black – lead metal for the salt of Saturn version or urine-soaked, dung-enriched soil for the saltpetre version – and he had managed to turn it into something white. He had successfully transmuted mortification into purity. The next phase of the recipe was to turn the white elixir into the red elixir. The final red elixir, however, never appeared in the Philosopher's Egg. Another attempt would have to await the appropriate planetary conjunctions.

To understand why it did not appear, we have to consider the nature of his experiment. Sir Robert managed to make the white elixir as well as drugs and pigments. In fact, alchemical successes in military, medical and colour technologies were so widespread they encouraged the ruthless exploitation of nature. Francis Bacon compared nature to a lion that, when caged, could be safely 'vexed'.[121] Following Bacon, many saw science as a cold and impersonal way of representing and manipulating reality. But more recently, modern science has been described as a 'performance' in which equipment works across the 'border' between scientists and the world (the scientists having withdrawn from the world into their laboratories). As the performance unfolds, repeatedly criss-crossing the border, the materials under study and the person studying them are both changed. First, the materials are subjected to the scientists' experiments, then the scientists are subjected to materials' unpredictable responses. There is a give and take between the people and the things they study with each gradually becoming 'tuned' to the other, but never quite knowing what will come next as the experiments proceed. The scientific experiment has been described as a 'mangle' through which the experimenter and the experimented upon eventually emerge inextricably entwined.[122]

A very similar idea underpinned traditional apprenticeships, which could last seven years at formative stages of life. Master craftsmen knew that working with clay 'made' the potter, just as lead made the plumber and gold, the goldsmith. Sir Robert would have understood this completely. He was steeped in the tradition of experiment as theatrical performance and he understood that border crossing – from observer to observed and back again – was why the Book of Nature was open to so many readings.[123] Anyone's reading of the world was bound to be coloured by their own reflection in the mirror of the world. In the fullness of time, the Royal Society's belief that isolated laboratory experiments were immune from ambiguity and scripture-like multiple interpretations would prove overly optimistic. The enduring entanglement of experimenter and the experimented upon revealed itself in the quantum world with Heisenberg's uncertainty principle, wave-particle duality, Bell's theorem and more.

The successful military, medical and colour technologies could be seen as products of the alchemical labyrinth's outer circles. The territory Sir Robert explored could also be compared to a mountain, with military, medical and colour technologies as fruits of the surrounding foothills. Then, the red elixir at the heart of the labyrinth would correspond to the mountain's summit and to get there you had to raise your game. The spiritual dimension became increasingly important and, as one adage put it, 'only the true can reach the truth.' Perhaps the failure was with Sir Robert's character rather than with the chemicals in the glass vessel. Unless the experimenter's body, soul and spirit were in tune with each other, then there was no hope of being in tune with the rest of the universe.

Sir Robert continued to experiment for decades, but the red elixir remained elusive. None of the ripples emanating from his laboratory materialized into gold. The failure of this extraordinarily expensive, time-consuming and hazardous experiment must have been devastating. Understandably, it caused rifts between Sir Robert, Clayton and Henshaw. Once upon a time, letters had been encouraging and full of confidence, but slowly their tone changed as doubts crept in. Defensively, Henshaw claimed to have faithfully acquainted Sir Robert with 'all the real or seeming truths [he] could discover in so obscure and winding a labyrinth'.[124] There were also recriminations about details that may have been withheld or spoken about too openly. If you were not very careful, alchemy could transmute friendship into strife. Its 'ignivomous dragons' took many forms.

While details were shared cautiously, the underlying principles were elaborated upon openly in numerous texts; indeed, their publication multiplied tenfold between 1650 and 1680.[125] One such was *Atalanta fugiens* by Michael Maier, a contemporary of Drebbel and one-time fellow alchemist to the court of Rudolph II in Prague. This treatise expounded upon the relationships of sulphur, mercury and salt. It was essential background reading for trying to understand why the recipe may have failed. Maier's book title meant 'Atalanta Fleeing'. It is almost certainly no coincidence that the *Paston Treasure* conspicuously displays a mounted shell cup with a very clear image of Atalanta in the act of running.[126] It is as if Sir Robert had put this shell in the painting to draw attention to a book that guided his alchemical journey.

Atalanta fugiens was divided into fifty parts, each with an epigraph, most which were mythological and required a very good grounding in the classics, which, thanks to Westminster and Trinity, Sir Robert possessed. Some of the non-mythological epigraphs are quite straightforward. For example: 'Nature, reason, experience and study must be the guide, staff, spectacles and lamp for those following chemical affairs' (Epigraph 42). Others are more obscure: 'Two eagles come together, one from the East, the other from the West' (Epigraph 47). Most of the required background knowledge has now been lost, but Sir Robert would still have been able to at least start to decipher *Atalanta fugiens*. For example, when reading 'Put a toad to a woman's breast that she may suckle him till she die and he becomes gross with her milk' (Epigraph 5), he would have had a few solid reference points from which to start. He would have known that the 'toad' may have had something to do with the extraction of disease or the spontaneous generation of low forms of life. He would also have known that the 'woman's milk' may have had something to do with his recipe's snow-dome-like insoluble white crystals or with the artists' pigment lead white.[127] Yet even with all his background knowledge, he was still unable to journey beyond the white elixir to obtain the red elixir. (The section of Ripley Scroll at the front of this chapter shows a toad in a 'double pelican' glass-flask; the text beneath it reads: 'here is the last of the whyt stone And ye beginyng of ye red stone'.)

It would appear that Sir Robert's quest failed to reach its goal. Certainly, he did not make the Philosopher's Stone or gold. However, he may have found riches, albeit not in the way he initially anticipated.

Sir Robert and Rebecca struggled through a hostile political landscape. They must have felt like an embattled couple taking on the whole world. In marked contrast, his experiments earned him fellowship with a group of like-minded friends. He belonged to an invisible college dedicated to exploring the unknown and sharing whatever they found, no matter how strange. He was a founding member of an active network of Norfolk scientists that thrived for over 150 years as well as the Royal Society, which continues to thrive.[128] Experiments in separate laboratories (and artists' studios) each found little pathways through nature, and, through letters and social engagements, virtuosi like Sir Robert were joining up all those little pathways and, slowly but surely, starting to map nature's labyrinth. Together, the community to which he belonged was laying the foundations for a future that would, in time, make a radically different world. In the 350 years since his brother-in-law bought the book found at the bottom of a well, the scientific enterprise that Sir Robert and his friends were building has flourished beyond belief. He cannot have known when he started in the shadow of Civil War, but in that respect his quest was an outstanding success.

As a postscript, it must be observed that Sir Robert, Clayton, Henshaw, William and Brickenden's collective efforts in Oxnead do not seem to have contributed much significant detail to modern science's view of the world. However, science's strength depends on keeping an open mind. The success of the scientific enterprise depends on acknowledging that, for example, the iron-eating ostriches in Sir Robert's family crest may indeed have held one of nature's secrets and even that, over a thousand years earlier, Wayland the smith may have been privy to that secret. Even today, no one knows where the next piece of the jigsaw will be found. For example, a delicate Amazonian herb whose habitat is endangered by logging may be the source of a drug that cures cancer. Finding that plant depends on keeping an open mind and exploring other cultures' remedies, the premise of scientific disciplines like ethnobotany and ethnopharmacology. Of course, there is also the question of how those cultures discovered the herb's properties in the first place. Perhaps shaman-like *nagualli* found them while possessed by the spirit of a parrot. And perhaps European myths about heroes like Sigurd – who killed a dragon using another of Wayland's swords and subsequently understood the language of the birds – hint that our own culture once had similar insights.[129] Today, some people still say 'a little bird told me [a secret]', but Wayland did not get his metalworking secrets from his chickens; he acquired them while living with two dwarves.[130] However, Wayland did once make a contraption from birds' feathers that allowed him to fly to freedom, away from an ill-disposed king to settle in a farm where he and the king's daughter had a child.[131] Perhaps he too was a shaman.

Such myths – like the almost unbelievable realities of Polynesian navigation – suggest that modern science provides just one of many possible routes through nature's labyrinth. In other words, it is possible that Sir Robert's cryptically documented labours in his Oxnead laboratory may yet prove fruitful.[132] His alchemy represents a path that others may have chosen not to follow, but it remains there, ready to be picked up again, to lead who knows where.

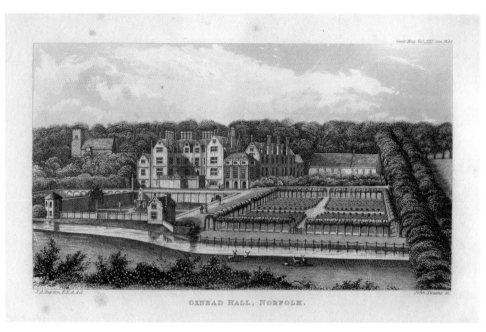

'Oxnead Hall, Norfolk', John Swaine after John Adey Repton,
from *The Gentleman's Magazine* (January 1844).

six

The Scattering

Ciphers – Customs Farms – Robert's childhood gift – hospitality – Charles ii's visit – food and diets – melancholy – Charles ii's daughter – party politics – 1st Earl of Yarmouth – William Paston – Gough's pews – James ii, William and Mary – Walpole and Catherine the Great – recycling

According to modern science, lead cannot be transmuted into gold, and Sir Robert's long and extraordinarily expensive alchemical experiment was destined to fail. However, as we have seen, the science of his day was not quite so sure. There were some in his circle who warned him against the quest and some may even have thought it rather foolish. None, however, would have gone so far as calling him 'a Paston fool' – he was not a victim of the Bromholme curse. On the other hand, he could reasonably be accused of being unrealistic, or at least too idealistic, in his alchemical adventures. But at least he was true to himself, since he was also idealistic in the political arena.

The impressionable teenage Royalist had been acutely affected by Charles i's execution, yet if he had been tempted to think Oliver Cromwell was a monster who had been overcome, he soon learned that he was wrong. Cutting off heads – whether from living monarchs or disinterred corpses – changed little because, hydra-like, the body politic simply sprouted more heads. Like all bodies, the body politic keeps changing, and those who want to ride it have to keep up with its twists and turns. In many respects, the political landscape that Sir Robert had to navigate was more complex than that of his ancestors. Centuries ago, as the Pastons struggled through the Wars of the Roses, they sought patronage by attaching themselves to the limbs of a body with either a Lancastrian or a Yorkist head. When the head changed, Sir Robert's ancestors repositioned themselves as the body politic mutated into something with a broadly similar structure. However, the competing forces in Sir Robert's time were very different. On the one hand, there was the familiar shape of a monarchy

– this time with a Stuart head – and on the other was the new and constantly shape-shifting parliamentary organism.

Sir Robert's approach to politics was deeply coloured by alchemy. For him, politics engaged in the workings of history – God's action in the moral world – just as alchemy engaged in the workings of matter, which were God's actions in the natural world.[1] In the natural world, order always seemed to emerge from chaos, so he had every reason to be optimistic after the traumatic upheavals of his youth. Sir Robert remained politically active all through his alchemical experimentation, and if one activity would not produce gold, then ultimately maybe the other would do so, from King Charles II. For the Pastons, the king was a living breathing 'hieroglyph' that pointed towards the end of their money troubles.

Alchemy had been Sir Robert's true calling, but politics was Rebecca's calling and they worked well as a team, conferring in coded letters when separated. Luckily for us, their ciphers were quite old-fashioned. They did not use the complex systems that John Wilkins recommended in his *Mercury, or, The Secret and Swift Messenger*. Nor did they use the new pocket-sized digital gadgets that Samuel Morland designed to undertake mathematical calculations and encrypt alphabets. Morland called them 'digital' because their mechanisms were manipulated with digits, or fingers. They were made from silver, brass and crystal by clockmakers like Humphrey Adamson and were advertised in 1666 for £3 10s., making them comparable to today's top-of-the-range mobile phones.[2]

One of the Pastons' simple ink-on-paper ciphers offers a clue to what they thought of their king. The key for coded letters sent in the late 1670s contains mainly alchemical and astrological symbols that represented thirty people, from the king downwards. As an alchemist, Sir Robert knew very well that the king was a solar figure, associated with fire and gold, while the queen was a lunar figure, associated with water and silver. (In this respect, European and Andean metallurgical and dynastic symbolisms were in perfect accord.) It is therefore quite surprising that their cipher did not represent the king with symbols for either gold – a circle with a dot in the centre – or fire, an upright triangle. Instead, Sir Robert and Rebecca chose to represent him with the symbol of fire's exact opposite, water, an upturned triangle.[3] Their cipher for the king was contrary to what symbolism the world over would have led one to expect. Indeed, in an earlier set of correspondence that used different ciphers, the upturned triangle referred, much more appropriately, to Lady Danby, an influential woman whom they courted assiduously.[4]

Yet the Pastons were far from ignorant, so there must have been reasons for their apparent idiosyncrasy. In terms of Sir Robert's *Phoenix Hermetica* and 'Manna' recipe, their hieroglyph for Charles II – the upturned triangle – referred to water or the 'volatile'. In order to make the red elixir or gold, this had to be united with fire or the 'fixed', which was symbolized by the upright triangle. However, none of the other 29 people in their cipher key was represented by an upright triangle. This seems even stranger than inverting the usual associations of kingship. It was like having a list of symbols that included *yin* but not *yang*, even though Sir Robert knew very well that the 'volatile' could not exist without the 'fixed', just as *yin* could not exist without *yang*. The absence of an upright triangle in the cipher suggests that the person who represented the 'fixed' would never appear in the text of any letters. Perhaps one of the letter writers themselves represented the 'fixed principle'? If so, the family's political 'fixer' would have been Rebecca – the ambitious daughter of an ambitious merchant and faithful follower in the tradition of strong Paston women, like the indomitable fifteenth-century Margaret who took on mercenaries and marauding duchesses.

Their late 1670s cipher suggests that Sir Robert and Rebecca saw Charles II as unstable and unpredictable, a moving target that needed to be pinned down if they were ever to capitalize on court connections. Robert was knighted in 1660 but progress up the ranks had been slow. Sir Robert's political big break – and his chance to come back to the king's attention – happened in 1664, the year after his father's death. As luck would have it, Sir Robert's established position and apparent lack of political ambition made him an attractively independent-looking mouthpiece for the administration.[5]

Chief Minister Edward Hyde, the First Earl of Clarendon, approached Sir Robert and asked if he would propose the then enormous sum of £2,500,000 to supply the king in preparation for war with the Dutch. Whatever appearances may have suggested, Sir Robert did not lack ambition and saw this as an excellent opportunity to raise his profile. He accepted the challenge and proposed the unprecedented sum to the Commons. The House was temporarily stunned into silence by the proposal's almost unbelievable audacity. After they recovered and it was put to a vote, those in favour made a reasonable noise, those against made relatively little noise and many remained silent. The bill was therefore passed.[6] The king was understandably delighted and Sir Robert enthusiastically wrote to his 'dear heart' that he looked forward to 'not being denied anything in His Majesty's power'.[7]

Still, advancement was not quick, although his actions did gain the support of important factions in Parliament who pushed through a bill that enabled him to profit from developments in Great Yarmouth, in the face of local opposition.[8] He also found other ways to try and claim his reward. In the seventeenth century, well-placed individuals could collect the duties payable on imported goods in return for paying rent to the Crown. In 1665 Sir Robert applied for one such 'Farm on the Customs' on all imported wood, stone, earth and glass and associated wares, plus oranges, lemons and pomegranates. The lease on custom duties of these items was for 21 years, to start from 1667. The annual rent for this privilege was originally set at £2,700 but was renegotiated by the Crown up to £6,500 per annum. Nonetheless, he still hoped to make £3,000 a year on the deal.[9] This is how the Pastons profited from the Great Fire of London – the city's reconstruction required lots of imported wood.

Income from the Customs Farm was unpredictable and Sir Robert spent the money before it materialized, so he had to pursue numerous other projects.[10] (Technically, the word 'project' means 'to extend' and it links Sir Robert's business and alchemical activities.) In 1669 Sir Robert and his brother-in-law, Clayton, received support to build lighthouses at Great Yarmouth, Cromer and further up the east coast. Unfortunately, the scheme, another 'tax farming' arrangement, floundered.[11] Ill omens abounded. For example, Henshaw wrote of people being killed by lightning and the sun being darkened by a vast

black cloud of 'ant flies' that stampeded cattle and then died, covering the streets four inches thick with their bodies.[12] With these and
many other difficulties, Sir Robert found that he could not meet his
mortgage repayments. As an MP, he was immune from arrest but
he feared the sheriff's arrival, and Henshaw recommended that he
hide his treasures to prevent their seizure. He was eventually bailed
out by his in-laws, who lent him £13,000 to pay off the mortgages.
The money arrived just in time, because 1671 proved a very expensive year.[13] The Pastons' eldest son, William, was on his Grand Tour
complaining about how much everything cost. Since his grandfather's
Grand Tour, guidebooks had been published and young William's
expedition to France was more like a package holiday that included
fencing and dancing lessons.[14] At the same time, their eldest daughter, Margaret, was costing them a fortune in fashionable clothes.[15]
She also had an unsuitable suitor – half-Spanish, Roman Catholic
and penniless – who, when he discovered her £4,000 dowry, proved
rather hard to dislodge.[16]

Sir Robert was desperate for money but his hands were tied
because of a much earlier, and extraordinarily impulsive, transaction.
During the Interregnum, the teenage Robert pledged money to
support his exiled king. Much later, in his funeral sermon, it was
acknowledged that he had generously 'supplied his Majesty with
money whilst in Exile . . . he borrowed to give, fearing that his
Sovereign might want'.[17] Robert promised a massive £10,000. This
was more than all his father's Civil War losses – more than the seques-
tration of rents, the fines for 'delinquency' plus the plundering of silver
plate to pay troops. The young Robert's gesture was in keeping with
his actions later in life and reinforces the impression of a man who was
genuinely kind and good-natured, if financially naive. Robert's father
had to send £10,000 to France, raised by selling off two estates, including Fastolf's Caister. Sir William was furious, because in addition to
the enormous expense he had reached an accord with Cromwell and
had much to lose if his son's gift had ever become public knowledge.
The price Sir William extracted was to transfer most of the remaining
family estates from Robert and pass them over to his eldest grandson. Sir William also provided Margaret's dowry. The idealistic and

youthful Robert's impulsive gift defined the financial trajectory of the rest of his life. He was effectively a powerless tenant on his father's lands and then a powerless tenant on his son's lands. However, he grew up to become very adept at paying off one debt with another and today would have been a master at juggling credit cards.

Sir Robert may have taken a back seat when it came to politics at court, leaving the machinations to his wife, but he took great interest in another form of politics – entertaining and hospitality. There was significant political leverage in the provision of food, and when Robert was a child Queen Henrietta Maria and Elizabeth Cromwell, First Ladies from the opposite sides of the political spectrum, both published cookbooks. Barbed comparisons were made between their recipes, motivated more by ideology than gastronomy.[18] Around the same time, mirroring the court, Sir Robert's father had employed a celebrity chef in Oxnead's kitchens. The chef, Robert May, had spent five years on the Continent studying French, Italian and Spanish recipes before returning to cook for the English. His book – the first English illustrated cookbook – was dedicated to a handful of nobles, including Sir William, who were 'well known to the Nation for their admired Hospitalities'.[19]

When Sir Robert became the head of the family, Oxnead's hospitality continued in the style he had experienced as a child. He knew that offering food helped maintain the body politic. It has always been thought that 'you are what you eat', and paintings even tied the social order to the natural order by, for example, showing peasantry eating lowly beans while the gentry ate lofty birds.[20] Increasingly, through the sixteenth and seventeenth centuries, trade put a wider range of foods on the plate. Some, like Sir Robert's oranges, peaches and grapes, had been traded for a long time, and had surprisingly wide circulation through society, so ordinary people's diets could be much richer than we might suppose. The evidence comes from archaeologists who heroically pick their way through the contents of historic latrines and cesspits to identify discarded bones and evacuated seeds.[21] Imported foods were received selectively. For example, two foods related to England's poison of choice – belladonna, or deadly nightshade – arrived from the New World, and while the tomatoes were avoided, the potatoes were accepted.[22] None of the food on Sir Robert's table is from the New World, but his use of another related New World import, tobacco, is evident in the paper twist and clay pipe near the *Paston Treasure*'s hourglass. Tobacco – which is also related to belladonna – was described as a (literally) 'outlandish weede [which] spends the Braine, and spoils the seed: It dulls the spirit, it dims the sight, it robs the woman of her right.'[23] Nonetheless, like the potato, it was a hit.

The *Paston Treasure*'s food does not look as if it is laid out for a meal, but it certainly alludes to Oxnead's continuing tradition of hospitality. Not surprisingly, the most spectacular political meal that Sir Robert ever presented was in honour of the king. Charles II's brief tour of Norfolk in 1671 was the first royal visit for nearly a century. He was a regular autumn visitor to Newmarket in Suffolk, and enjoyed its horse racing, hunting and hawking, but had not ventured the extra day north, off the heath and through the forest, to Norfolk. But that year, towards the end of September, the royal entourage divided at Newmarket and the king proceeded to Great Yarmouth. He was accompanied by his brother, who had an interest in the port, which would be of strategic importance in any attack on the Dutch. Charles II named a ship *James* in his brother's honour and attended a banquet. He was welcomed into Great Yarmouth with a 1,200-gun salute, a reception that cost £1,000 and gifts that included a gold chain featuring four gold herrings with ruby eyes.[24] That particular gift acknowledged the truth of Nashe's assessment of Great Yarmouth as 'principall metropolis of the redde fish'.

The following day the king made his way to Norwich, while the queen left Newmarket, also destined for Norwich. There was some difficulty co-ordinating the arrival of their entourages since they arrived from different directions. The queen arrived first from the south and it started to rain, so all the dignitaries were soaked to the skin by the time they could split up to greet the king, coming in from the east. Norwich's reception was even greater than Great Yarmouth's and was presided over by the mayor, the corporation and Duke of Norfolk. The king and queen were united in the Duke of Norfolk's palace, which had been specially converted for the occasion.

The indoor tennis court had become a kitchen and the vast bowling alley was turned into five separate dining halls. The queen's retinue had 55 people, the most important of whom also had their own private attendants. The king's retinue was even bigger yet everyone managed to spend the night in the palace. The king started the next day with a tour, touching people afflicted with the king's evil (a skin disease), followed by a visit to the cathedral, then the guildhall and a packed market square. He then joined the queen for a banquet.[25]

Sir Robert accompanied the king through all the Norwich pomp. When the entourage left town, Sir Robert headed for Oxnead. The king and queen went to the home of Sir John Hobart in Blickling, five miles from Oxnead. This was an attempt at reconciliation with Hobart, who had been a staunch supporter of Cromwell. The king and queen dined there, after which the king's retinue made the short trip to Oxnead while the queen's returned to Norwich. This split was because, much to Sir Robert's distress, Oxnead was not big enough to offer hospitality to everyone for the night. Indeed, a letter planning the whole operation described him as being 'in the greatest trouble and confusion I ever saw'.[26]

Only five miles separated Blickling and Oxnead, but politically the Hobarts and the Pastons were worlds apart and, on arrival, the king said he now felt 'Safe in the House of A Friend'. These seven short words were a sign of the recognition that Sir Robert had craved ever since proposing the king's £2.5 million war chest seven long years ago. The king enjoyed a fabulous meal in Oxnead's new banqueting hall. It must have been extraordinarily extravagant, even by Sir Robert's standards, because it cost 'three times more' than the dowry for an earl's daughter and was later described as one of the greatest events of his life.[27] The king retired for the night and the following morning the queen's retinue returned from Norwich to join them in Oxnead. In the afternoon, the king visited Lord Townsend, the Lord Lieutenant of Norfolk, while the queen remained at Oxnead, playing cards with her hostess, Rebecca.[28]

Nothing could be too much for the king, and when he was at Oxnead, Sir Robert apologized for the relative dearth of silver plate, reminding Charles that the family's silver had been plundered 'by the trunksfull' in the Civil War.²⁹ The cost of the single dinner was so enormous that he was still paying it off the following year, for example giving £60 to the pewterer, £40 to the confectioner and £20 to the hatter.³⁰ Sir Robert's extraordinarily conspicuous expenditure infuriated his creditors, including his father-in-law, who discovered that his loan had funded the dinner rather than paid off the mortgage. Sir Robert was used to juggling debt, but he was deeply upset by the angry exchanges with his father-in-law so – in desperation – he even tried to sell some of the very little land that was not held in his son's name. Unfortunately, nobody would buy.³¹

The cost of all that entertaining was also personal, because, as we have seen, Sir Robert was seriously overweight (letters suggest he had a sweet tooth). Seven years before Charles II's visit, immediately after his political triumph of proposing money for the Dutch wars, he told his wife that he had been lampooned in a Dutch cartoon. He described a picture of the House of Commons with 'a burly fellow out of whose mouth comes two millions and a half'.³² Sir Robert's enormous size became satirical shorthand, and other jokes were made about Hyde, the Earl of Clarendon, and Sir Robert's proposal of a colossal war chest

> Whose very bulk may represent its Birth,
> From Hyde and Paston, burthens of the Earth,
> Paston, whose Belly bears more Millions,
> Than Indian Carracks and contains more Tons.³³

Carracks were three-masted cargo ships, like the vessels commanded by his ancestor Sir Clement.

By the time the *Paston Treasure* was painted, Sir Robert no longer rode but travelled by carriage and had recurring, very painful episodes of gout. He would have been fully aware that his sorry physical condition was due to his lavish entertaining because of the close traditional relationship between diet and health. As an alchemist who made his own medicines, he knew that what connected diet and health were the four elements – fire, air, water and earth; the four qualities – hot, cold, wet and dry; and the four humours – choleric, sanguine, phlegmatic and melancholic. The elements, qualities and humours were 'a moral theatre, in which the human body was the stage for a never-ending drama'. Constant harmony was the ideal, constant change was the problem, and the dominance of one element, quality or humour was the constant danger.[34] Foods were chosen for their elemental qualities and were combined to balance the humours or correct disorders associated with imbalance. Remnants of these ideas still circulate today since we refer to peppers as 'hot', lemons as 'sharp' and martinis as 'dry', adjectives which refer to Aristotelian rather than literal properties.

Since many of his health issues were related to diet, Sir Robert might have benefited from the old strict traditional coupling of diet and medicine. His family doctor would have given dietary advice; however, in print, Browne seemed more interested in questions of historic dietary restrictions. He observed that no flesh was eaten in Eden, or before the Flood, or in the age of Saturn, or by Pythagoreans or even by contemporary Indians.[35] (At least Christian Europe still observed enough meat-free days to keep Yarmouth's fishermen busy.) Over the hundred or so years leading up to the painting's execution, quite what you were able to eat might have been freeing up, but at the same time exactly how you ate it was tightening up. Meals were becoming increasingly ritualized. Self-governance and manners grew in parallel with increasing levels of governance by the state, and bodily processes like eating became the focus of self-imposed correct 'table manners'.[36] The body politic's regime spread into the body's regimen.[37] As the Civil War's battle of the cookbooks suggested, personal, domestic and national identities were inextricably intertwined.

Some regulation of diet – whether of political, religious or alchemical origin – would have been beneficial for the seriously overweight Sir Robert. Unlike the political, religious and economic affairs that swirled chaotically around him, eating was something that seemed to lie within his control. It was therefore a sad irony that the effects of eating started to control him. As a boy he had been too fat to play sports and, in time, he turned into a living example of the unregulated eating that made 'our bellies sovereign to our brains'.[38] Gluttony, or being governed by one's appetite, was likened to submission to a foreign power that would ultimately enslave the nation.[39] The body politic and the physical body both had 'constitutions' that needed to be governed. The word 'economics' initially meant the management of a household or a family and Sir Robert understood it as such, as well as scaled up to the nation's body politic and scaled down to his own, admittedly large, physical body. Sir Robert's unconstrained appetite ultimately constrained him.

In April 1676 an obese Sir Robert thanked God that he had no gout and wrote to his wife that he would 'endeavour to husband my body as well as I may', reporting that he had drunk no more than six glasses of wine. Two days later he reiterated that there had been 'no hard drinking' at Oxnead. In early May, though, he told his wife that he was 'confined with the gout to my chamber' even though he had 'observed all the temperate methods I can'. Yet a week later, he told his wife that her 'letters are such cordials that they are able to set a gouty man on his legs again' and – having also 'swinged my body with physick' including 'my owne salt' – his gout was gone.[40]

As a direct result of his lavish hospitality and entertaining, his personal constitution was seriously out of balance. It seems that he was rarely free of pain and his body's unhappy condition added to the burdens on his soul. It was said that 'The soul must be careful of the body and make it a fit instrument for herself . . . slackening and sometimes winding up according as necessity require.'[41] According to contemporary medical theory, the body worked by 'harmony and rhythm' in a kind of 'silent music'.[42] But, over the decades, Sir Robert had failed to make his body a 'fit instrument' for his soul. And as he became more and more sedentary, he had more and more time to ponder his 'out of tune' condition. He would have felt just 'How sour sweet music is / When time is broke and no proportion kept!'[43]

Sir Robert suffered from melancholy, as did Browne.[44] Under medical guidance he would have taken various remedies, some of which he made himself, which was not at all uncommon. A Norfolk contemporary, Elizabeth Freke, had a vast and well-documented store of homemade medicines.[45] For melancholy, Browne would have recommended the oil of hypericum that Margaret helped make in his Oxnead laboratory as well as Sir Robert's homemade 'Hart's

Horn Water'.[46] These were not necessarily seen as drugs, which were a relatively new concept in the seventeenth century, part of the new medicine which implied patients could be treated as chemical machines.[47] As an alchemist, Sir Robert would have had faith in hart's horn water's ability to rebalance his humours. He would have had no difficulty getting the ingredients, since venison was regularly on his menu and an inventory listed over fifty stag's heads on Oxnead's walls.[48] Traditionally, the body-soul-spirit was treated as a self-regulating organism that could be fine-tuned both internally and externally. Health management had been based on maintaining balance in the humours by altering the mix of warm, cool, wet and dry qualities in a patient's diet or environment. For example, stags were cold and dry, and thus related to melancholy, which was a cold and dry condition.[49] The older medicine recognized that music or colour could also be manipulated to strengthen the patient's body and help treat 'accidents of the soul'. Medicine could be received through the eyes and ears as well as through the mouth.

Sir Robert took *alkermes*, an ancient Arabic cordial, a major ingredient of which was dried kermes insects, relatives of the cochineal that provided the red for the *Paston Treasure*. You could take kermes or cochineal by mouth to influence the body. You could also take them in through the eyes – gazing upon red paint – to influence the soul. Sir Robert did both. Painters knew, and presumably used, these properties. As one artists' manual said, 'colours have different qualities, therefore they cause diverse effects in the beholders.'[50] The verdigris of the servant's tunic and Margaret's chair in the *Paston Treasure* was in the cheaper version of the *zenexton* that hopefully averted plague. Orpiment was in more expensive *zenexton* and depicts the glittery gold of the shell cup mounts in the *Paston Treasure*. Blue lapis lazuli was also used in the painting and the mere sight of it was widely believed to purge melancholy.[51] The overlap between medicine and art reinforced the value of a painting such as the *Paston Treasure* in the treatment of melancholia. Simply gazing upon it was therapeutic.

Yet all the while, money worries continued. Having failed to sell land, the Pastons reverted to the old family tactic of seeking rich partners for their offspring. Margaret grew up to be very strong-willed, just like her fifteenth-century namesake. The Pastons had managed to dislodge the persistent half-Spanish suitor and were hoping to arrange a marriage with Sir John Godolphin, but within six months she was on the brink of marrying a secretary at the Italian embassy. Girolamo Alberti di Conte came from Venice and Sir Robert had presumably known him through his dealings with the Customs Farm (it included taxes on glass and, of course, the best glass came from Venice). Margaret, Sir Robert's beloved apprentice alchemist, was marrying into an Italian family, and his contact with her was destined to be reduced to distant letters. Worse still, she was entering a Roman Catholic family, and while Sir Robert was very respectful of religious differences, who knew whether his daughter's in-laws would prove equally accommodating of her Anglicanism? It would have been a deep cause for concern for a loving father. Anyway, Sir Robert had no control over her dowry, so he just had to hope, for her sake, that Girolamo's family were as open and accepting as he was.[52]

Margaret's match, however, did not benefit the family's finances and the Pastons hoped to do better when finding a wife for William. In 1672 they had been negotiating with a London merchant, who also happened to be a creditor, for his daughter's hand. When this fell through they tried to arrange a marriage with another merchant heiress.[53] But then one of the king's illegitimate daughters, Charlotte Jemima Howard, became available, and in 1673 she and William were married. Sir Robert was rewarded with the titles Viscount Yarmouth and Baron Paston, and the following year was made High Steward of Great Yarmouth. Yet whatever economic and political manoeuvrings lay behind the match, William and Charlotte's marriage proved to be a happy one. The couple lived in London and enjoyed visiting Oxnead. Their eldest son was born in the king's palace in Whitehall and his godparents included the king.[54] Positions and titles accumulated and status seemed assured but money was still tight. Charles II gave Charlotte an annual grant of £500 and William lodgings at the court and a coach and horses plus £1,000 per annum (a sum that was eventually tripled). On the other hand, the wedding had been very expensive and by this time Sir Robert's debts amounted to a massive £30,000.[55]

Oil paintings look like static images so it is perhaps surprising that the *Paston Treasure* provides physical evidence of goods flowing out of Oxnead as the family either divided up assets or paid off debts. However, when the painting was examined in the conservation studio, an X-ray showed that, where a fashionable 1660s clock now hangs on the wall, the painting had originally featured a large silver platter. The details of this silver platter were completely finished but it was then painted over. Could it have been obliterated because it left Sir Robert's collection while the painting was being completed and he did not want to be reminded of its loss?[56]

When the finely wrought silver platter had been made, the cost of the silver and the workmanship would have been approximately equal. So, if the plate was recycled for its metal content – as earlier Paston plate had been – then melting it down would halve its value.[57] Cromwell must have been quite desperate to convert the Pastons' highly worked silver into cash for his troops. When Parliament proposed melting down silver from the Jewel House in 1644, the House of Lords ruled that the workmanship was worth more than the metal.[58] In fact, silver was so expensive that when Margaret outgrew the dress she wore for the *Paston Treasure* the silver thread in its appliqué ribbons would have been recycled. In the eighteenth century it even became fashionable to unravel silver and gold thread from clothes that people were still wearing. Presumably, well-dressed women had to pretend they did not mind others dismantling their dresses. Extracting silver and gold thread from tassels, fringes and lacework was called 'drizzling' and was an imported Continental custom that could prove quite lucrative for the pushy socialite who moved in the right circles.[59]

Sir Robert's painter replaced the image of the silver platter with the image of a young woman. Her exotic costume rivalled that of the servant on the other side of the painting. She wore ribbons and leaves or feathers in her hair, a pearl necklace, a green shawl and a rich red laced bodice.[60] Like the silver platter, her image was also highly finished – with blushing cheeks and blue eyes – but, in turn, she too was painted over. The painting's final black clock covers both the woman and the silver platter, yet if you look very closely, hints of the woman are still visible. A ghostly suggestion of her face shows in the wall to the left of the clock and two eyes peer out of the picture at the viewer.[61] Across the clock-face, a curve of bumps corresponds to her hidden chain of pearls. We cannot know who she was or why she was painted out.

A silver platter and an unidentified woman disappeared from the painting, and the children were being married off, but life went on. Outside Oxnead, Sir Robert had to respond to political affairs in Norfolk while Rebecca continued with her efforts at court. The king's futile and expensive wars, combined with his extravagant life-style and numerous illegitimate offspring, polarized Parliament into two factions. And Norfolk politics proved even more difficult to negotiate as local politics was driven by a very obscure mixture of self-interest, deeply held belief and extreme confusion. The situation – a legacy of the previous century's Reformation and the previous decade's Interregnum – got so bad that it led to a completely new way of doing politics.

Previously, political allegiances had been built on the strength of personal connections, so patronage, propaganda and force were all exercised locally, conducted around the homes of those who vied for power. More often than not, the cause of local troubles was simply an abrasive personality. Then, in the 1670s, responding to Parliament's polarization, the old tools of local politics – patronage, propaganda and force – started to be used at a national level. The interests of widely differing localities were made to coalesce into a brand new kind of grouping – a political 'party'. Fluid personal allegiances became frozen into ideological allegiances and commitments switched from change-able, or 'volatile', individuals to unchangeable, or 'fixed', ideas. This shift in the temper in the body politic meant that Sir Robert had to adapt from attempting to tie his fate to the fickle person of Charles II (for all his faults) to making an attachment to the eternal idea of 'monarchy'. Multifaceted personalities were rapidly conscripted into one-size-fits-all mass movements at exactly the time Sir Robert was engaged in a contest with his neighbour, Lord Townsend.[62] The local conflict between two men morphed into a fight between two national parties, and the body politic – which had been a mirror of God's action through history – mutated into a one-dimensional game.

Sir Robert's political style was inclusive. He had always tried to keep everybody happy. On the other hand, the whole idea of the new-style party politics was to exclude the other party from power. At the time, Norfolk was the most deeply divided county in England as Lord Townsend's increasingly unpopular stewardship had widened divisions in the county, and in 1675 Sir Robert was asked to challenge him. Sir Robert had reservations because he was essentially a quiet family man who knew the role entailed maintaining a court that he could ill afford. Nonetheless, he accepted the fight and it turned out to be very bitter.

In the end, Sir Robert won and his friends were elated. 'We are . . . in an ecstasy . . . What good can we not expect?'[63] It was thought that with Sir Robert – now Viscount Yarmouth – as Lord Lieutenant, Norfolk would be restored to harmony. Rebecca – now Viscountess Yarmouth – was in London when victory was declared and Sir William Doyly wrote to her, saying that the parade which greeted her husband was greater than any except the one that celebrating the king's return from exile. He recorded forty coaches filled with gentlemen 'of the best rank', eighty clergymen and over a thousand gentlemen on horseback.[64] She got at least three other letters that same day describing her husband's rapturous reception from the people of Norwich. Sir Robert himself claimed 45 coaches with 'the prime of the gentry' and 1,500 on horseback so that 'the King himself could not have been more honoured'. He said the sight 'elevated an ambitious heart' but, at the same time, he still had to confess to 'many melancholy thoughts'.[65]

For well over a month, Sir Robert was so hard pressed by well-wishers that he could not leave home, providing one sumptuous feast after another. He worked vigorously to reap the benefits of his popularity. While trying to be conciliatory to supporters of the defeated Townsend, he appointed his friends in positions of authority and consolidated his power base. Meanwhile, back in London, Rebecca tried to cement relations at court, reinforced in the knowledge that the 'loyal party' was thriving in Norfolk. However, allegiance to favourites was no longer sufficient – principles were what mattered. The Crown had learned from the bitter partisan politics of Townsend and Paston. Sir Robert continued to work tirelessly on behalf of the king while also trying to get his son established in politics, and in 1679 William became MP for Norwich. But local politics was becoming even more bad-tempered, so in 1681, suffering from ill-health, Sir Robert retired to London.[66] Just as the weather played a part in Charles II's entry on to the political stage, it seemed to play a part in Sir Robert's exit. 'A strange storm of hail' the previous year was seen as 'a warning by the King of Kings'.[67]

England's Civil War had been just one of nearly fifty rebellions against state authorities across Europe and Asia over Sir Robert's lifetime.[68] Numerous states had escalated their militaries to unsustainable levels but natural disasters added to the mix. As Sir Robert's fortunes ebbed away, he would have seen the weather mirror his increasingly chilly predicament. Practically every decade of his life saw biting winters, cold summers and failed harvests, and it has been said that 'the seventeenth century experienced extremes of weather seldom witnessed before and never (so far) since.'[69] Modern commentators argue about whether or not a global seventeenth-century crisis could be blamed on the weather.[70] Either way, Sir Robert's increasingly fraught political and economic circumstances definitely reflected the passing climate change – the seventeenth century's Little Ice Age.[71] The fraught meteorological backdrop was like a literary 'pathetic fallacy', but was fact, not fiction, reinforcing an impression of God's parallel actions in the realms of politics and nature. At the bottom of Oxnead's stately gardens, the River Bure froze, through Norwich the Waveney froze, and through London even the Thames froze. Likewise, because of the young Robert's spontaneous gift to the exiled Charles II, his father had frozen most of his assets.

Money worries must have contributed significantly to Sir Robert's poor state of health and his health worries must have been very serious indeed to make him leave Oxnead. He was saying goodbye to a house he loved and to Thomas Browne, close neighbour, lifetime friend and trusted doctor. Though scarcely able to walk, he remained politically active in London, attending the House of Lords to oppose the exclusion of the Catholic Duke of York from the succession. However, in 1683, within two years of leaving Oxnead, Sir

Robert died. He was only 51. His beloved daughter, Margaret Alberti, wrote a subtly barbed letter to her mother saying, 'perhaps if my dear father had contented himself with the wholesome air of poor Oxnead without troubling himself with affairs of state ... your ladyship would not now be a widow.'[72]

History had repeated itself and Sir Robert had worn himself out by constant struggles, just like family patriarchs generations before him. As his wise doctor once said, 'every man is his own Atropos, and lends a hand to cut the thread of his own days.'[73] However, unlike previous patriarchs, no monument was raised for him, nor for that matter were monuments made for any of his children or grandchildren.[74] The same year, two of his children, Margaret and Jasper, died. The following year William's wife, Charlotte, died. Another daughter, Elizabeth, died in 1687.

Meanwhile, on the national stage, Charles II died suddenly in 1685. He was buried in Westminster Abbey with minimal pomp and ceremony. His Catholic brother, James II, ascended to the throne, but as an unloved authoritarian his reign was to prove short. In 1688 William and Mary's forces, which had assembled in Holland, were helped by a 'Protestant wind' from the east that delivered five hundred ships to England while simultaneously trapping James II's ships for three days. The 'Protestant wind' came after a sustained westerly that would have favoured James II, and was called a 'Popish wind' only by those who dared defy Dutch magistrates who were threatening heavy fines. This easterly Protestant wind came a hundred years after a similarly providential westerly Protestant wind saved the English from the Spanish Armada in 1588, when 'God blew and they were scattered'.[75]

Upon Sir Robert's death, William Paston became the head of the family, but he turned out to be an unreliable helmsman and the family's downward spiral accelerated. Three years after Charlotte's death, William married Elizabeth Wiseman and, thanks to his new wife's connections, became treasurer of the royal household and proved his loyalty to James II by converting to Catholicism. After James II was deposed in 1688's Glorious Revolution, William faced ruin and converted back to Anglicanism. Under William and Mary's rule, he was suspected of being a Jacobite and was imprisoned in the

Tower but released in 1690. Despite all these tribulations, William's second marriage must have been happy, because Elizabeth asked, and was permitted, to join her husband in the Tower. William was briefly recommitted to the Tower in 1692 and, out of favour at court, they were reduced to living off Elizabeth's dowry.

The Pastons' climb had taken centuries but their fall from grace was extraordinarily fast. Tensions grew between William and his ageing mother, who had no place at court or Oxnead. She was living in a run-down thatched cottage, struggling to pay her rent and harassed by a landlord who sought numerous ways to evict her – 'but she will understand none of them, not knowing where next to go'. The description of her sad predicament went on: 'Her son gives her no respects or holds any correspondence with her, though she lives not above two miles from him.'[76] She died in her early sixties in 1694, eleven years after her beloved husband, and was buried beside him at Oxnead church.

The family's spectacular decline would have been a fantastic source of gossip. The story would have been a very short-lived topic in the febrile court but would have run and run in Norfolk. Unfortunately, there is little record of Norfolk gossip as the Pastons sank, yet stories of how everyday lives unfolded were recorded by a contemporary of Sir Robert's, Richard Gough, who wrote a book about who-sat-where in his parish church in Shropshire. However unlikely Gough's subject-matter might seem, a rich picture of life in a rural community emerges from his book. Where people sat in Gough's church was determined by where they lived outside the church – if a family's place of abode changed, they changed pews. It is clear that about half the people Gough knew lived in the same property for two or three generations. The other half were either upwardly or downwardly mobile, with movements around the village faithfully reflected in seating arrangements in church. Thanks to farmer Gough's gossip about the people in one pew, the fate of the Pastons' Oxnead house can be compared to the fate of Balderton Hall, which was built in Shropshire around the time Sir Clement rebuilt Oxnead.

Balderton Hall's first owner was 'addicted to projects', speculating in timber and charcoal, which ultimately 'proved his ruin'. He had to sell up to pay off his creditors. The Hall was bought by a man who left the country and, according to different accounts, was either never heard of again or returned as a beggar, seen sitting by the barn one day and found dead the next. A family member inherited the Hall but he was 'addicted to idleness' and, worse still, had 'lewd consorts' who could 'resemble ugliness itself'. He was sued by family members and the Hall passed to a wealthy merchant. This man eventually had to mortgage some of it to another merchant, who then also had cash flow problems, forcing both to sell on to a pious rector who died soon after buying it. The Hall passed to the rector's widow and sons, the eldest of whom sold up just before being killed fighting for Charles I. The Hall was bought by a man who was 'born to no estate' but amassed a fortune working the land. His daughter married 'a reasonable good husband' who moved into the Hall but slowly declined into 'cocking, racing, drinking and lewdness'. By these 'ill courses' he 'consumed his estate' and had to sell. So, in less than a hundred years Balderton Hall and its estates had changed hands five times.[77]

Compared to Balderton Hall, the Pastons' Oxnead was a picture of stability. Its loss after centuries was not due to 'idleness' or 'lewdness' but to a combination of economic mismanagement and conscience – the family's religious and political sympathies being at odds with the time and the place. William Paston was unable to stem the flow but his evident charm enabled him to live on credit. He submitted to King William in 1696 but was accused of conspiracy the following year. However, he had become so politically insignificant that the matter seems to have just faded away. He retrenched and remortgaged but was forced to deal with very hard-nosed lenders and had to accept punitive compound-interest loans that were shortly to be declared illegal.[78] It seems he was also taken advantage of in business. Friends helped by taking over his properties to save them from the lawyers, but their moves only delayed the inevitable. By 1708 he had accrued 'vast' debts, and while the family's dire financial state was not completely beyond repair, William could not be persuaded to put 'his affairs into a better posture'. He overstepped the balance, tipped into chaos and the family's goods were put up for auction in 1709. By 1713 they were living in Westminster and an eviscerated Oxnead was starting to decay.[79]

William's two daughters married into Norfolk families that had been long-term opponents of the Pastons, but – despite being on the winning side – these once-prominent families were destined to disappear within a few generations. Charles, William's eldest son, married the daughter of a porter and an apple-seller in Gravesend and died in 1718. By then William's two other sons had already died and none had left any children. William himself died on Christmas Day, 1732. In the absence of offspring to ensure the succession of generations, the family line failed.[80] His death was 'universally lamented by all that had the happiness to know him'.[81]

The fifty years between the painting of the *Paston Treasure* and the complete dispersal of the family's collections and estates was littered with inventories and auction price lists. One inventory showed that Oxnead used to have 79 rooms, including several galleries. The Lower Gallery had '36 large pictures', the Withdrawing Room had '10 middling and 40 small pictures' and the Great Dining Hall had a portrait of the king, family portraits, more statues and gilt heads. The Great Hall had a large landscape over the chimney-piece, two crocodiles hanging over the stone table, two gilt statues, six gilt heads and fourteen carved heads – in addition to over fifty stag heads – on the walls. An inventory of *c.*1670 was more detailed, but covered only a fraction of the house. It listed a 'great picture of Magdalen, in a great carved frame', a 'fine picture of Andromeda, chained to a rock' and family portraits by Sir Peter Lely, Michael Wright and Samuel Cooper. A shelf-by-shelf list of plate and jewels mentions the *Paston Treasure*'s 'shell engraven with the story of Atalanta, standing upon an Eagle's foot of silver'.[82] Everything, including the fireplaces, was up for sale.

The portrait of Sir Robert's father with a crocodile was bought by the Windhams of Felbrigg Hall, neighbours and old Parliamentarian foes. Some of Nicholas Stone's statues and the graceful garden fountain were bought by the Hobarts of Blickling, another neighbouring old foe. The statue of Hercules is still recognizable, but the others were later broken up to fill a pond.[83] Many paintings went to Sir Robert Walpole, yet another political opponent, to swell his already vast collection at nearby Houghton. Of these, over two hundred eventually went, via Catherine the Great, to Russia, where many now hang in the Hermitage. Sir Robert Walpole's youngest son, Horace, took the *Paston Treasure*'s 'nautilus mounted in silver gilt, with satyrs and the arms of Paston' from Houghton to Strawberry Hill, west London. It was sold in 1842 for £37 16s., and the mount – with a new shell, the original presumably having been broken – is now in the Rijksmuseum, Amsterdam.[84] Another *Paston Treasure* shell cup is at the Mauritshuis, The Hague, while a third is in the Castle Museum, Norwich. If the others survive, their locations are unknown.

Some of Sir Robert's drawings are in the Louvre, and his once highly fashionable family portraits by Lely went on to the market and are now hanging, many unidentified, in galleries and houses across the Western world. Around the time the Paston line ended, a portrait by Godfrey Kneller – the fashionable society portrait painter equivalent to Lely – could cost around £30 and its frame around £20. The cost of these pictures was comparable to a carved stone fireplace, a year's tax on a London townhouse, four silver candlesticks, sixteen bottles of good wine or 250 china soup plates.[85] As the Paston pictures of comparable quality were auctioned off, they would have been much cheaper.

Meanwhile, an issue of the *Female Spectator* reported that a fashionable tea-table – equipped with silver tea-pots, silver kettles, silver cream-boats, silver milk-jugs, silver spoons, silver sugar-tongs and silver sugar-basins as well as cups and saucers – could cost more to maintain than two children and a nanny.[86] Elsewhere, the *London Gazette* repeatedly published calls for Paston creditors, producing a final list in 1760, some 77 years after Sir Robert's death. Four years later, the family's debts were finally settled at 11s. 6d. to the pound, a return of 53 per cent. This final tranche of debts amounted to about £16 million in today's money. The debts that had previously been paid off are impossible to estimate, but they were doubtless very significant.[87]

All the connections between the treasures in Sir Robert's painting were severed. The family's possessions were picked off and reassembled according to other people's interests. Seven of their portraits of kings, for example, ended up (via the son of Walpole's chaplain, a Cambridge college and a university librarian) in the collection of the Society of Antiquaries of London. The Buxtons – a family distantly connected to the Pastons who lived on the other side of Norwich – bought the contents of one room, including the *Paston Treasure*.[88] Unlike Balderton Hall in Gough's Shropshire village, Oxnead was not reoccupied, which reinforces the impression that neighbours had conspired to bring about the family's catastrophic downfall.

In 1744 the ancestral home at Oxnead was sold in ruins. Parts of the servant's wing were converted into smaller dwellings while the rest became an overground quarry. Oxnead's stones and timbers were carted off to build other houses, just as an old Shoreditch theatre had supplied the timbers for Shakespeare's Globe. Oxnead's lead was melted down and turned into more roofing or plumbing, or even into the cheap silver substitute pewter. Its copper, brass and bronze – including a vast candelabrum weighing 166 pounds – was melted down, just as upon the Dissolution of the Monasteries church bells had been turned into Henry VIII's armaments. Oxnead's ornate wrought ironwork would have been turned into ploughshares and horseshoes.[89]

The sea-faring Sir Clement Paston had rebuilt the church at Oxnead with, amongst other materials, ancient tiles and bricks salvaged from ruins of the neighbouring Roman settlement of Brampton. A generation later, William's great-great-great grandfather, another William, had built the great barn at Paston with stone scavenged from two victims of Henry VIII's Dissolution – St Benet's Abbey, about fifteen miles down the River Bure, and Bromholme Priory, just two miles away. Henry's 'royal whirlwind' had left the skeletal remains of one thousand years of history on the Pastons' doorstep – poignant reminders of impermanence, but also useful sources of building material.[90] The Pastons had repeatedly recycled the past in order to build their futures and it was their turn to be recycled. The late eighteenth-century William Paston reaped what the early fifteenth-century William Paston had sown. The Prior of Bromholme had cursed the predatory Pastons, prophesying 'a fool, till [the family] is become poor'. The peasant family that started its journey to riches riding on the backs of neighbouring peasants, elderly widows and the clergy had eventually become poor.

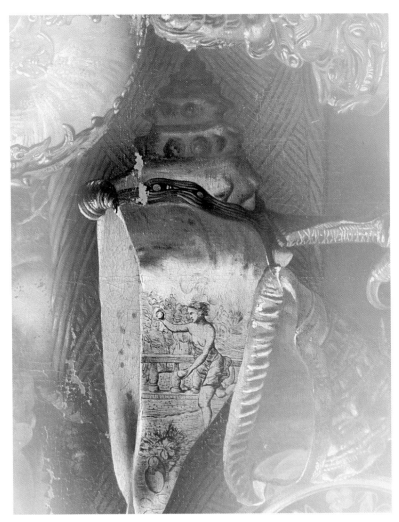

Anon., *Paston Treasure*, detail (rotated 90° counterclockwise) of 'Atalanta Fugiens'
(Atalanta Fleeing).

seven

Repentance

Fortuna – wonder – the patience of Job – shipwrecks – the single eye – Cézanne – Thomas Browne – *The Garden of Cyrus* – harmony – orchards – Sir Walter Raleigh's cordial – belonging – Indra's net – *sylva* – Atalanta fleeing – the hourglass – shells and the whirlwind ·

At the end of the century in which the Paston line died out, Goethe said:

> One must see [a seventeenth-century Dutch still-life paint-ing] in order to understand in what sense art is superior to nature and what the spirit of man imparts to objects when it views them with creative eyes . . . if I had to choose between the golden vessels or the picture . . . I would choose the picture.[1]

As Sir Robert's 'golden vessels' were sold off, one hopes he may have felt the same. This chapter considers what 'the spirit of man' might impart to the *Paston Treasure* when viewed by someone with 'creative eyes' like Sir Robert.

The picture was created at the family's zenith and the paint had hardly dried before the Paston story took its tragic turn. A trag-edy is defined as a story in which all the threads unravel – illustrated in this case by the onward journeys of Oxnead's treasures to col-lections across Norfolk, the Rijksmuseum, Louvre, Hermitage and beyond. Yet one person's loss is another's gain, so we could see the shell cups' journeys as either the dismantling of one collection or as the assembling of other collections.[2] From the Hobarts', Walpole's or Catherine the Great's perspectives, the shell cups' journeys would be parts of comedies, since comedies are stories in which initially disparate threads come together.[3] A traditional comedy was not nec-essarily full of laughs but it left the audience feeling good because, as the plot unfolded, the cast collectively achieved balance in its proper 'humour'. Comedies always start in a state of disorder, and the power of even the stand-up comic's punchline comes from its restoration of order, albeit order seen from an unexpected point of view. Next to any other seventeenth-century Dutch still-life painting, the *Paston Treasure* looks extremely disorderly, so is there any point of view from which the picture's apparently chaotic composition makes sense?

With threads simultaneously diverging and converging, whether we see a story as a tragedy or comedy depends in part upon when the curtain rises and falls or, in the case of a painting, upon what is inside or outside the frame. Global trade accounted for how things got into the picture but it does not account for how they were arranged. This chapter speculates about what might have influenced the way in which the *Paston Treasure* was composed, and it does so in a manner that Sir Robert, hopefully, would have recognized. The word 'specu-lation' comes from the Latin *speculum*, or mirror, and Sir Robert would no doubt have seen his painting as a mirror on to his world. However, unlike the overwhelming majority of seventeenth-century still-life paintings, the *Paston Treasure* does not try to look like an optical reflection of a scene. Indeed, as it stood in the studio awaiting its conservation treatment, one of the things that intrigued me about it was that it just looked 'wrong'. I felt the need to pull together its many unruly threads.

Of course, 350 years earlier, as the painting slowly emerged in Oxnead's makeshift studio, Sir Robert could not have known his family's fate. Death spared him the details.[4] Also, he could not have known that modern science would dismiss his attempts to make gold. He would have been very surprised, because modern science emerged from Robert Boyle's chemistry and Isaac Newton's physics, both of which had significant alchemical components.[5] He had seen omin-ous shadows threaten his world since he was a boy, and his habitual response might seem to have been naive, idealistic or just plain irre-sponsible. He just wanted the people around him to be happy, but with the benefit of hindsight we might think his actions ill-judged.

However, in genealogical terms, the family was well established and secure. There was less need to invoke possibly fictitious ancestors like Wulstan because, through marriage, the Pastons were connected to practically every aristocratic family in East Anglia. In 1674 their extensive network of relations was sufficiently impressive to be worth recording. Five years later, the earldom seemed to seal their position.[6] Sir Robert had seen greater changes than most and he knew that responsibility for his family's fate would soon pass to his son. In the ways that he thought best, he had done everything possible to prepare his son for the future. While the family's finances were weak, their blood ties could not have been stronger. By the time the *Paston Treasure* was painted, the die had been cast and the trajectory set. There was nothing for Sir Robert to do but watch events unfold. He knew the wheel of fortune was spun by the blindfolded and impartial Lady Fortuna, and he knew that positions changed. As a letter from his friend Henshaw said, every day shows us Fortune's inconstancy and warns us 'not to be too fond of her smiles and caresses'.[7] Lady Fortuna's presence was reinforced by living in the midst of ancestral heirlooms that were constant reminders of the family's vicissitudes. In the century that followed the suppression of religious relics, merely historical relics had started to take on almost religious significance. Those near the bottom might hope to rise, but those near the top can expect to fall. In a world of inversions, Sir Robert knew that while mysterious forces raised sea beds to mountain tops, rivers returned them to the sea.

Money worries and the repeated failure of his financial activities would have been a source of confusion. The world was evidently trying to tell him something. His alchemy yielded no gold, his politics provided no advancement, and his hospitality won no respite. All his life he had tried, but he had found few solutions to the many problems he faced. He seemed to be labouring under a serious misapprehension, to which we will turn in the Epilogue. Here, however, we explore what the *Paston Treasure* might tell us about how he understood his world as a great family patriarch.

Some people have seen still-life paintings as displays of control, as showing pride in the ability to bring the world to one's tabletop. Others have seen them as displays of anxiety, as raising concerns about disruption of the status quo.[8] Of course, control and anxiety are just two sides of the same coin, like European merchants' bluster that masked fear of missing out in the East. Sir Robert must have felt the tensions between control and anxiety more keenly than most, as his own exotic goods became the property of others. He had welcomed what was foreign and made it domestic – he had taken in the strange but was now becoming estranged.

As well as being 'cabinets of curiosity', still-lifes are also 'cabinets of wonders'. Wonder was associated with the peculiar, the mixed and paradoxical. Wonder could be delightful or dreadful, beautiful or horrible, but it could not be grasped and it could be the first step towards knowledge.[9] A sense of wonder marked lack of knowledge and spurred inquiry. Sir Robert still enjoyed the medieval fascination with wonder and could embrace the beauty of mystery. In fact, it was one of the things that made him dispensable to the Royal Society. After helping found it, he was expelled in 1682.[10] Mainstream science was shifting its course and leaving him behind. Sir Robert's sense of wonder was going out of fashion and the idea of nature as a symbolic labyrinth was being replaced by nature as a mechanical system. Of course, mechanical systems have some advantages over symbolic labyrinths, but systems only work if they are closed, and labyrinths always lead on to something else.[11]

Sir Robert's old-fashioned sense of wonder stopped his treasures being pinned down into cut-and-dried categories. Indeed, like Great Yarmouth's red herrings, the *Paston Treasure* was neither one thing nor the other. It was a *pronk-vanitas*, showing off in full knowledge that showing off was vain. It celebrated an insoluble conflict, as a rich thing made, in part, to denigrate riches.[12] We might see it as revelling in the profane in the light of the sacred, because today we see the sacred and the profane as two opposite realms – the world of religion and everything that lies outside religion. But while this division – like that between art and science – seems quite natural to us, it was brand new in the seventeenth century.[13] Separating the sacred from the profane had been an expedient way of neutralizing the religious tensions that had torn Europe apart for over a century. The separation of Church and state had been a novel political idea, but it was a complete anathema to Sir Robert.[14] For him, religion embraced all – body and soul, the body politic, the natural and the supernatural, the comprehensible and the incomprehensible. Religion embraced the wonder that allowed escape from the mundane world's twists and turns.

In his alchemical laboratory Sir Robert had gone through the 'mangle', and if base metals did not change into gold as he might have wished, then in the Hermetic attempt, maybe he himself changed. He entered into the alchemical quest with at least a part of him like Ben Jonson's Sir Epicure Mammon – wanting money – but it is entirely possible that he ended his quest more like William Shakespeare's Prospero. The inveterate border-crossing Hermes had a tendency to blur boundaries but he also had a habit of shifting the goalposts. Sir Robert did not find material gold, but he may have hit upon spiritual gold. That, after all, was exactly what the average seventeenth-century Anglican alchemist was aiming for – personal transformation. Sir Robert pursued a book of secrets from a bottom of the well to try and 'prove' gold and, in the process, he may have 'proved' himself.

Henshaw warned that one of Sir Robert's alchemical procedures would need 'the patience of half a dozen Jobs'.[15] Since Sir Robert had an undeniably great household and was pre-eminent in East Anglia, he may even have identified with the biblical Job, who was 'the greatest of all the men in the East' with a 'very great household'. The Devil bet he could undermine Job's faith by inflicting misfortune, and he seemed to win as Job descended into self-pity and self-righteousness. However, the wallowing Job was admonished for his limited perspective by someone who pointed out that his understanding was restricted by the vantage point of a mere individual creature. Job took this to heart and accepted his lot, acknowledging that only the Creator could see all creation. The story ended with God addressing Job 'out of a whirlwind', whereupon Job repented, and his repentance, or literally 'rethinking', was rewarded with even greater riches (Job 1–42).

The *Paston Treasure*'s X-rays revealed Sir Robert's ability to 'rethink', because, technically, the hidden silver platter, woman and ostrich egg are known as *pentimenti* or 'changes of mind'. The biblical Job had experienced a transformative 'whirlwind', and, in a letter to

Rebecca, Sir Robert described his 'whirlpool of misadventures' that may well have also proved transformative.[16] In his own terms, his life turned into a shipwreck. This was a very apt analogy since many merchants were ruined by their ships being sucked down by whirlpools, swamped by tempestuous waves or foundered on hidden shoals. But shipwrecks are also very apt beginnings for comedies because they throw threads into disarray, providing the chance that loose ends will eventually be tied up.

Everything changes. Even those parts of Sir Robert's collection that did not seem to change – like the individual shell cups that travelled to other collections – were capable of change. Shells were valued as objects of contemplation because of the way they unfolded, their spirals plotting the passage of time through space. Yet if their shapes expressed an orderly unfolding through time, then their material could express the disorder associated with time's passing.[17] Sir Robert was evidently very fond of shells' iridescent inner matter, their mother-of-pearl, and in the *Paston Treasure* his daughter, the servant and hidden woman all wore pearls. The painting featured the Pacific, but his whirlpool analogy acknowledged that oceans could be far from pacific. They could be catastrophically changeable. Sir Robert also knew how Shakespeare used the changeable sea in a play that explored – amongst other things – Europe's interaction with the New World.[18] *The Tempest* (classified as a comedy in the first folio of Shakespeare's plays) opens with a shipwreck, announced by Ariel, who sang:

> Full fathom five thy father lies.
> Of his bones are coral made;
> Those are pearls that were his eyes;
> Nothing of him that doth fade
> But doth suffer a sea-change
> Into something rich and strange.[19]

For Shakespeare's contemporaries, and for Sir Robert some fifty years later, the line 'Those are pearls that were his eyes' would have added a sinister twist to the song's overall grace and charm. The disturbing effect of that line is lost on us because we are no longer familiar with its graphic allusion to an age-related disorder, an unwelcome sign of the passage of time. Ariel's 'pearls' referred to cataracts, the apparent mineralization of the eye.[20] In the shipwreck caused by his 'whirlpool of misadventures', Sir Robert would undoubtedly have suffered a 'sea-change'. However, did that sea-change involve creeping blindness? Or might it have been a changed vision of 'something rich and strange', a change of perspective that could bring order to his state of chaos? This chapter explores that last possibility.

The *Paston Treasure* contains strong hints that Sir Robert may indeed have become more Prospero-like. His friend Thomas Browne, however, had always been more of a Prospero.[21] Browne said, 'I am [at home] everywhere . . . I have been ship-wrecked, yet am not enemy with the sea or winds; I can study, play or sleep in a tempest.'[22] Browne's accepting temperament, not to mention his professional bedside manner, would have helped Sir Robert put both the collection's dispersal and the family's decline into perspective. Browne also collected art and exotica, so he could empathize with its loss. In fact, he wrote a satire on the whole phenomenon of collecting called the *Musaeum clausum* or *Bibliotheca abscondita*, the 'Closed Museum' or 'Flown Library'.[23] And he also understood the cyclic nature of families because, some twenty years earlier, he had written: 'Generations pass while some trees stand, and old Families last not three Oaks.'[24] As one who was happy in a shipwreck and could 'sleep in a tempest', Browne was the ideal companion for Sir Robert in his 'whirlpool of misfortunes'. Indeed, there is a hint of Browne-like guidance in a letter Sir Robert sent Rebecca. He counselled, 'wink at things you cannot help,' and maybe he took his own advice.[25] In his alchemical laboratory he actively navigated deeply confusing territory and laboured to put things in place. Maybe, after his son came of age and project after project failed, he learned to accept being buffeted by fate and to simply allow things to just fall into place, recognizing, like Prospero, that 'my ending is despair, unless I be relieved by prayer.'[26]

The *Paston Treasure* itself looks a bit of a shipwreck and there must be reasons why someone who grew up surrounded by great art should have chosen to make it look so unlike any other painting. I think his still-life was a way of trying to understand the world, just like a literary creation.[27] After all, neither painting nor literature was seen as radically different from science, in which 'facts' were creatively conjured up by particular people at particular times and in particular places, not to mention the support of 'immense amounts of labour'.[28] Scientific facts are social constructions, just like literature and art. The *Paston Treasure* was Sir Robert's personal experiment in making his knowledge visible, and in the attempt he was in good company. After all, it was Galileo's artistic skill that allowed him to interpret the moon's 'strange spottedness' and, while his pockmarked moon may have implied the heavens' imperfection, he chose circles – not ellipses – for the planets' orbits because he felt circles were the more perfect figure. His scientific convictions and his aesthetic judgements 'obeyed ... the same controlling tendencies'.[29] Likewise, Sir Robert's painting would have been the product of his alchemical understanding of the world.

The *Paston Treasure* brought together disparate things – in a theatrical tableau, a staged shipwreck – as a way of exploring their relationships. If the new idea of science was, paradoxically, to find truth through artifice – withdrawing from the world in order to study it through experiments – then so was Sir Robert's picture. Today we equate pictorial depth with 'truth', but at the same time we know that the paint film is less than a millimetre thick. We should not complain if the *Paston Treasure* tabletop fails to create a convincing illusion of depth, because it is simply being true to itself as a piece of stretched canvas. The girl might seem squeezed in as an afterthought and the tabletop might seem askew, yet all our technical investigations – X-rays, paint samples and the like – proved that these apparent oddities were actually planned right from the very start.

Left to his own devices, the painter would almost certainly have approached the task very differently. Objects on the table would have been arranged to overlap each other with a single focus and there would be more space for the eye to rest. The painter was very skilful and everything about the painting that looks 'wrong' – apart from its faded colours – must be attributed to Sir Robert. Yet it would be a mistake to attribute the painting's suffocating busyness and apparent confusion to the patron's artistic naivety. He knew all about linear perspective, but purposefully avoided it.[30] Why?

Linear, or single-point, perspective visually reinforces our impression that the world is coherent and orderly. But, of course, that impression is only a comforting illusion, and in reality the world is neither coherent nor orderly. After all, the Forest of Arden looked very different to Duke Senior, Jacques, Touchstone and Corin, while England looked very different through Royalist and Parliamentarian eyes. Sir Robert also respected the fact that Catholics, Anglicans and Puritans had different perspectives. Through the Civil War and its aftermath, he had visceral experience of the world's fragmented and unstable nature. Acknowledging that fragmentation and avoiding the illusion of stability in his painting was a brave move.

In perspective paintings, objects in the foreground are bigger than, and often obscure, those in the background. Perspective privileges the foreground and it also privileges one position from which to view the picture. Or, to be precise, it privileges one eye. We are now so used to seeing the world through a single eye – the carefully directed film, TV or phone camera lens – that the *Paston Treasure*'s composition appears awkward.[31] But that need not stop us from trying to see what Sir Robert was trying to say.

Perspective in Inigo Jones's theatrical stage-sets privileged a single position in the auditorium. There, the optical effect had metaphysical significance, turning the source of the masque's riches, Charles I, into its focus. However, in domestic settings, the single viewing position for perspective paintings had no such significance and not everyone approved. Earlier in the century, while Inigo Jones used perspective, England's top miniature painter, Nicholas Hilliard, purposely avoided it. He thought perspective deceived both 'the understanding and the eye'. Perspective was seductive and illusory, because it offered a very restricted technical 'accuracy' that could be – and is now regularly – confused with 'truth'.[32] Hilliard thought that perspective pictures masqueraded as objective statements and, inevitably, masked the subjectivity inherent in any representation. Such tensions between subjectivity and objectivity also informed the work of Sir Robert's contemporary the metaphysical poet Thomas

Traherne, who used the idea of linear perspective as a stepping stone towards all-seeing vision.[33] Sir Robert was not ignorant and his scribe-like painter was not incompetent. The *Paston Treasure* refused to obey the dictates of illusory perspective on purpose.

I think the *Paston Treasure*'s composition is a heroic aesthetic experiment, just as Sir Robert's attempt to make the Philosopher's Stone was a grand Hermetic experiment. The painting has a medieval flavour – it focuses on many distinct things rather than aiming for a single unified effect – that is perfectly consistent with Sir Robert's alchemical interests.[34] He knew he was looking for truth through artifice in his laboratory and I think he was doing exactly the same in his painting. The relationships he was exploring in the *Paston Treasure* were not merely optical; they went beyond the realm of everyday appearances.

Sir Robert's extraordinarily original painting was what, centuries later, Pablo Picasso would call the lie that tells the truth.[35] Picasso's experiments with pictorial space were revolutionary, but we could usefully compare the *Paston Treasure* with Paul Cézanne's equally uncompromising but less assertive paintings. Statements by Cézanne, together with analysis of his paintings, suggest that he was deeply engaged in experiments with perspective.[36] Our visual worlds are now so conditioned by perspective that it is worth briefly considering what an alternative system of representation might offer.

When Cézanne painted a still-life he regarded his apples – as well as his plates, bowls and jugs – as 'gentlemen' who spoke to one another and exchanged 'confidences'. He said that his fruits enjoyed 'having their portraits painted'.[37] If he had used perspective then he would have shown how that particular 'group portrait' looked from a artist's frozen point of view. Yet Cézanne wanted more. He did not want to use the 'miserable trick' of perspective to make distant apples shrink when he knew full well they were all the same size.[38] He also wanted to show how one apple – or plate, bowl or jug – would appear when 'seen' by its neighbours. He added clues about how the scene looked when seen from other vantage points and he removed clues that privileged one vantage point over others. He managed to imply multiple viewpoints within a single viewpoint by turning towards what he called 'the intelligence of the *Pater Omnipotens*' and was later called the 'view from everywhere'.[39] Cézanne achieved this by acknowledging the tactile aspects of visual scenes – he imagined how objects could be grasped in the hand, and how he might navigate a route through the objects, or assembled 'gentlemen'.[40] Cézanne spent a lifetime on his experiments with vision but, as far as we know, Sir Robert only composed one painting. However, both Sir Robert and Cézanne were influenced by medieval ideas of space, as in Villard de Honnecourt's architecture.[41] It is therefore worth considering the *Paston Treasure* as a medieval interior and group portrait.

Luckily, we know a lot about one man with whom Sir Robert could have discussed his ideas for the painting – his lifelong friend Thomas Browne. Browne was some 25 years older than Sir Robert, but the two men died within six months of each other, Sir Robert describing Browne's last illness in a letter to Rebecca.[42] He was the son of a London silk merchant who was educated at the universities of Oxford, Montpellier, Padua (he arrived in Italy the year Galileo's *Dialogue Concerning the Two Chief World Systems* was published) and Leiden. He moved to Norwich when Robert was about six years old and was knighted when Charles II visited Norwich in 1671, and his house was described by Evelyn as 'a Paradise and Cabinet of rarities'.[43]

Browne had interesting opinions about most things and could 'look a whole day with delight upon a handsome picture'.[44] In the 1630s he made spirited defences of painting in his *Religio medici*, or 'Religion of a Doctor', written during Charles I's generous patronage of foreign painters. Later, in his *Pseudodoxia epidemica*, or 'Widespread Falsehoods', his approach to paintings was quite different. *Pseudodoxia* first came out in 1646, so Browne was writing it while Robert was in his early teens. As a family friend, he would have known that Robert was in Westminster when the schoolboys defended the Abbey against a mob intent on destroying its art. At the same time, he would also have known all about the much greater destruction caused by William Dowsing. In 1643, as an ordinary citizen, Dowsing took issue with the 'blasphemous crucifixes ... superstitious pictures and relics of popery' all over Cambridge.[45] Within months he became the official parliamentary 'Iconoclast General', and travelled the length and breadth of East Anglia destroying art with great enthusiasm in a very systematic and well-documented campaign.[46] But, again within a few months, support faltered, doubt set in and his zeal waned before he could destroy even more. He did not need to visit Norwich, because the locals were happy enough to smash sculptures and slash and burn paintings all on their own.

It is not surprising that Browne's approach to art changed during the Cavalier winter. Typically, he took paintings to task when he felt that they were not literally true – he was offended, for example, that Adam was depicted with a navel when only those born of a woman were scarred with navels.[47] Yet, at the same time, he also took people to task for only interpreting things literally.[48] Between the 1630s and the 1640s, he swung from an unconditional concept of the 'Beauty of Holiness' towards a more cautious conditional defence of paintings as long as they were 'correct'.[49] There can be little doubt that Browne and Sir Robert had conversations about paintings, and a letter from Clayton alluded to just such a conversation with their mutual friend Henshaw. Sir Robert had been planning to convert a room and paint 'a history' on its walls. Clayton wrote of how he and Henshaw 'resolved over a glass of claret' that the appropriate subject for this painting would be 'the woman of Samaria giving Our Saviour a drink' (John 4:7). This was because the room was 'a buttery transmuted into a chapel', so the image would be 'hieroglyphicke as well as history'.[50] Assuming that Sir Robert and Browne engaged in similar conversations over the odd glass of claret, our understanding of the *Paston Treasure*'s strange composition might benefit from comparison with one of Browne's books, *The Garden of Cyrus*. They are strictly comparable because images and texts were fundamentally connected by an idea that profoundly informed early seventeenth-century English painting. Browne even used that idea – *ut pictura poesis*, or 'as is painting so is poetry' – in his defence of images through the iconoclasm.

The full title of Browne's book was *The Garden of Cyrus, or The Quincunciall, Lozenge, or Net-work Plantations of the Ancients, Artificially, Naturally, Mystically Considered*. It is a treatise on the 'quincuncial' order, a pattern of five things, one in the centre surrounded by four in a square – like dots on the side of dice. It was written about five

years before the *Paston Treasure* was painted and contains stream-
of-consciousness imagery even dizzier than its title. Robert Boyle
damned it with faint praise, calling it 'no ordinary book'. Twentieth-
century commentators went on to describe it as 'radically bad',
'tiresome' and the 'least important' of Browne's books. Some para-
graphs have been called 'the finest he ever wrote', yet much of it is
deemed 'almost unreadable'.[51] Many of his readers threw up their
hands in horror at what seemed to some a 'haphazard cull from reading and notebooks'.[52] So far, so similar to the shipwreck-like *Paston
Treasure*. Indeed a modern scholar has said that Browne's books are
'a literary version of ... the cabinet of natural and antique curiosities
... assemblages ... held together ... by the taste and inclination of
the collector'.[53]

The *Garden* provides the perfect comparison for Sir Robert's
picture, which in some respects might seem the worst painting produced by an otherwise perfectly capable artist. Although dismissed
by many, the *Garden*'s admirers included Thomas De Quincey, Jorge
Luis Borges and W. G. Sebald, who presumably appreciated Browne's
interest in the profound order that sustains a superficial appearance
of chaos. We can treat the book as one side of a conversation with Sir
Robert and approach the picture's strange visual structure in terms
of literary structures.

For example, the slightly disturbing effect of this idiosyncratic
still-life – with its strange juxtapositions, like a lobster emerging from
a girl's head – is like a visual equivalent of literary catachresis. This
technique involves mixed metaphors and exaggerated comparison,
such as 'His complexion is perfect gallows.'[54] Catachresis initially
creates confusion and, if dwelt upon, evokes heightened emotion, a
sense of alienation, disorientation and tension. Sir Robert may well
have suffered all these feelings as the world around him spiralled out
of control, but we cannot know if he intended this effect in the picture.
The overwhelming majority of seventeenth-century still-life paintings
do not have an air of catachresis. Yet, as an aside, while they do not
aim for catachresis, they do aim for catechesis, or religious instruction.
Still-life painters were, and still are, popular because their catechesis is
not preachy. The spiritual dimension sits there, quiet and unassuming

and easily overlooked. It patiently awaits your notice, rewarding attention but not asserting itself. Still-life paintings celebrate life's riches
in full knowledge of their transience.

Browne's *Garden* used another literary style – the paratactic
or 'side by side' style where phrases are added to each other without
conjunctions to coordinate or subordinate them. A famous example is
Caesar's 'I came, I saw, I conquered,' where there is no hierarchy and
all components are treated as equally important. Parataxis has musical
rhythms that we can imagine transformed into visual rhythms. The
Paston Treasure seems to emulate this paratactic style. The things in it
are 'side by side'; their margins touch and overlapping is minimized.
Of course, there are some overlaps – the girl's head obscures part of
the lobster and porcelain bowl – but the bowl's rim just skims the
bottom of the silver tankard, glances off the globe's equatorial rim and
is perfectly aligned with the top of the girl's chair.[55] The lute's body
also glances off the globe while its neck runs along the clock's edge
and its head just touches the picture frame. This visual version of parataxis is most obvious with the shell cups, which all touch each other,
an arrangement that would have been impossible if Sir Robert had
allowed the painter to use strict perspective. It may be significant that
these shell cups were the first items to be completed in the process of
painting the *Paston Treasure.* Perhaps the picture's items touch each
other to imply something like the 'exchange of confidences' between
'gentlemen' in Cézanne's apple paintings?

Together, the arrangement of shell cups could be thought to
resemble notes in written music, with which, of course, Sir Robert
was very familiar. The 'staff notation' in the *Paston Treasure*'s songbook,
for example, visually represents pitch within an immaterial musical
space, referring to things and relationships between things that exist
completely outside the everyday dimensions of space. While music
may 'touch' us, it does not do so with fingers. As one would read a
musical score, from left to right, the shell cups seem to gradually rise,
peak above the globe, then rapidly fall after touching the hourglass.
Each item is purposely given its own space, as we might expect in
an abstract diagram rather than in a scene of things on a tabletop.
Like musical notes on a staff, together they refer to relationships in

some metaphysical space. The shell cups rise and fall like the notes in Kepler's *Harmonices mundi* that show the 'harmonies' sung by heavenly bodies.[56] The pattern also follows the Paston family's slow, gathering ascent followed by its rapid, scattering descent.[57] We cannot know what the pattern meant to Sir Robert, but we cannot doubt that it had some meaning since, in his view, such visual and musical structures resonated with the structure of the world and of the mind.[58]

Now we tend to think of harmonies as notes played simultaneously, but Sir Robert knew otherwise. The root of the word 'harmony' is *ar*, which means 'to join distinct parts', and words sharing the same root include 'arm', 'artisan', 'artist' and 'articulate', which is the joining of distinct sounds into words or sentences. When notes are played simultaneously they are no longer distinct since their individual identities are swallowed by the chord's identity. Yet when notes are joined in sequence they become a 'harmony' while at the same time remaining distinct. Such harmonies are instances of 'making one out of many' and, crucially, they respect each note as an individual, each with its own unique possibilities. They are like the harmonies that Sir Robert strove for throughout his entire political life – making one Norfolk out of separate Royalist, Parliamentarian, Puritan, Anglican and Catholic factions, uniting them in community while respecting their differences.

Of course, painted shell cups are not musical notes, but our understanding of the *Paston Treasure*'s odd composition can be helped by the equally odd *Garden* in which Browne wanted 'to read the book of nature without recourse to the book of Scripture'.[59] The *Garden* was intended as a guide to reading the Book of Nature, which Browne described as 'that universal and public manuscript, that lies expans'd unto the eyes for all'.[60] It was an extraordinarily ambitious aim so it is not surprising that he lost some of his readers along the way. He followed Plato's *Timaeus* in describing the material world as an imperfect imitation of the perfect immaterial world. Browne also recognized that the *Timaeus* could not be 'true' since, as Plato himself said, it was just 'a likely story' – no more was ever possible.[61] With such an attitude towards God's work in making the world, and Plato's work in telling its story, Browne would have had a lot to say to the person who designed the *Paston Treasure*. He knew that a still-life copied nature and therefore had to be imperfect. The more it tried to look real, the more illusory it inevitably became – it could not escape its true nature as pigment and oil on canvas. As he made clear in his *Pseudodoxia*, the tragedy of iconoclasm was that people looked for literal truth in pictures where there could be none. As he said of his *Garden*, 'expect herein no mathematicall truths'.[62] The inevitability of imperfection gave him licence to play.

Browne would probably have agreed with Sir Henry Wotton's general views on art, condemning Dürer for slavishly expressing 'that which was' and Michelangelo for idealistically expressing 'that which should be'. In Wotton's opinion, both painters produced 'a kind of Rigidity' that left no room for the strangeness and imperfections that were required for the viewer to engage with the picture.[63] For him, great paintings – like tragic heroes – must have faults.[64] The *Paston Treasure* certainly has some strangeness and imperfection, yet, according to Browne, nothing in the world was 'ugly or mis-shapen . . . nature is not at variance with art, nor art with nature, they both being servants of His providence.'[65] So, what may strike the modern eye as confusing or wrong may actually be intentional since many, including Browne, were convinced that the world required 'unriddling'.[66]

Browne found the *Garden's* five-point 'quincunx' everywhere – in nature, Egyptian hieroglyphs and Greek philosophy. The pattern proliferated in such a chaotic profusion that it made his assertion of underlying order seem ludicrously optimistic.[67] But this was simply his way of making his own book mirror the Book of Nature, in which an inscrutable order is hidden beneath what looks like disorder. Indeed, the *Garden* was recently called 'as disorderly a text as can be imagined, whose argument is endless order'.[68] After many apparent digressions, Browne eventually revealed the five points' spiritual significance by relating the pattern to the Crucifixion, with four wounds in Christ's extremities and one at his centre.

In spite of its naturally chaotic structure and profoundly spiritual message, the book starts with a very orderly and pragmatic example of the pattern. The quincunx is, he says, the best way to plant an orchard. For us, an orchard may not seem an obvious place to start, but Browne probably knew Ralph Austen's *Treatise of Fruit Trees*, which has been described as 'as much a revolutionary manifesto and a spiritual autobiography as . . . a technical handbook'.[69] Austen also wrote *The Spiritual Use of an Orchard or Garden of Fruit Trees*. Yet, even without Austen's work, orchards may have been an obvious starting point for Browne since he had chosen to spend most of his life in Norwich, which an English gazetteer said was 'either a city in an orchard, or an orchard in a city, so equally are houses and trees blended in it'.[70] Classically, he would have seen orchards through Virgil's *Georgics*, and biblically, of course, they represented Eden.[71]

An orchard's trees, Browne said, should be planted to allow 'commodious radiation in their growth, and a due expansion of their branches, for shadow or delight'. (Note his entirely characteristic wordplay on 'light' and a tree's pleasure.) In the pattern of a quincunx, trees enjoy 'the fructifying breath of Heaven' and each is 'fairly exposed unto the rayes of moon and sunne'.[72] Together, the trees 'frameth a penthouse over the eye, and maketh a quiet vision' and, in so doing, they imitate Providence, which 'hath arched and paved the great house of the world'.[73] The 1658 edition of the *Garden* had a frontispiece showing the ideal plantation – a diaper-lattice pattern of circles, each connected with lines to four other circles. The trees in his orchard were strictly paratactic.

For Sir Robert and Browne, much of the cosmic harmony embodied in Charles I's court lived on, at a comfortable distance from the cut-throat expediency of Charles II's court. Any conversation between them about the painting could be expected to dwell on the interconnections between things. In fact, like the *Garden*, the structure of the *Paston Treasure* may be an attempt to imitate the structure of the cosmos, as reflected in the Oxnead collection, an exploration of the Pastons' relationship with the cosmos. For Sir Robert and Browne, the 'self' was a microcosm which reflected, and was reflected in, the macrocosm. For both men, the gold in the shell cups' mounts, for example, was linked with the sun in the heavens and the heart in the body, as well as with the king in the realm.

That, of course, was why Browne investigated, and why Sir Robert made and took, *aurum potible*. Browne's Leiden professor called medicine 'a search for self knowledge',[74] and believed that health arose naturally from achieving balance with the rest of the world. This approach is made clear by the ingredients of Sir Walter Raleigh's famous 'Royal cordial'. The cordial's animal-based ingredients were hart's horn, bezoar stone and musk from the land, as well as pearls and ambergris from the sea. Its vegetable ingredients were ten roots, including angelica; six whole plants, including mint; six flowers, including elderflower; and six fruits, including nutmeg; five barks, including cinnamon; and six woods, including aloe. The mineral ingredients included gold (of course), bole and loadstone. These were all prepared in spirit of wine – known as the 'key of the philosophers' – together with alkermes, the traditional medicine made from the dye-producing insect kermes, and attar, the fragrant oil extracted from rose petals.[75] Raleigh's son, who was in Sir Robert's circle of friends, had another version, and Sir Robert's notebook contains the recipe for yet another.[76] All played with ideas of sympathy between the microcosm and macrocosm.

Sir Robert was very familiar with such ideas. He did not labour under ideas like that of gravity as an impersonal force. For him, and Browne, things were still driven by internal desires, so fire, for example, always rose because it wished to get above the realm of air, its proper home in the ideal world. Cold, impersonal forces simply did not exist, because everything was interconnected. Even the movement of heavenly bodies could be personal, as demonstrated by the weather, eclipses and comets that portended change in the body politic. So, the arrangement of objects in Sir Robert's picture need not have been determined by dry laws, like the physical law of gravity or the optical law of perspective. The *Paston Treasure*'s strange composition arose from something much, much richer than such merely 'mathematicall truths'. Things in the *Paston Treasure* relate to each other in ways that owe more to the reasoning implied by the ingredients of Raleigh's cordial than to the optical laws.

In the old cosmic harmony, the heart, the sun and gold 'belonged together' in the way that mutually besotted lovers 'belong together', and not at all in the way contractually obliged parties 'belong together'. Such cosmic relationships were not imposed 'from without', as with legally bound parties who are 'held responsible' to each other. The relationships were mysteriously created 'from within', like the bonds between those who are in love and who 'take responsibility' for each other.

As the product of a long line of lawyers and as a politician, Sir Robert may initially have been inclined towards legalistic interpretations of 'belonging'. On the other hand, Browne, as a rather old-fashioned doctor, would have been strongly inclined to the other interpretation, the understanding that Dante described as 'the love which moves the sun and the other stars'.[77] Yet how could 'love' move the sun or arrange things in a picture?

For Dante, the sun and stars were moved by their love of God, just as suitors are moved by the one they desire and the hungry are moved by food. The arrangement in the picture does not represent the appearance of Sir Robert's collection at any one time or from any one place. Rather, it is an attempt to express his emotional relationship with his collection, quite possibly including pride at its gradual assembly and resignation at its inevitable dispersal. The paratactic picture makes visible how the collection touched him.[78] The laws of single-point perspective would have imposed a legalistic 'belonging together' in the *Paston Treasure*. On the other hand, the 'belonging together' of lovers allowed the painted things to move around the canvas freely, reflecting their relationships in Sir Robert's eyes.

The shift from one view of 'belonging' to the other is utterly transformative. It is a 'repentance' or change of mind so deep that it could be called a change of heart.[79] The shift of belonging is the kind of altering of perception that could result from going through the alchemical 'mangle' of suffering that Sir Robert endured. He might have started to put the *Paston Treasure* together as a celebration of family and wealth, but he had time to ponder on it as his family and wealth started to slip away. In that time, any hint of Sir Epicure Mammon in him may have undergone a sea-change into a Prospero. That sea-change would change absolutely nothing in the outside world – plague would still rage, London would still burn and political machinations would still grind on. However, their psychological impact would be incomparably different – anxieties would evaporate in the face of acceptance. If 'the love which moves the sun and the other stars' also moved the items on Sir Robert's tabletop, then the *Paston Treasure* would be a constant reminder of cosmic laws, beside which mere laws of the land pale into insignificance.

Such a subtle yet profound shift in perspective marks the turning-point at which the potentially dark and obsessive acquisitive nature of a *pronk* can turn into the liberating recognition of a *vanitas*. It also suggests how the painting's cut-and-paste appearance of multiple, separate items might be brought together – not with an overarching optical unity imposed by perspective, but with much more personal connections. And Sir Robert's radical rethinking (or repentance) of standard seventeenth-century pictorial composition also opens up the possibility of a happy ending to his story. This is because a suitor might be moved by the one they desire, but their movement is an expression of distance from their beloved. A suitor's love is therefore tinged with longing while, as we shall see, Sir Robert's repentance allowed any such longing to be banished by belonging.[80]

The things in the picture touch each other, cheek-to-cheek. More subtly, they are also linked by light, because, where appropriate, each piece reflects its neighbour's colour. For example, the nautilus shell above the globe has the warm reflection of the golden recorder and the back of the lute takes on the colour of the red chair. With these reflections, one object shares the colour of its neighbour, making connections between objects in the *Paston Treasure* like the 'confidences' exchanged by the 'gentlemen' in Cézanne's apple paintings. The shared colours are everywhere and were much more obvious before the pigments faded.[81] They lend another dimension to the *Paston Treasure*'s connection with the quincuncial lines and circles on Browne's *Garden* frontispiece. (See the beginning of the Epilogue.) If repeated mutual reflections are imagined in Browne's pattern, then it becomes like a section of a spider's web with dewdrops at each junction and with each drop reflecting the others.

There is an Eastern version of this image – Indra's net – which has the same pattern in three dimensions rather than two.[82] At each knot of the net there is a dewdrop-like pearl or a multifaceted jewel in which every other pearl or jewel is reflected. The image conveys the idea that all things depend upon, and are found in, each other. Sir Robert may not have known Indra's net, but exactly the same ideas were in the European tradition. For example, Nicholas of Cusa claimed, 'Everything [is] in everything.'[83] Glimpses of Indra's net are also in the metaphysical poetry of Sir Robert's contemporary Andrew Marvell, and in the *Divine Comedy* where Dante described an 'eternal power which has made for itself / So many mirrors on which to break itself / And yet remains One as before.'[84]

As an aside, we could note that the *Divine Comedy*'s image throws more light on Sir Robert's interest in the forms, and transformations, of shells. There is only one true form, and that is unmanifest unity. The multiplicity of manifest things – like shells – consists of innumerable temporary unions of form and matter. Each partner brings something to their union, and the transformation of shells – whether by nature or by a craftsperson – is an additional temporary weaving together of other aspects of form and matter. In Dante's image, the 'eternal power' chose to 'break itself', and Sir Robert would have seen the many changing things, like shells, as ways in which the unchanging One 'articulated' itself, both hiding and expressing its truth.

In the *Paston Treasure* the reflected patches of colour on neighbouring objects hint at their interdependence and interpenetration, and those connections reinforce the fact that each of the depicted objects was, of course, part of the family's one great treasure trove. Some seventeenth-century painters even explicitly acknowledged these Indra's net-like connections extending beyond their paintings. The enigmatic Clara Peeters, for example, filled some of her exquisite still-life paintings with minute fragmentary portraits – either of her as the painting's creator, or of us as the painting's viewer – reflected in ornate silverware. More obviously, Velázquez painted two people – either the sitters he was ostensibly painting, or us as the painting's viewers – reflected in the mirror of his *Las Meninas*. The *Paston Treasure*'s painter did not include reflections of himself or the viewer. But, as Sir Robert's alchemical experiences showed, the observer inevitably coloured his or her view of what they observed and, in turn, they were coloured by what they observed. Although the still-life is very big, its almost obsessive fine detail draws in the viewer in a mangle-like experiment, one that Sir Robert used to help strengthen the links of friendships within his learned circle.

The painting's reflected colours were due to light playing with a multitude of materials and – from his experience with the painter and his own pigment recipes – Sir Robert knew a lot about those materials. After all, as we know, the red curtain was painted with cochineal extracted from real red cloth. Yet he also knew – from his alchemical studies – that while the painting, and the whole world, seemed to be made of many different materials, they were all really just different forms of one matter, *prima materia*. Both he and Browne were very interested in that one, universal matter. It provided the physical continuity that underpinned the Indra's net-like world in which all things belonged together, paratactically bound by love.

In comedies disparate threads eventually come together. Sir Robert's shift in point of view – represented by his breaking free of the strictures of linear perspective – provided a different way of looking at the world that had clarity, simplicity and order. It offered a cosmic, and comic, resolution. In the *Paston Treasure*'s strange composition, the multiple parts of the world could be seen as just so many mutual reflections of the One. Similarly, the painting's multiple materials were just so many variations on *prima materia*. And, like the *Divine Comedy*'s 'eternal power' that chose to 'break itself', *prima materia* also had an Eastern equivalent – it was 'the Way', or Tao, and 'she was generated before heaven and earth'.[85] *Prima materia* was the seething substrate of reality, pregnant with innumerable possibilities. So, it is entirely appropriate that *prima materia* was known by many different names. Names can assume disproportionate significance in comedies – like Dr Subtle and Sir Epicure Mammon in Jonson's *The Alchemist* – and one of *prima materia*'s names, *sylva*, would have held significance for Sir Robert.

Sir Robert knew *Sylva* as a paper presented to the Royal Society, a year or so before the *Paston Treasure* was painted. Its full title was *Sylva, or, A Discourse of Forest Trees and the Propagation of Timber*. Browne knew it as a book by his friend John Evelyn that covered territory related to Austen's *Spiritual Use of an Orchard* and his own *Garden of Cyrus . . . Plantations of the Ancients*. Evelyn meant *Sylva* as wood, plantation or forest – as in Transylvania, the land 'beyond the forests' – but *sylva* was also the Latin version of the Greek *hyle*, so it also meant Aristotelian matter, water or the alchemical 'principle of volatility'. Theoretically, *sylva* was formless matter, or pure chaos, which of course could not be represented. *Sylva* was therefore usually represented as matter with a little form, or chaos with a little order. Critically, the matter that was chosen to represent chaos had to have the potential for more form or more order. Medieval metalwork explored forest, orchard and vine-like motifs as ways of representing *sylva* in cast metal sculpture. They were usually cast in bronze although, of course, it would have been more appropriate to cast *sylva* in silver.[86]

Sylva punned with silver. And silver was related to quicksilver, 'live-silver' or mercury, the alchemical principle of volatility, as well as water and Aristotelian matter. They were all variations on the theme of *prima materia*. Silver was also tied to the waxing and waning moon, the heavenly body connected to the tides, earth's quintessentially changeable waters, and 'governess of the floods'.[87] In trade silver was the embodiment of financial liquidity, the principle of volatility in economic realms. This was why Pliny called silver a 'madness of mankind'.[88] Shape-shifting silver was the constant that flowed through businesses as water flows through ever-changing rivers. So, upon reflection, it was not surprising that 'trunksfull' of silver left Oxnead to be melted down and that a painted silver platter mysteriously vanished from the *Paston Treasure* to remain only as a ghostly X-ray. It is the very nature of silver/*sylva* to be restless – to expect otherwise would be to deny the fundamental hylomorphic nature of the cosmos.[89] Someone who secretly identified his shifty, expedient king with the hieroglyph for water or the principle of volatility would not make the mistake of thinking silver/*sylva* could be relied upon.

Losing the family silver was undoubtedly a hard lesson, but it could have been a very effective teacher. As an Anglican, Sir Robert knew his psalms and knew that silver, as well as having a relationship with *sylva*, could also represent divine communication. 'The words of the Lord are pure words: as silver tried in a furnace of earth, purified seven times' (Psalm 12:6). As Bede had said, whereas gold represented wisdom, silver represented 'the brightness of words'.[90] If silver was the protean *sylva*-like substrate of the economy then, biblically, it was lucid eloquence and glittering rhetoric. Through the movement of silver, God was trying to tell Sir Robert something.

Silver may have flowed out of Oxnead, but *sylva* flowed everywhere and the *Paston Treasure* celebrated that flow. Not only did objects come from around the world to Sir Robert's tabletop, but the materials with which those objects were depicted also flowed around the world. The presence in Oxnead of materials that had travelled the world – like Peruvian or Mexican cochineal – could not help but reinforce Sir Robert's awareness of *sylva*'s restless nature. He had observed the *Paston Treasure*'s painter at work; he had worked in his laboratory and possibly been instructed by a master wood-turner. He would have been fully aware that each and every material was 'apt and good for' some things but not for others.[91] Silver was a material that was astrologically and alchemically tied to water and the everchanging moon. It was most certainly not 'apt and good for' staying in one shape or one place.

Even if they were not melted down, silver platters needed regular polishing as they tarnished, so they could be dark as well as bright. In his *Garden* Browne noted that there were two sides to everything, even light itself, so that the 'light that make things seen, makes some things invisible'. He went on to explain that 'were it not for darkness . . . the noblest part of creation [would be] unseen, and the stars in Heaven [would be] invisible.' And he was far from being alone in declaring that the 'greatest mystery of religion' was expressed by darkness or nothingness.[92] As the gloom gathered and Sir Robert's family fortune started slipping away, Browne might have reminded him of the hidden light that could be revealed only by darkness. That 'silver lining' was evident in a classical myth that Sir Robert already knew very well.

In his quest for the Philosopher's Stone, Sir Robert would have read Michael Maier's *Atalanta fugiens* or 'Atalanta Fleeing'. He was obviously interested in the myth that lay behind the book's title, because the *Paston Treasure* shows a mounted shell cup engraved with a very prominent image of Atalanta in the act of running.[93] Maier's alchemical interpretation was extraordinarily complex but Atalanta's story was quite simple. As a baby, she was abandoned by her father and raised by bears. She grew into a beautiful woman who, upon returning to civilization, wished to remain single. Having been raised in the wild, she could run extremely fast so challenged all her suitors to a race – if they won she would marry them, but if she won she would kill them. Many died until a suitor sought Aphrodite's advice. The goddess gave him three golden apples and each time Atalanta started to overtake him, he threw one away and she ran off to collect it. He won the race and they were married.[94]

At one level, Atalanta's story is of a woman trapped into marriage by attraction to worldly riches. And a direct connection between her riches and Sir Robert's own trappings – his outward signs of status – is implied in the *Paston Treasure* by the engraved image of a nautilus shell in the shade of the bush at her feet. The painting shows that Sir Robert knew his trappings could entrap. In fact, Henshaw mentioned Paston's 'cursed gold', suggesting that many could see riches as two-sided.[95] The double meanings of words like 'trapping' were part of the Janus nature of reality that Sir Robert explored in his laboratory. After all, Hermes presided over both secrecy and communication so himself embodied a Janus nature. It was also evident in everyday life, since Great Yarmouth's fishermen chased 'shoals' (of herrings) around 'shoals' (the North Sea's notorious shifting shallows). Shoals were the source of riches and the place of wrecks – they could both make and break. Indeed, the Janus nature of Sir Robert's treasures was precisely the point of the *pronk-vanitas*.

As Sir Robert's collection slipped through his fingers, Atalanta's myth would have offered him hope. She had lost her freedom acquiring glittering baubles. Perhaps losing his glittering baubles might help him acquire freedom?

Losing his treasures could be seen as an echo of the biblical *felix culpa*, or 'lucky fault'. Sir Robert's 'whirlpool of misadventures' was like Adam's 'fortunate fall' from Eden – it was a necessary step on the path towards self-knowledge. After all, as an alchemist, Sir Robert knew that base lead had to be reduced to *prima materia*, or *sylva*, before it could be transmuted into noble gold. Existing order had to be sacrificed before a higher order could be attained. Certainties had

to be relinquished and uncertainties acknowledged before understanding could be reached. The 'lucky fault' and the 'fortunate fall'
recognized that the material and the spiritual could have completely
opposite trajectories, and Sir Robert chose to depict those opposite
trajectories in his *Paston Treasure*. He did so with the least glamor-
ous of all its objects, the possibly part-homemade hourglass, perfect
counterpart to the exotic shell cup engraved with Atalanta. In keeping
with the idea of surreverence, the picture's most symbolically charged
object was also its most humble.

The painting shows sand falling through an hourglass. It does
not show air's accompanying ascent. In Greek, air is *pneuma* and is
synonymous with spirit. So, as matter falls to the lower glass, spirit
rises into the upper glass, their paths crossing in a narrow neck that
opens into an expansive 'other'. Sir Robert knew the symbolic significance of his hourglass – the 'narrow' neck, for example, was the
'strait' gate 'which leadeth unto life' (Matthew 7:14). The lower glass
corresponded to the terrestrial globe shown in the *Paston Treasure*,
while the upper one corresponded to its sister, the celestial globe
which Sir Robert had in his collection but did not show in his picture. Structurally, the hourglass echoes the contact and intercourse
between heaven and earth, the invisible and the visible, the spiritual
and the material. And humans, alone in all creation, could be equally
at home in both realms, which is why Thomas Browne called humans
'that great and true Amphibium'.[96]

At rest, the upper globe of the hourglass contains air while the
lower contains both air and sand. The upper globe can therefore par-
ticipate in unity, while the lower only ever participates in diversity.
Now, diversity requires distinction between parts, and – remembering
the etymology of 'harmony' as well as Dante's image of 'many mirrors'
– it can therefore be articulated. On the other hand, there is no distinction in unity so it cannot be articulated.[97] Unity is indescribable.
Is that why Sir Robert had his terrestrial globe painted, but left the
celestial one unpainted? Is that why he made the half-lifted curtain
reveal the things below but conceal the things above? Great art contains many possibilities. Did his painted curtain allude to the temple
veil, an ancient Greek art joke, or his interests in dyestuffs and the

textile trade? The only thing about which we can be certain is that the curtain is open to more than one interpretation. The painting therefore successfully reflects the richness of reality, which never lends itself to a single explanation. Therein lay the *Paston Treasure*'s power to foster cohesion in the aftermath of divisive Civil War.[98]

Sir Robert oversaw the painting of a *pronk-vanitas*. As an Anglican, he knew about the vanity of worldly possessions, and unlike most English patrons of the arts, he actually wished to be reminded of it. He may not have included the celestial globe in the picture, but he knew it was implied by the terrestrial one. He also knew the changeable nature of worldly goods could illuminate the unchanging nature of heavenly truths and that globes and maps were symbols of guidance for our passage through life. As sailors returned home with ever more accurate information, maps were constantly being updated, so even his globe's inaccuracies were reminders of worldly transience.[99] Of course, maps were made for many purposes, some of which might be unexpected. For example, Sir Clement Paston's contemporary, Raleigh, had been told about a non-existent island on a map, discovering that it had been added by the cartographer for his wife where 'she, in imagination, might have an island of her own'.[100] Maps and globes do not acknowledge the extraordinary labour and skills that inform them, so – as Hilliard said of perspective pictures – their 'technical accuracy' can be mistaken for 'truth'.[101]

Whatever faith Sir Robert placed in his globes, a late seventeenth-century book of trades counselled, 'to measure the course of the sky high above seems very significant; but it is far more useful to investigate the course of life and what is going to happen at its end.'[102] The music book in the girl's hand explicitly reinforces the *Paston Treasure*'s interest in what happens at life's end. It is a dialogue sung between a recently deceased supplicant and Charon, the boatman who ferries souls across the River Styx, the boundary between this and the underworld. The parrot's claw points to the words 'Bring death's black seal'.[103]

The music score and hourglass were absolutely standard *vanitas* motifs. The shell cup engraved with Atalanta running, on the other hand, was a very personal way of expressing *vanitas*, the relative poverty of the fabulous Oxnead collection when seen from a spiritual perspective. And Sir Robert also included another innovative reference to *vanitas* – an almost completely black mirror. Mirrors are made to reflect things, yet this one seems to reflect nothing at all. In the seventeenth century a jet-black mirror might evoke an obsidian fortune-telling scrying glass, such as the one from Mexico that allegedly belonged to Dr John Dee. However, these were usually oval and the very faint reflection of vine leaves hints that the *Paston Treasure's* rectangular mirror is an optical device, not a divinatory tool. It is likely to be a biblical reference to the worldly glories that look like mere reflections in a 'dark glass' when compared with heavenly glory (1 Corinthians 13:12). According to Sir Robert's 'speculative' view of the world the mirror was the symbol of symbols, so it was bound to have many meanings.

It has been said that collectors like Sir Robert were interested in things for their own sake rather than their utility. Yet it might be more accurate to say that virtuosi were interested in things as reflections of themselves, as parts of the macrocosm that illuminated parts of the microcosm, as one gem in Indra's net that reflected another gem. According to Dante's Adam, God is 'the true mirror / Which makes itself the image of other things'.[104] And images seen in mirrors were potentially transformative since 'beholding as in a glass the glory of the Lord, [we] are changed into the same image' (2 Corinthians 3:18). The blackness reflected in the *Paston Treasure's* mirror alluded to the unknowable mysteries of God. Its inscrutability was the perfect complement to all the newly acquired knowledge that swirled around Sir Robert's worldly riches. It was a wonder-filled means of escaping the worldly labyrinth.

Of course, other sources of wonder in the *Paston Treasure* were the precious shells. Shortly before his death, Newton described himself as 'a boy playing on the sea-shore [who found] a prettier shell than ordinary, whilst the great ocean of truth lay all undiscovered before me'.[105] He compared the elegance of his mathematical theories to the elegance of seashells. Sir Robert also appreciated many a 'prettier shell', and would have been the first to acknowledge that 'the great ocean of truth lay all undiscovered' before him. He could compare the way snails made their shells to the way the heavens rotated and the way life unfolded. In the final analysis, though, he knew that no matter how stimulating life's twists and turns might be, they were all vanity. Most of the shells in the *Paston Treasure* were polished or engraved, down to the iridescent mother-of-pearl. Their rough outer surfaces had been worked away to reveal what nature had hidden, reinforcing the fact that the snail had been born into a thing of sublime beauty. However, snails could escape only through death and spent their lives imprisoned in 'gilded cages'. An accident of birth also gave Sir Robert great riches accompanied by great burdens, so he may well have sympathized with snails' fates.

Once snails died, their shells became the ornate packaging of nothing. Shells are empty, and the word *vanitas*, as a classical scholar like Sir Robert knew only too well, is Latin for 'emptiness'. Like nostalgia, propaganda, progress and probability, 'vanity' is a word whose meaning has changed. Today to be vain is to be shallow and lacking in substance. In the seventeenth century vanity's original meaning (Ecclesiastes 1:2) was still in circulation. But it was being diluted by related ideas – like 'nothing', 'nobody' and 'nowhere' – that were becoming the stuff of jokes.[106] However, in Eastern traditions, vanity's positive side, 'emptiness' or 'nothingness', could not be more explicit: for example, 'Possess something to make it profit you; Take it as nothing to make it useful for you.'[107] The idea of 'nothing's' usefulness was illustrated with the emptiness at the centre of a pot, a wheel or a door. The pot's value lay in its ability to receive water, the wheel's value was in its receipt of an axle and the door's, a visitor. The porcelain, the spokes and rim, and the door frame just enclosed the emptiness upon which their usefulness depended. Sir Robert's hourglass also demonstrated the value of emptiness. As the sands of time ran through it, the upper globe was emptied of sand and filled with spirit.

One common sign that a painting is a *vanitas* is the presence of a skull, a now empty vessel which once carried a spirit that no longer requires physical protection. Like a snakeskin or chrysalis case, the skull remains behind after the spirit has been liberated from its gilded cage. Human skulls and snail shells are both mineral residues – forms of apatite and calcite – left by the cycle of life. In the absence of a skull, the *Paston Treasure*'s empty shells are the clearest reference to its status as a *vanitas*. And one of the clearest indigenous statements about the value of emptiness was written – not far from Bishop's Lynn – around the time Margery Kemp was born and the first Clement Paston worked his hundred acres. The unknown author of *The Cloud of Unknowing* suggested we should

> Let go this 'everywhere' and this 'everything' in exchange for this 'nowhere' and this 'nothing' . . . Our inner self calls it 'All', for through it he is learning the secret of all things, physical and spiritual alike, without having to consider every single one separately on its own.[108]

Shells' emptiness added immeasurably to their richness as spiritual symbols, contrasting a giddy material rim with an unmoving immaterial centre. Empty shells evoked spiral staircases and whirl-winds, vehicles of elevation analogous to prayer and meditation. They echoed the divine disorientation that accompanies access to the dizzy-ing heights of contemplation. Browne said, 'I love to lose myself in a mystery, to pursue my reason to an *oh altitudo* [spiritual exaltation].'[109] Like the mirror's blackness, the shells' emptiness pointed 'hieroglyph-ically' to repose in the silence that resides beyond the busy world of signs. Indeed, Raleigh reminded his readers of their significance by opening his *Passionate Man's Pilgrimage* with a 'scallop shell of quiet'. Shells offered paths of escape from the clutter of the ever-changing world to give glimpses of eternity.

While the shell cups themselves could continue their journeys beyond Oxnead, the ever-receptive and fruitful emptiness to which they pointed remained at hand. Things can be lost, but nothingness cannot be lost – *they* may be absent, but *it* is ever-present. As the shell cups moved on, any trace of Epicure Mammon in Sir Robert would have felt pangs of longing. Yet as *pronk* transmuted into *vanitas*, his Prospero-like part would have known the peace of belonging.

For eyes that preferred cosmic parataxis to optic perspective, everything about the *Paston Treasure* – including the 'whirlpool of misadventures' into which it was inextricably woven – was exactly as it should be. However, over 350 years, Sir Robert's picture has changed. Blood has drained from the girl's cheeks, the once succulent-looking lobster is now ghostly and the shell cups' golden mounts have lost their glitter. These changes are all due to fading pigments, yet they add to the painting's value by highlighting its venerable age. They are also a reminder that the tabletop laden with Sir Robert's riches is just an illusion, conjured up with oil on canvas.[110] The twenty-first-century version of the *Paston Treasure* is still exactly as it should be.

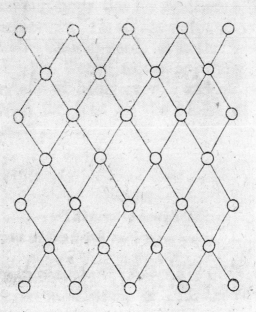

Quid Quincunce speciosius, qui, in
quam cunqꝫ partem spectaueris,
rectus est. Quintilian: //

Detail of Thomas Browne, *The Garden of Cyrus . . .* (1658), p. 86.
The text reads: 'Again, is beauty an object of no consideration
in the planting of fruit trees? Quintilian.'

Epilogue

I t is an old adage that while spiritual gifts look after you, you have to look after material gifts. Sir Robert inherited some gifts that he was unable to look after. *Sylva*-like silver may have slipped through his fingers but – given what we know about his attitude to science, philosophy and religion – it is entirely possible that he bore his losses with equanimity. He may have seen his fate in accord with the soul's cosmic ascent through life, a commonplace summarized by Sir Walter Raleigh, in which

> infancy is compared to the Moon, in which we only seem to live and grow . . . the second age to Mercury, wherein we are taught and instructed; our third age to Venus, the days of love, desire and vanity; the forth to the Sun, the strong, flourishing and beautiful age of man's life; the fifth to Mars, in which we seek honour and victory, and in which our thoughts travel to ambitious ends; the sixth age is ascribed to Jupiter, in which we begin to take account of our times, judge ourselves and grow to the perfection of our understanding; the last and seventh to Saturn, wherein our days are sad and overcast.[1]

The blows of fortune that Sir Robert received in his seventh age were 'the tool of God and the educator of man'.[2]

Sir Robert repeatedly borrowed and failed to pay off mortgages. Yet it would be unfair to call him selfish, lazy or reckless – all the evidence suggests that he was public-spirited, conscientious and calculating, although from a financial perspective his calculations proved disastrously wrong. Change was in the air and he either failed to read the signs or chose to ignore them. However, it would be wrong to think he was left behind by the relentless march of progress. History does not travel in a straight line. As he knew, it unfolds like a snail's shell.

For example, at the beginning of the seventeenth century, cosmic prophecies were central to political propaganda and almanacs were bestsellers; a century later, Jonathan Swift felt able to belittle astrology as 'deceits . . . to laugh at and despise'.[3] But astrology did not go away, because another of the changes that Sir Robert lived through was the gradual uncoupling of elite and popular culture. Astrology simply became unfashionable amongst the elite. Today, upmarket newspapers do not carry horoscopes – or they relegate them to a magazine section – but newspapers with greater circulation still do. Sir Robert's God-fearing world might seem to have succumbed to the cold light of reason but, actually, the old world-view lives on.

Other old ideas were also being slowly eased from centre stage. Alchemy was not suddenly found to be 'wrong', but the Norwich science of Arthur Dee, Thomas Browne and Robert Paston was quietly sidelined by the London science of the Royal Society. The differences were mainly social and political. The Norwich practitioners read signs, like Polynesian canoeists, Yarmouth's fishermen and Navy tars, while the London practitioners started to use instruments and charts, like naval officers.

London's post-Civil War natural or experimental philosophers were deeply insecure, and upon the Restoration they sought out the king as a patron, even though he found many of their activities laughable. Yet they knew that his position was also precarious so they built additional support structures. Together, their lectures, rehearsed demonstrations and vetted publications provided mechanisms for creating new forms of authority. They had lived through alternate forms of government and they saw ways to apply the lessons they had learned to control alternate stories about nature.[4] They saw that people could choose their own narrators for stories about reality. Some preferred stories told by authorities like Moses and Aristotle, but there was also room for those told by institutionally validated authors like Boyle and Newton. Through the Civil War, natural philosophers had experienced shifts in ways of asserting power, and they responded by shifting ways of asserting truth. English magic peaked with Elizabeth 1's magus, Dr John Dee, but by the time his son Arthur had settled in Norwich, it was morphing into the new science. The old magicians and the new scientists both pursued knowledge in order to exert their will over nature; they simply employed different rhetoric.[5]

Sir Robert failed to embrace the rhetorical shift and was just too open about his heartfelt beliefs – he should have either kept them to himself or put more effort into repackaging them for public consumption. Not noticing, or not caring about, alchemy's slow side-lining would simply have turned Sir Robert into just another English eccentric, but failing to respond to another change helped ruin his family. Strangely, that change also happened in a Hermetic realm. Hermes was a late arrival in the Greek pantheon of gods, appearing in the sixth century BC, a time of great political upheaval in Greece when the old agrarian kingships came into conflict with new mercantile democracies.[6] Public marketplaces had just appeared in Greek cities and in them strangers could meet and strike deals with each other. The deals they made might have been perfectly fair, and both sides might have been happy but – according to the old guard – such deals were immoral or even criminal. They felt that goods should only be exchanged between people who were related to each other. The exchange of goods between strangers was akin to theft, which is why Hermes became the god of thieves as well as the god of merchants.

Sir Robert was studying the *Phoenix Hermetica* through another time of economic and political upheaval, when methods of doing business were changing yet again. He found himself in the old guard. His family's accelerating decline was in part due to his failure to recognize, or his choice not to adapt to, the unspoken rules of the new emerging economy. Sir Robert was comfortable operating in systems of largesse. With lavish hospitality, he continued to invest in the old system of visible power, and tried to use that power indirectly to persuade people. Yet all around him, money was becoming more important, the agents of power were increasingly becoming invisible, and they were being used to influence people directly, to buy them off.[7] Sir Robert overlooked what Lord Cutler Beckett told

Elizabeth Swan – the cold fact that loyalty was no longer the currency of the realm and 'currency' had become the currency of the realm.[8] Through the seventeenth century, as elite and popular cultures drifted apart, the boundaries between hospitality and charity, and the mutual obligations of host and guest – which had been purposely blurred – were becoming increasingly sharpened.[9] Hermes was stirring up the market, much as he had done in ancient Greece (and is doing again in the digital realm, where today's messengers, merchants and thieves play). When Hermes entered the Greek pantheon, the trust established between kith and kin had been extended to strangers. While the *Paston Treasure* was being painted, that same trust was being extended to institutions and corporations.

Sir Robert's behaviour suggests he was deeply committed to the old economy of gift-exchange. Traditionally, gifts involved three obligations – to give, to receive and to reciprocate.[10] Giving created a debt, yet that debt was not hard, commercial and impersonal like a mortgage; it was closer to the 'belonging together' of lovers than of business associates. Gifts created soft, social and personal bonds of indebtedness. Crucially, reciprocation was not necessarily expected to involve the original donor. If gifts were transmitted to third parties, then more people, or more families, could be woven into the web of mutual obligations.

Gifts could be small, like items of food. The exact status of these small tokens could be ambiguous, so a hen, for example, could be owed as part of a tenant's rent or it could be a gift. And a hen demanded by the landowner as rent could be cooked and shared in a meal with the tenant, turning the rent into a gift.[11] Such presents were quickly consumed, which allowed donors to give again and create a dialogue. Of course, care had to be taken since too many unsolicited offerings might create the wrong impression, as someone who gave Sir Robert's mother several cakes was all too aware.[12] Food gifts could also be bigger, like the venison that – if one overlooked poaching – was 'neither bought nor sold . . . but maintained only for the pleasure of the owner and friends'.[13] The lavish hospitality offered by the corpulent Sir Robert was at the very top of the scale of this tradition of gift-exchange.[14]

The aggressive ancestral Pastons had grown rich by the exercise of law and the acquisition of land, but they eased their progress by persuasion. Reciprocal gifts were extremely deep-rooted in the family and they even involved giving and receiving children. The first William Paston looked after a ward around 1434, and, of course, his grandson Sir John went to the court while John III went to the Duke of Norfolk.[15] Wardships could bring problems, but by the time Sir Clement rebuilt Oxnead, the process was administered through a Court of Wards in a 'spirit of generosity [without] mercenary or financial motives'.[16] The 'spirit of generosity' ran deep: 'generosity' is etymologically related to words like 'genitals' and 'gentry', so the act of giving was closely related to procreation and family.

Girls and boys were usually given away in their early teens and circular exchanges embodied the idea that reciprocation need not be directed to donors.[17] One ring of exchange included Queen Elizabeth, to whom children were 'present-ed' and then 'a-ward-ed' court positions, and one of her gift letters blurred the acts of giving and receiving to such an extent that it is impossible to distinguish benefactor from beneficiary.[18] In a world that also blurred boundaries between the natural and the supernatural, wardship could even involve fairies. However, it has been suggested that stories of children taken, or given, by the fairies were knowingly accepted 'white lies'.[19] They enabled victims of rape and abandoned or illegitimate children to live in the community free of shame. When Shakespeare's Old Shepherd found a baby on the beach, he introduced it to his family as a 'changeling'.[20] She was accepted as such and grew into a princess.

The practice of child gift-exchange continued through the seventeenth century, especially with girls, but its power as a mechanism for social cohesion waned. Boys were increasingly sent off to school and university, which acted *in loco parentis*, or 'in place of parents'. Ceremonial admission to university was a matriculation, a word that has its origins in the word 'matrix', meaning uterus. For a happy few years, Cambridge had been Sir Robert's womb from womb, and when he left it became his *alma mater* or 'nourishing mother', not his *alma pater* or 'nourishing father'. Schools, colleges and universities were institutional surrogate mothers and what they offered was personified by female deities – successful studies led to wisdom, represented by the goddess Sophia.

The money economy gained ground in part because the gift system had been weakened by the abuses of Charles I's father, James I.[21] Yet Charles II explicitly used gift-exchange conventions to delay reciprocating services, saying, 'it would look too near a contract' if Sir Robert was rewarded too soon.[22] The money economy was, of course, simultaneously boosted by burgeoning trade, which, as Dryden said, 'like blood, should circularly flow'.[23] Connections between the circulation of blood and money were reflected in William Harvey's anatomical discoveries and the establishment of the Bank of England, in 1628 and 1694 respectively, which framed Sir Robert's life. Trade, blood and money also undermined the reciprocal gift systems that had operated in the wider world, perverting the South American *mit'a* system, for example. Sir Robert clung on to the gift system tenaciously – at least with his gentlemen friends – but around him, the concept was becoming more and more impoverished. Europeans only rediscovered the potential richness of gift systems – at least in theory – three hundred years later, and they did so by studying distant cultures, systematically exploring the kind of travellers' tales that had fascinated Sir Robert.[24]

The *Paston Treasure*'s globe shows New Guinea just above Margaret's roses. To the east of New Guinea, but too small to mark, are the tiny Trobriand Islands, home to the Massim. In the 1910s Bronislaw Malinowski visited this scattered community and observed their exchanges of shell jewellery. In canoe journeys of hundreds of miles, red-shell necklaces moved clockwise and white-shell armbands moved anti-clockwise around a ring of about twenty islands. The shells were given as gifts and, after a while, were given again, gradually moving from family to family around the archipelago, maybe returning to the original island after a decade. These exchanges were called *kula*, and they were governed by a very strict but unspoken decorum. In stark contrast to the Massim's noisy bartering, their gift-giving was undertaken in silence with no hint about when a gift might be given in return, to whom it might go or how it might compare with the one that had just been received. Numerous intricate social barriers prevented all the calculations that characterize commodity exchange and the gift system strengthened bonds between individuals, households and islands.[25] The *kula* ring inspired Marcel Mauss to develop his theory of reciprocal gifts as the fundamental mode of social and political exchange.

However, European gift systems were not completely destroyed. A seventeenth-century misunderstanding of the related North American *potlatch* system spawned the idea of the 'Indian gift', or a gift with strings attached. This shows how Western gift-exchange polarized, splitting into the supposedly disinterested 'free' gift, on the one hand, and the completely self-interested market, on the other.[26] Just as magic went out of fashion in the scientific mainstream, reciprocal gifts went out of fashion in the economic mainstream. Yet they found other places to thrive.

For example, Sir Robert's personal calling, Hermetic alchemy, was entirely based upon gift-exchange. It was why the 'invisible college' could take the word of unpaid virtuosi but not that of paid alchemists.[27] John Wilkins created a social environment in which bright boys – even the most reclusive and egotistical – could happily work together in a spirit of free exchange.[28] As Newton once said, 'If I have seen further, it is by standing on the shoulders of Giants.'[29] Sadly, of course, not all scientists were generous and the Oxford chymist Robert Plot (he of the 'ignivomous dragons') was happier to take than to give. He was more interested in 'experiments of fruit' from which he could profit than 'experiments of light' from which others might benefit.[30]

Luckily, Plot was an exception and a spirit of generosity still thrives in today's academic community. Now, the whole academic world still relies on intersecting gift-exchange rings in which individuals take ideas freely from others and, in return, give ideas freely to others.[31] For example, we only know that the *Paston Treasure*'s hidden woman had blue eyes, wore ribbons in her hair and had a red-laced bodice because a scientist, Francesco Paolo Romano, built specialist software and hardware and air-freighted it from the University of Catania, Sicily, to the Castle Museum, Norwich. He spent a week surveying the painting and then freely shared all his findings with other scientists and art historians.

Gift-exchange also thrived in the arts, which, of course, were not distinct from the sciences. Edmund Spenser's *Faerie Queene* was a gift to Queen Elizabeth.[32] The poem features a number of children who were freely given just as, in conception, they had been freely received. After all, a poet's 'conception' of their poem is linked to a mother's 'conception' of their child, just as 'genitals' are related to 'genius'. Having received the queen's blessing, Spenser dedicated his 'labour' to her, giving the poem in the hope it would flourish with her. The spirit of both the maker and giver was embodied in, and added value to, the gift. Sir Robert's shell cups' value came from the 'careful Indian' or 'keen Ethiopian' who obtained the shells, the courageous mariners who conveyed them, and the skilful engravers and silver-smiths who embellished them. As a *vanitas*, the *Paston Treasure* was a reminder that the objects passing in and out of Sir Robert's collection would be as sterile as the sands that ran through his hourglass if stripped of their spiritual significance. Their spiritual significance naturally included the spirit of the gift.

Ralph Waldo Emerson said people's gifts conveyed their biographies, because a gift is 'a portion of thyself . . . Therefore the poet brings his poem . . . the sailor, coral and shells; the painter his picture.'[33] Of course, we all recognize pictures as products of gifts, since we say artists are 'gifted'. Artists' gifts are part talent and part acquired. Talents are inherent inclinations or values, the origins of which are mysterious or God-given. The acquired part of an artistic gift is the assimilation of, and response to, an established tradition. In the case of the *Paston Treasure*'s painter, it involved training with a master whose role was to pass on the skills that he himself had acquired from his master in a chain that went, via St Luke, all the way back to Hermes. The craft guilds had religious functions and trained those with aptitude, in accordance with the biblical 'parable of the talents' – 'unto them that hath [aptitude] shall be given [training]' (Matthew 25:29). Above all, the craft guilds imparted 'mysteries'.[34]

The *Paston Treasure*'s painter had not yet lost the 'mystery' of his craft and, according to a seventeenth-century artist's treatise, his creativity was a subtle, boundary-crossing fluid endowed with the 'generative' power of nature.[35] However, along with Sir Robert's alchemy, the everyday crafts were slowly sidelined and Europeans who wished to rediscover their profound significance could eventually have to find guidance from China. For example, acknowledging the significance of small repeated acts in the transmission of understanding, Confucius said, 'I do not create, I only tell of the past,' and Laozi talked of 'Grasping the Way of old so as to guide the beings of today'.[36]

In the *Paston Treasure*, Sir Robert and the unknown painter were engaged in making a part commodity, part gift.[37] Whereas commodities grow profits, gifts grow relationships. Gifts enrich the flow of time, establishing connections and using periods of indebtedness to generate reciprocal action at a distance. The gift part of an artwork is an enduring 'present', subsuming both past and future. Thanks to that present, long-gone relationships – such as those between masters and apprentices and between the unknown painter and Sir Robert – are still evident in the picture. Traces of those relationships are visible in the brush-strokes that record the artist's fleeting gestures, captured in paints whose flow properties were determined by centuries-old traditions. The overlapping paint layers are signs that record the artist's systematic movement around the canvas as well as the patron's changes of mind. The present *Paston Treasure* also contains the seeds of its future, yet because of our limited perspective we do not recognize them. As a thing of pigment, oil, canvas and wood, we know it will turn to gas and ash, and its ultimate future is as plant food, but details of its more immediate and culturally interesting future are shrouded in mystery.

Inevitably, gift giving continues. So, in the mid-twentieth century, hundreds of years after the family treasures were dispersed by auction, Sir Robert Paston's distant relative Maud Buxton gifted the *Paston Treasure* to Norwich Castle Museum.[38] Sir Robert's attachment to the gift system may have contributed to his family's demise, but the spirit of the gift created the *Paston Treasure* and the spirit of the gift has ensured its safe passage down to us.

References

Prologue

1 A number of possible artists have been suggested – Franciscus Gijsbrechts, Carstian Luyckx and Peeter Boell as well as painters in the circle of Pieter Gerritsz. van Roestraeten including Goddard Dunning, Gaspar Smits and Jan Frans van Son and Jopris von Son. See R. Wenley and A. Moore, 'The Master of the Paston Treasure', in *The Paston Treasure: Microcosm of the Known World*, ed. A. Moore, N. Flis and F. Vanke (New Haven, CT, 2018).
2 C. Tilley, *Material Culture and Text: The Art of Ambiguity* (London, 2014).
3 Robert Burton, 'Democritus to the Reader', in *The Anatomy of Melancholy* (Philadelphia, PA, 1883), p. 24.
4 Mary Midgely, *Science and Poetry* (London, 2001).
5 The painting is on permanent display at Norwich Castle Museum and Art Gallery.
6 *The Anatomy of Riches* was written whilst an exhibition dedicated to the *Paston Treasure* was being prepared. Those who want more detail should consult Moore, Flis and Vanke, eds, *The Paston Treasure*.

one Ancestors

1 F. Worship, *Account of a Manuscript Genealogy of the Paston Family* (Norwich, 1852).
2 John Stow, *A Summarie of our Englysh Chronicles* (London, 1566), fols 136v–138, in L. M. Matheson, 'The Peasants' Revolt through Five Centuries of Rumour and Reporting', *Studies in Philology*, xcv/2 (1998), p. 121.
3 Raphael Holingshed, *The Chronicles of England, Scotland and Ireland* (London, 1557), vol. ii, pp. 1024–5, in Matheson, 'Revolt', p. 129.
4 Matheson, 'Revolt', pp. 121–51.
5 R. B. Dobson, *The Peasants' Revolt of 1381* (London, 1982), pp. 160–62.
6 W. M. Ormrod, 'The Peasants' Revolt and the Government of England', *Journal of British Studies*, xxix/1 (1990), p. 3.
7 H. Eiden, 'Norfolk, 1382: A Sequel to the Peasants' Revolt', *English Historical Review*, cxiv/456 (1999), pp. 370–77.

8 Thomas Walsingham, *Historia Anglicana* (2:70), in Dobson, *Peasants'*, pp. 334–5.

9 J. Gairdner, 'Introduction', in J. Gairdner, ed., *The Paston Letters* (London, 1901), p. xxxv.

10 B.M.S. Campbell, 'Agricultural Progress in Medieval England', *Economic History Review*, XXXVI/1 (1983), pp. 26–46.

11 H. Castor, *Blood and Roses* (London, 2004), p. 16.

12 D. Stoker, '*Innumerable letters of good consequence in history*: The Discovery and First Publication of the Paston Letters', *The Library*, 6th ser., XVII (1995), pp. 107–55. See also the Bibliography for sources for the Paston letters.

13 Margery Kempe, *The Book of Margery Kempe*, trans. B. A. Windeatt (Harmondsworth, 2004).

14 C. Richmond, *The Paston Family in the Fifteenth Century: The First Phase* (Cambridge, 1990), pp. 34–7.

15 Castor, *Blood*, pp. 14–20.

16 R. W. Ketton-Cremer, *Norfolk Portraits* (London, 1944), pp. 55–6.

17 Dante, *The Divine Comedy* (Inferno, VII), trans. C. H. Sisson (Oxford, 1988), pp. 72–6.

18 Richmond, *Paston*, pp. 53–5, and H. S. Bennett, *The Pastons and their England* (Cambridge, 1922), pp. 5–7.

19 Richmond, *Paston*, p. 41.

20 R. M. Faurot, 'From Records to Romance', *Studies in English Literature*, V/4 (1965), p. 682.

21 R. H. Britnell, 'The Pastons and their Norfolk', *Agricultural History Review*, XXXVI/2 (1988), pp. 132–44.

22 Richmond, *Paston*, p. 48.

23 Faurot, 'Romance', pp. 678–9. The story was turned into a swashbuckling movie in 1948, which was in turn remade for TV in 1985.

24 Bennett, *Pastons*, pp. 9–10.

25 Richmond, *Paston*, p. 20.

26 J. Broadway, 'Symbolic and Self-consciously Antiquarian: The Elizabethan and Early Stuart Gentry's Use of the Past', *Huntington Library Quarterly*, LXXVI/4 (2013), pp. 541–58. Two centuries later, in 1652, parodying this perceived need, an impoverished member of the Scottish gentry, Sir Thomas Urquart, published his family's genealogy in *Pantochronachanon* where he named 153 generations all the way back to Adam.

27 Letters took between three and six days to get between Norwich and London, depending on weather. Bennett, *Pastons*, p. 157.

28 Ibid., pp. 14–15.

29 Ibid., p. 15.

30 Ibid., pp. 83–4.

31 Ibid., pp. 64 and 17.

32 C. F. Buhler, 'Sir John Paston's Grete Booke: A Fifteenth-century "Best-seller"', *Modern Language Notes*, LVI/5 (1941), pp. 345–51.

33 MS 285, British Library, London.

34 P. R. Coss, 'Aspects of Cultural Diffusion in Medieval England', *Past and Present*, CVIII/1 (1985), pp. 54–5.

35 W. E. Simeone, 'The May Games and the Robin Hood Legend', *Journal of American Folklore*, LXIV/253 (1951), p. 266.

36 Bennett, *Pastons*, p. 44; H. Castor, 'Richard Calle', *Oxford Dictionary of National Biography*, www.oxforddnb.com, October 2006.

37 Bennett, *Pastons*, p. 46.

38 R. W. Ketton-Cremer, *Norfolk Assembly* (London, 1957), p. 17.

39 D. Loades, 'Clement Paston', *Oxford Dictionary of National Biography*, www.oxforddnb.com, October 2006.

40 Ketton-Cremer, *Portraits*, p. 23.

41 Ketton-Cremer, *Assembly*, p. 19.

42 Ibid., pp. 18–20.

43 Paston School's most famous pupil was Horatio Nelson, and in the 1960s it was one of a number of schools that felt it necessary to expel the comedian Stephen Fry.

two Growing Up

1 A. Fletcher, *Growing Up in England, 1600–1914* (New Haven, CT, 2008).

2 L. Pollock, *Forgotten Children* (Cambridge, 1983), pp. 260–61.

3 W. L. Spiers, 'The Note-book and Account Book of Nicholas Stone', *Walpole Society*, VII (1919), p. 68. The costs were between two and five times the annual expenditure of the average Englishman.

4 W. E. Simeone, 'The May Games and the Robin Hood Legend', *Journal of American Folklore*, LXIV/253 (1951), pp. 270–73.

5 S. Greenblatt, *Will in the World* (London, 2016), p. 40.

6 R. Strong, *The Tudor and Stuart Monarchy: Pageantry, Painting, Iconography* (Woodbridge, 1995–8).

7 K. Sharpe, *Image Wars* (New Haven, CT, 2010).

8 Strong, *Monarchy*, vol. III, p. 185.

9 Lucy Hutchinson, *Memoirs of the Life of Colonel Hutchinson* (London, 1906), p. 69, in S. Orgel and R. Strong, *Inigo Jones: The Theatre of the Stuart Court* (Berkeley, CA, 1973), p. 51.

10 Edward Phillips, *A New World of Words* (London, 1658).

11 D. Woodman, *White Magic and English Renaissance Drama* (Cranbury, NJ, 1973), pp. 73–86.

12 V. Hart, *Art and Magic in the Court of the Stuarts* (London, 1994), p. 17.

13 Johannes Kepler, *Harmony of the Worlds* (v, vi), trans. C. G. Wallis (Chicago, IL, 1990), pp. 1039–40.

14 V. Hart and R. Tucker, '"Immaginacy Set Free": Aristotelian Ethics and Inigo Jones' Banqueting House at Whitehall', RES *Anthropology and Aesthetics*, XXXIX (2001), pp. 151–67.

15 A. B. Seligman et al., *Ritual and its Consequences* (New York, 2008).

16 G. Martin, 'The Banqueting House Ceiling', *Apollo* (February 1994), pp. 29–34.

17 S. Orgel, *The Illusion of Power* (Berkeley and Los Angeles, CA, 1975).

T. Demaubus, 'Ritual, Ostentation and the Divine in the Stuart Masque', *Literature and Theology*, XVII/3 (2003), pp. 298–313.

18 Inigo Jones, *Tempe Restored*, ll. 356–60, in Orgel and Strong, *Jones*, p. 50.

19 Jones, *Restored*, ll. 361–4, ibid., p. 62.

20 S. Foister, 'Foreigners at Court', in D. Howarth, ed., *Art and Patronage in the Caroline Courts* (Cambridge, 1993), p. 42.

21 J. Field, *The King's Nurseries* (London, 1987), pp. 39–43.

22 13 May 1661, in *The Diary of John Evelyn*, ed. E. S. de Beer (Oxford, 1955), vol. III, p. 287.

23 L. L. Peck, *Consuming Splendor* (Cambridge, 2005), p. 6.

24 J. Spraggon, *Puritan Iconoclasm during the English Civil War* (Woodbridge, 2003).

25 Samuel Hering, 1653, in Spraggon, *Puritan*, p. 55.

26 J. Walter, 'Abolishing Superstition with Sedition?', *Past and Present*, CLXXXIII (2004), pp. 79–123.

27 Field, *Nurseries*, p. 35.

28 Westminster Abbey Muniments (WAM) 33693, in J. D. Carleton, *Westminster School* (London, 1965), p. 10.

29 R. W. Ketton-Cremer, *Norfolk Assembly* (London, 1957), p. 28.

30 R. W. Ketton-Cremer, *Norfolk Portraits* (London, 1944), p. 25.

31 Ketton-Cremer, *Assembly*, pp. 27–35.

32 Ketton-Cremer, *Portraits*, p. 25.

33 C. H. Hull, *The Economic Writings of Petty* (Cambridge, 1899), vol. I, p. 105, in P. Slack, 'Material Progress', *Economic History Review*, new ser., LXIII/3 (2009), p. 587.

34 Edward Hyde, Earl of Clarendon, *The History of the Rebellion* [London, 1646], ed. W. Dunn Macray (Oxford, 1888), vol. I, p. 93, in R. A. Anselment, 'Clarendon and the Caroline Myth of Peace', *Journal of British Studies*, XXIII/2 (1984), p. 37.

35 Hamon L'Estrange, *The Reign of King Charles* (London, 1656).

36 Anselment, 'Peace', pp. 37–54.

37 E. Miner, *The Cavalier Mode from Jonson to Cotton* (Princeton, NJ, 1971), pp. 282–8.

38 Extensive psychological research has demonstrated that the ease with which novel external stimuli are assimilated depends upon pre-existing internal beliefs, irrespective of the stimuli's veracity or the beliefs' origins. At the time of writing, political exploitation of this phenomenon involves 'fake news' and 'alternative facts'. It is interesting that – whilst politicians and the media dutifully chase red herrings – the nature of the practice is recognized in the arts by, for example, Adam Curtis (*Hypernormalisation*, 2016) and Wolfgang Tillmans (Tate Modern, 2017).

39 Ketton-Cremer, *Assembly*, pp. 19–26.

40 *The 19 Years Travels of William Lithgow* (§VII) (London, 1632), p. 314.

41 Portrait now in Felbrigg Hall, Norfolk. See Ketton-Cremer, *Assembly*, p. 214.

42 S. R. Gardiner, *History of England, 1603–1642* (London, 1884), vol. VIII, pp. 147–8, in Orgel and Strong, *Jones*, p. 49.

43 ACAD, A Cambridge Alumni Database, http://venn.lib.cam.ac.uk.
44 MS Osborn fb255, Beinecke Library, Yale University, New Haven, CT, p. 56.
45 P. Hammond, 'Dryden and Trinity', *Review of English Studies*, XXXVI/141 (1985), p. 51.
46 John Wilkins, *Mathematical Magick, or The Wonders that may be Performed by Mechanical Geometry* (London, 1648).
47 Cornelius Agrippa, *Vanitie and Uncertaintie of the Arts and Sciences*, trans. James Sanford (London, 1569).
48 John Dee, 'Preface', in *Euclid's Elements*, trans. Sir Henry Billingsley (1570), in L. A. Jacobus, '"Thaumaturgike" in *Paradise Lost*', *Huntington Library Quarterly*, XXXIII/4 (1970), p. 389.
49 Cicero, *De re publica* (VI, 19), trans. C. W. Keyes (London, 1970), p. 273.
50 Aristotle, *De anima* (407b–408a), trans. W. S. Hett (London, 1964), pp. 45–7.
51 J. Brooks and J. Wainwright, 'Dialogues in the *Paston Treasure*', *The Paston Treasure: Microcosm of the Known World*, ed. A. Moore, N. Flis and F. Vanke (New Haven, CT, 2018). I. Payne, 'Robert Ramsey', *Oxford Dictionary of National Biography*, www.oxforddnb.com, October 2006.
52 S. Hutton, 'The Cambridge Platonists', *The Stanford Encyclopedia of Philosophy*, 11 November 2013, https://plato.stanford.edu.
53 William Prynne, *Histrio-Mastix, or The Scourge of the Players* (London, 1633).
54 John Aubrey, *Brief Lives*, ed. A. Powell (London, 1949), p. 101.
55 S. Orgel, *The Illusion of Power* (Berkeley, CA, 1975), pp. 43–4.
56 J. Hildeyard, *A Sermon Preached at the Funeral of the R. H. Robert, Earl and Viscount Yarmouth* (1683, p. 20), in R. Wenley, 'Robert Paston and The Yarmouth Collection', *Norfolk Archaeology*, XLI/2 (1991), p. 117.
57 Hildeyard, *Sermon*, p. 24, in J. Agnew, 'The Bankrupt Bibliophile', in *A Verray Parfit Praktisour*, ed. L. Clark and E. Danbury (Woodbridge, 2017), p. 150.
58 B. Worden, 'Providence and Politics in Cromwellian England', *Past and Present*, CIX (1985), pp. 55–99.
59 R. Zaller, 'Breaking the Vessels: The Desacralization of Monarchy in Early Modern England', *Sixteenth Century Journal*, XXIX/3 (1998), pp. 762–6.
60 *Eikon Basilike*, ed. P. A. Knachel (Ithaca, NY, 1966), p. 179, in Zaller, 'Breaking', p. 770.
61 *King Charles, His Speech Made upon the Scaffold at Whitehall-Gate* (London, 1649).
62 C. Holmes, 'The Trial and Execution of Charles I', *Historical Journal*, LIII/2 (2010), p. 316.
63 J. Woodward, *The Theatre of Death: The Ritual Management of Royal Funerals in Renaissance England* (Woodbridge, 1997).
64 *Charles II's Escape from Worcester: A Collection of Narratives Assembled by Samuel Pepys*, ed. W. Matthews (Berkeley, CA, 1966).

65 Sir Walter Raleigh, *The History of the World* (I, i, 1), in *The Works of Sir Walter Raleigh . . .*, ed. W. Oldys and T. Birch (Oxford, 1829), vol. II, p. 3.

66 C. Blagden, 'The Distribution of Almanacs in the Second Half of the Seventeenth Century', *Studies in Bibliography*, x (1958), pp. 107–16.

67 J. Friedman, 'The Battle of the Frogs and Fairford's Flies', *Sixteenth Century Journal*, XXIII/3 (1992), p. 421.

68 *Religio Medici* (II, 2), in K. Killeen, ed., *Thomas Browne* (Oxford, 2014), p. 63.

69 Lucretius, *De re natura* (VI, 95–120), trans. W.H.D. Rouse (London, 1975), p. 501.

70 L. Hutchinson, *The Translation of Lucretius* (II, 123, VI, 171–3, and 'Dedication'), ed. R. Barbour and D. Norbook (Oxford, 2011), pp. 91, 393 and 7.

71 V. Jankovic, *Reading the Skies: A Cultural History of English Weather* (Manchester, 2000).

72 G. Parker, *Global Crisis: War, Climate Change and Catastrophe in the Seventeenth Century* (New Haven, CT, 2013), pp. 13–16.

73 P. J. Willis, '"Tongues in Trees": The Book of Nature in "As You Like It"', *Modern Language Studies*, XVIII/3 (1988), pp. 65–74.

74 Even after its desacralization, the Book of Nature is still open to partisan readings, as shown by the current acceptance and simultaneous denial of climate change.

75 Friedman, 'Frogs', pp. 425–7.

76 *Mirabilis Annus, or The Year of Prodigies* (London, 1661), p. 49.

77 *The Pack of Autolycus, or Strange and Terrible News*, ed. H. E. Rollins (Port Washington, NY, 1969), pp. 37–8.

78 *Autolycus*, pp. 42–3.

79 Friedman, 'Frogs', p. 430.

80 *Autolycus*, pp. 81–6.

81 H. Rusche, 'Prophecies and Propaganda, 1641–51', *English Historical Review*, LXXXIV (1969), pp. 752–70.

82 Samuel Thurston, *Angelus anglicanus, or A General Judgement of the Three Great Eclipses of the Sun and Moon Which Will Happen in the Year 1652* (London, 1652).

83 W. E. Burns, '"The Terriblest Eclipse That Hath Been Seen in Our Days": Black Monday and the Debate about Astrology', in *Rethinking the Scientific Revolution*, ed. M. K. Osler (Cambridge, 2000), pp. 143–5.

84 K. Sharpe, 'Private Conscience and Public Duty in the Writings of Charles I', *Historical Journal*, XL/3 (1997), pp. 643–65.

85 Friedman, 'Frogs', pp. 429–30.

86 F. F. Madan, *A New Bibliography of the Eikon Basilike* (Oxford, 1951).

87 Actually, the storm happened three days earlier, but the two events were conflated in Royalist mythology. *Evelyn*, ed. de Beer, vol. III, p. 220.

88 *Diary of Thomas Burton Esq*, vol. II: *April 1657 – February 1658*, ed. J. T. Rutt (London, 1828), pp. 516–30.

89 *Mercurius Politicus*, 25 November 1658, pp. 30–32.

90 *Evelyn*, ed. de Beer, vol. III, p. 224.

91 Ketton-Cremer, *Assembly*, p. 39.
92 *The Age of Wonders, or Miracles are Not Ceased* (London, 1660), in Friedman, 'Frogs', pp. 436–7.
93 *Diary of Samuel Pepys*, ed. R. Latham and W. Matthews (Berkeley, CA, 2000), vol. II, p. 88.
94 John Ogilvy, *The Entertainment of His Most Excellent Majestie Charles II, in His Passage through the City of London . . .* (London, 1662), pp. 1–2, in S. J. Gerard Reedy, 'Mystical Politics: The Imagery of Charles II's Coronation', in *Studies in Change and Revolution: Aspects of English Intellectual History, 1640–1800*, ed. P. J. Korshin (Menston, 1972), p. 23.
95 Aurelian Cook, 'Epistle Dedicatory', *Titus Britannicus* (London, 1685), in Reedy, 'Mystical', p. 24.
96 *St George Day Sacred to the Coronation of His Most Excellent Majesties Charles the II* (London, 1661), pp. 1–4, in Reedy, 'Mystical', p. 20.
97 Cook, *Titus*, p. 9, in Reedy, 'Mystical', p. 28.
98 James Heath, *The Glorious and Magnificent Triumphs of the Blessed Coronation of His Sacred Majesty K. Charles II* (London, 1662), p. 2, in Reedy, 'Mystical', p. 30.
99 George Morley, *A Sermon Preached at the Magnificent Coronation of the Moste High and Mighty King Charles the IId* (London, 1661), pp. 57–60, in Reedy, 'Mystical', p. 30.
100 John Dryden, *To His Sacred Majesty, A Panegyrick on His Coronation* (London, 1661), p. 6, in Reedy, 'Mystical', p. 35.
101 Anon., *An Ode on the Fair Weather that attended His Majesty* (London, 1661), Anon., *A Poem Upon His Majesties Coronation* (London, 1661), Aurelian Cook, *Titus Britannicus* (London, 1685), pp. 279–80, in Reedy, 'Mystical', pp. 29–33.
102 Charles Patin, *Relations historiques et curieuses de voyage* (Lyon, 1674), p. 168, in L. Clymer, 'Cromwell's Head and Milton's Hair', *Eighteenth Century*, XL/2 (1999), p. 99.
103 Clymer, 'Head', pp. 100–102.
104 A. Smith, 'The Image of Cromwell in Folklore and Tradition', *Folklore*, LXXIX/1 (1968), pp. 36–8.
105 K. Pearson and G. M. Morant, 'The Wilkinson Head of Oliver Cromwell and its Relationship to Busts, Masks and Painted Portraits', *Biometrika*, XXVI/3 (1934), p. 109.
106 *Pepys*, ed. Latham and Matthews, vol. V, p. 297.
107 Clymer, 'Head', p. 110.
108 Abraham Nelson, *A Perfect Description of the Antichrist, and his False Prophet; Wherein is Plainly Shewed that Oliver Cromwell was Antichrist, and John Presbiter, or John Covenanter his False Prophet: Written in the Yeare MDCLIV . . .* (London, 1660); see W. Johnston, *Revelation Restored: The Apocalypse in Later Seventeenth-century England* (Woodbridge, 2011).

three Going Home

1   H. Trevor-Roper, '*Eikon Basiliké*: The Problem of the King's Book', *History Today*, I/9 (1951), pp. 7–12.
2   K. Sharpe, 'Private Conscience and Public Duty in the Writings of Charles I', *Historical Journal*, XL/3 (1997), pp. 643–65.
3   H. W. Randall, 'The Rise and Fall of a Martyrology: Sermons on Charles I', *Huntington Library Quarterly*, X/2 (1947), pp. 135–67.
4   J. Miller, *Charles II* (London, 1991), p. 97.
5   *Poems on Affairs of State*, ed. G. de Forest Lord (New Haven, CT, 1963–75) vol. I, p. 424, in R. Zaller, 'Breaking the Vessels: The Desacralization of Monarchy in Early Modern England', *Sixteenth Century Journal*, XXIX/3 (1998), p. 775.
6   John Oldham (1682), in Zaller, 'Breaking', p. 775.
7   *Diary of Samuel Pepys*, ed. R. Latham and W. Matthews (Berkeley, CA, 2000), vol. II, p. 86.
8   See, for example, Meric Casaubon, *Treatise Concerning Enthusiasm* (1655) and John Spencer, *A Discourse Concerning Prodigies* (1663), in P. J. Korshin, 'Figural Change and the Survival of Tradition in the Later Seventeenth Century', in *Studies in Change and Revolution*, ed. P. J. Korshin (Menston, 1972), pp. 107–8.
9   S. Pincus, 'Coffee Politicians Does Create', *Journal of Modern History*, LXVII/4 (1995), pp. 807–34.
10 J. Daly, 'Cosmic Harmony and Political Thinking in Early Stuart England', *Transactions of the American Philosophical Society*, LXIX/7 (1979), p. 34.
11 Richard Gough, *The History of Myddle*, ed. D. Dey (Harmondsworth, 1981), p. 249.
12 K. Park and L. J. Daston, 'Unnatural Conceptions', *Past and Present*, XCII (1981), p. 35.
13 John Aubrey, *Three Prose Works*, ed. J. Buchanan-Brown (Fontwell, 1972), p. 203, in M. E. Lamb, 'Taken by the Fairies: Fairy Practices and the Production of Popular Culture in "A Midsummer Night's Dream"', *Shakespeare Quarterly*, LI/3 (2000), p. 281.
14 Geoffrey Chaucer, 'The Wife of Bath's Tale', in *The Canterbury Tales*, trans. N. Coghill (Harmondsworth, 1975), p. 299.
15 *Hydriotaphia or Urne-Buriall* (V), in *Thomas Browne*, ed. K. Killeen (Oxford, 2014), p. 545.
16 John Aubrey, *Brief Lives*, ed. A. Powell (London, 1949), pp. 333–4.
17 L. P. Smith, *The Life and Letters of Sir Henry Wotton* (Oxford, 1907), vol. I, pp. 486–7, in Daly, 'Cosmic Harmony', p. 31.
18 B. J. Sokol, *A Brave New World of Knowledge* (Cranbury, NJ, 2003), p. 17. S. Edgerton, 'Galileo, Florentine Disegno and the Strange Spottedness of the Moon', *Art Journal*, XLIV/1 (1984), pp. 225–32.
19 M. Nicolson, 'Cosmic Voyages', *Journal of English Literary History*, VII/2 (1940), p. 94.
20 Francis Godwin, *The Man in the Moone* (London, 1638).
21 A. Coppola, 'Retraining the Virtuoso's Gaze: Behn's "Emperor of the

Moon", the Royal Society, and the Spectacles of Science and Politics', *Eighteenth-century Studies*, XLIV/4 (2008), pp. 481–506.

22 *The Illustrated Journeys of Celia Fiennes, c. 1682–1712*, ed. C. Morris (London, 1982), pp. 136–7.

23 C. F. Dendy Marshall, *The British Post Office* (Oxford, 1926), pp. 8–11.

24 Most are held in the Bradfer-Lawrence Collection, Norfolk Records Office, Norwich. Selected letters are in J. Agnew, ed., *The Whirlpool of Misadventures: Letters of Robert Paston, 1663–79* (Norwich, 2017).

25 P. Gouk, *Music, Science and Natural Magic in Seventeenth-century England* (New Haven, CT, 1999), pp. 56–60.

26 Plato, *The Republic* (IV, 422c), trans. D. Lee (Harmondsworth, 1974), p. 191.

27 J. Sargeaunt, *Annals of Westminster School* (London, 1898), p. 127.

28 *The Merchant of Venice* (V, i, 83–8).

29 Henry Peacham, *The Compleat Gentleman* (XI), ed. V. B. Heltzel (Ithaca, NY, 1962), pp. 110 and 116.

30 Plato, *Symposium* (186b–187c), trans. W.R.M. Lamb (London, 1967), p. 127.

31 Gouk, *Music*, pp. 116–21.

32 G. L. Finney, 'A World of Instruments', *Journal of English Literary History*, XX/2 (1953), pp. 87–120.

33 Peacham, *Gentleman* (XI), p. 116. Narcissus Marsh, 'Essay Touching the Sympathy between Lute or Viol Strings', in R. Plot, *Natural History of Oxfordshire* (Oxford, 1677), pp. 288–99.

34 Gouk, *Music*, p. 221.

35 Boethius, *Fundamentals of Music*, in Gouk, *Music*, p. 81. Physics dealt with material things in motion, like individual plucked strings. Mathematics dealt with the changeless aspects of those materials in motion, like the frequency of a particular string's vibration. Theology dealt with the changeless aspects of immaterial things, like the ratios or proportions between harmonious vibrations.

36 Charles Butler, *Principles of Musik* (London, 1636); Johannes Kepler, *Harmony of the Worlds* (V, vii), trans. C. G. Wallis (Chicago, IL, 1990), p. 1048.

37 Thomas Mace, *Musick's Monument* (X) (London, 1676), pp. 266–72.

38 Gouk, *Music*, p. 256.

39 See, for example, *Richard II* (V, v, 41–8 and 61–6), *Henry V* (I, ii, 180–83) and *The Merchant of Venice* (V, i, 60–65) respectively.

40 *Religio Medici* (II, 9), in *Browne*, ed. Killeen, p. 73.

41 Godfrey Goodman, *The Fall of Man* (London, 1616), p. 78, in J. Hollander, *The Untuning of the Sky* (New York, 1970), p. 127.

42 H. Love, 'The Religious Traditions of the North and Estrange Families', in *Writing and Religion in England, 1558–1689*, ed. R. D. Sell and A. W. Johnson (Farnham, 2009), pp. 419–20.

43 *The Life and Times of Anthony Wood*, ed. A. Clark (London, 1891–1900), vol. II, p. 465, in J. Uglow, *A Gambling Man* (London, 2009), p. 191.

44 Anon., *Upon His Majesties being Made Free of the Citty* (London, 1668).

45 *Pepys*, ed. Latham and Matthews, vol. VI, pp. 93–187.

46 19 June 1665, in Agnew, *Whirlpool*, p. 62.

47 M. van der Meulen, *Peter Paul Rubens, Antiquarius* (Alphen van den Rijn, 1975), pp. 12–13, 17–24, 166–7.

48 Robert Boyle, 'Usefulness of Natural Philosophy', 2, pp. 190–93, 'Reconcilableness of Specific Medicines', 5, pp. 103–4, and 'Advantages of the Use of Simple Medicines', 5, pp. 126–8, in M. Baldwin, 'Toads and Plague: Amulet Therapy in Seventeenth Century Medicine', *Bulletin of the History of Medicine*, LXVII/2, pp. 239–40.

49 Baldwin, 'Toads', pp. 227–47.

50 Johannes Hartemann, *Bazilica Chymica & Praxix Chymiatricae; or Royal and Practical Chymistry in Three Treatises* (London, 1669).

51 Johannes Baptista van Helmholt, *Ortus medicinae* (Lyon, 1647), p. 185.

52 Baldwin, 'Toads', p. 232.

53 MS Osborn fb255, Beinicke Library, Yale University, New Haven, CT, pp. 16 and 27.

54 MS 3777, Wellcome Library, London, fol. 18r–v.

55 Athanasius Kircher, *Scrutinium physico-medicum contagiosae luis quae pestis dictur* (Rome, 1658), pp. 199–201.

56 Helmholt, *Ortus*, p. 185.

57 Baldwin, 'Toads', p. 233.

58 William Boghurst, *Loimographia: An Account of the Great Plague of London in the Year 1665* (London, 1894), p. 10.

59 Robert Boyle, 'Experimental Discourse', 5, p. 62, in Baldwin, 'Toads', pp. 245.

60 M. Cipolla, *Fighting the Plague in Seventeenth Century Italy* (Madison, NY, 1981), pp. 89–110.

61 L. Cole, 'Of Mice and Moisture: Rats, Witches, Miasma and Early Modern Theories of Contagion', *Journal for Early Modern Cultural Studies*, X/2 (2010), pp. 65–84.

62 G. Hammill, 'Miracles and Plagues: Plague Discourses as Political Thought', *Journal for Early Modern Cultural Studies*, X/2 (2010), pp. 85–104.

63 *Pepys*, ed. Latham and Matthews, vol. VI, p. 93.

64 19 June 1666, in Agnew, *Whirlpool*, p. 74.

65 7 June 1666, ibid., p. 66.

66 A. Tinniswood, *By Permission of Heaven* (London, 2003), pp. 228–37.

67 29 May 1666, in Agnew, *Whirlpool*, p. 66.

68 14 January 1667/8, *Pepys*, ed. Latham and Matthews, vol. I, p. 24.

69 9 September 1671, in Agnew, *Whirlpool*, p. 135.

70 Anon., 'Robbery Rewarded' (1674), in *The Pack of Autolycus*, ed. H. E. Rollins (Port Washington, NY, 1969), pp. 168–71.

71 16 August 1675, in Agnew, *Whirlpool*, p. 165.

72 15 September 1675, ibid., p. 171.

73 17 September 1675, ibid., pp. 171–3.

74 1 and 4 October 1675, ibid., pp. 179–80.

75 C. A. Hanson, *The English Virtuoso* (Chicago, IL, 2009).

76 *Hydriotaphia or Urne–Buriall* (v), in *Browne*, ed. Killeen, p. 543.

77 Simon Jervis, in *The Paston Treasure: Microcosm of the Known World*, ed. A. Moore, N. Flis and F Vanke (New Haven, CT, 2018).

78 No documentation survives to say whether the commission did indeed come from Sir William but the circumstantial evidence is persuasive. Personal communication, Jean Agnew, February 2017.

79 P. O. Long, 'Power, Patronage and the Authorship of *Ars*: From Mechanical Know-how to Mechanical Knowledge in the Last Scribal Age', *Isis*, LXXXVIII/1(1997), pp. 1–41.

80 J. Connors, '*Ars Tornandi*: Baroque Architecture and the Lathe', *Journal of the Warburg and Courtauld Institutes*, LIII (1990), pp. 217–36.

81 Thomas Sprat, *History of the Royal Society* (London, 1667), p. 314.

82 Edward Phillips, *A New World of Words* (London, 1658).

83 L. Roberts, S. Schaffer and P. Dear, *The Mindful Hand: Inquiry and Invention from the Later Renaissance to Early Industrialization* (Amsterdam, 2007).

84 MS Osborn fb255, Beinecke Library, pp. 4 and 39.

85 12, 14 and 16 June 1666, in Agnew, *Whirlpool*, pp. 71–3.

86 J. Horden, 'Henry Peacham', in *Oxford Dictionary of National Biography*, www.oxforddnb.com, October 2006.

87 S. Alpers, *The Art of Describing* (Chicago, IL, 1983).

88 E. Wind, 'Shaftesbury as a Patron of Art', *Journal of the Warburg Institute*, II/2 (1938), pp. 185–8.

89 Alexander Browne, *Ars Pictoria* (London, 1675), p. 39, in R. Harley, *Artists' Pigment* (London, 1982), p. 17.

90 14 June 1666, in Agnew, *Whirlpool*, p. 73.

91 M. K. Talley, *Portrait Painting in England: Studies in the Technical Literature before 1700* (London, 1981), pp. 270–305.

92 On 3 March 1988 a double-decker bus fell into a crater caused by the collapse of one of these medieval tunnels.

93 Cennino Cennini, *The Craftsman's Handbook*, recipe no. VII (New York, 1960), p. 5.

94 J. S. Lee, 'Feeding the Colleges: Cambridge's Food and Fuel Supply, 1450–1560', *Economic History Review*, LVI/2 (2003), pp. 243–64.

95 *Sir Thomas Browne's Works*, ed. S. Wilkin (London, 1835), vol. I, p. 410.

96 When the room was damp, the painting's tension was maintained by the shrinkage of the canvas, and when the room was drier, the painting's tension was maintained by the glue's stiffness.

97 Anon., *The Excellence of the Pen and Pencil* (London, 1668), p. 92.

98 With thanks to Mr and Mrs Aspinall, who now run Oxnead Hall as a wedding venue.

99 See also S. Bucklow, *The Riddle of the Image* (London, 2014), pp. 42–72.

100 E. van de Wetering, *Rembrandt: The Painter at Work* (Amsterdam, 1997), p. 27.

101 MS Osborn fb255, p. 66.

102 P. H. Smith and T. Beentjes, 'Nature and Art, Making and Knowing', *Renaissance Quarterly*, LXIII (2010), pp. 128–79.

four The Gathering

1 J. Hochstrasser, 'Stil-Staende Dingen', in *Early Modern Things*, ed. P. Findlen (London, 2013), pp. 109–11.

2 N. Bryson, *Looking at the Overlooked* (London, 1990), pp. 120–21.

3 L. Salerno, 'Seventeenth-century English Literature on Painting', *Journal of the Warburg and Courtauld Institutes*, XIV/3–4 (1951), p. 246.

4 C. Gibson-Wood, 'Classification and Value in a Seventeenth-century Museum', *Journal of the History of Collections*, IX/1 (1997), p. 62.

5 *The Diary of John Evelyn*, ed. E. S. de Beer (Oxford, 1955), vol. IV, pp. 531–2; M. Hunter, *Science and the Shape of Orthodoxy* (Woodbridge, 1995), p. 140.

6 Sloane MS 3962, British Library, London, fols 196–203, in Gibson-Wood, 'Classification', p. 70.

7 Gibson-Wood, 'Classification', p. 72 (£2 = 480 *d.*).

8 Sir Henry Wotton, *The Elements of Architecture*, vol. II (London, 1624), p. 88.

9 See, for example, Adraen van der Spelt and Frans van Mieris, *Trompe-l'Oeil Still Life with a Flower Garland and a Curtain* (1658), currently in the Art Institute of Chicago.

10 Pliny, *Natural History* (XXXIII, 65), trans. H. Rackham (London, 1967), vol. IX, pp. 309–11.

11 M. Norton, 'Going to the Birds', in *Early Modern Things*, ed. Findlen, pp. 53–83.

12 J. B. Hoogenstrasser, *Still Life and Trade* (New Haven, CT, 2007), pp. 210–24.

13 C. Molineux, *Faces of Perfect Ebony: Encountering Atlantic Slavery in Imperial Britain* (Cambridge, MA, 2012), p. 22.

14 C. Ford, 'People as Property', *Oxford Art Journal*, XXV/1 (2002), p. 15.

15 W. C. Sturtevant and D. B. Quinn, '"This New Prey": Eskimos in Europe in 1567, 1576 and 1577', in *Indians in Europe*, ed. C. Feest (Aachen, 1989), pp. 61–140.

16 S. O. Beeton, *Anecdotes of Wit and Humour*, cited in J. D. Carleton, *Westminster School* (London, 1965), p. 9.

17 But see J. C. Scott, *Weapons of the Weak: Everyday Forms of Peasant Resistance* (New Haven, CT, 1985).

18 U. Priestley, *The Fabric of Stuffs: The Norwich Textile Industry from 1565* (Norwich, 1990), pp. 13–18.

19 E. Chadwick, '"This deepe and perfect glosse of Blacknesse": Colonialism, Scientific Knowledge, and the *Paston Treasure*'s Period Eye', in *The Paston Treasure: Microcosm of the Known World*, ed. A. Moore, N. Flis and F. Vanke (New Haven, CT, 2018).

20 K. Lowe, 'The Stereotyping of Black Africans in Renaissance Europe', in *Black Africans in Renaissance Europe*, ed. T. F. Earle and K.J.P. Lowe (Cambridge, 2005), p. 47. I. Habib, *Black Lives in the English Archives, 1500–1677* (London, 2008), p. 117.

21 *Othello* (I, i, 144).

22 F. Bethencourt, *Racisms* (Princeton, NJ, 2013).

23 I. Hanniford, *Race: The History of an Idea in the West* (Baltimore, MD, 1996); B. Isaac, *The Invention of Racism in Classical Antiquity* (Princeton, NJ, 2004).

24 They were Johan Picardt, *Korte beschyvinge*, and François Bernier, *Nouvelle Division de la terre par les differents espèces ou races qui l'habitent*, in C. Ford, 'People as Property', *Oxford Art Journal*, XXV/1 (2002), pp. 3–16.

25 H. L. Gates, *Figures in Black* (Oxford, 1990).

26 M. Neill, '"Mulattos", "Blacks" and "Indian Moors": Othello and Early Modern Constructions of Human Difference', *Shakespeare Quarterly*, XLIX/4 (1998), pp. 361–74.

27 *The Merchant of Venice* (II, i, 2–3).

28 *Masque of Blackness* (137–9), in S. Oldenburg, 'The Riddle of Blackness in England's National Family Romance', *Journal for Early Modern Cultural Studies*, I/1 (2001), p. 48.

29 *The Babylonian Talmud, Seder Nezikin*, trans. Rabbi H. Freedman (n.p., 1959), vol. II, p. 745, in Oldenburg, 'Riddle', p. 50.

30 Thomas Browne, *Pseudodoxia epidemica* (VI, 10 and 11), in *Thomas Browne*, ed. K. Killeen (Oxford, 2014), pp. 431–6 and 440–43.

31 *Religio Medici* (I, 15), in *Browne*, ed. Killeen, p. 18.

32 *The Tempest* (V, i, 183–4).

33 R. A. Donkin, 'The Insect Dyes of Western and West-central Asia', *Anthropos*, LXXII (1977), pp. 847–80, and R. A. Donkin, 'Spanish Red', *Transactions of the American Philosophical Society*, new ser., LXVII/5 (1977), pp. 1–84.

34 C. Singer, *The Earliest Chemical Industry* (London, 1948).

35 Pliny, *Natural History* (XXXIII, 184), vol. IX, p. 397.

36 D. Colwall, 'An Account of the English Alum Works', *Philosophical Transactions*, XII (1677–8), pp. 1052–6.

37 Bolognese MS, in M. P. Merrifield, *Original Treatises on the Arts of Painting* (New York, 1967), vol. II, pp. 432–54.

38 E. W. Bovill, *The Golden Trade of the Moors* (Oxford, 1968), p. 82.

39 H. Lechtman, 'The Significance of Metals in Pre-Columbian Andean Culture', *Bulletin of the American Academy of Arts and Sciences*, XXXVIII/5 (1985), p. 17.

40 H. Lechtman, 'Andean Value Systems and the Development of Prehistoric Metallurgy', *Technology and Culture*, XXV/1 (1984), pp. 1–36.

41 M. Rostworowski de Diez Canseco, *History of the Inca Realm*, trans. H. B. Iceland (Cambridge, 1999), p. 184, and B. S. Orlove, J.C.H. Chiang and M. Cane, 'Forecasting Andean Rain and Crop Yield from the Influence of El Nino on Pleiades Visibility', *Nature*, CDIII (2000), pp. 68–71.

42 N. J. Saunders, 'Stealers of Light, Traders in Brilliance: Amerindian Metaphysics in the Mirror of Conquest', *RES: Anthropology and Aesthetics*, XXXIII (1988), pp. 225–52.

43 Fra Bernardino de Sahagun, *Florentine Codex: General History of the Things of New Spain* [1569] (XII, 31), ibid., p. 239.

44 Sahagun, *Florentine* (XII, 31), ibid., p. 243.

45 G. Benzoni, *History of the New World* (London, 1857), ibid.

46 D. O. Flynn and A. Giráldez, 'Born with a "Silver Spoon": The Origin of World Trade in 1571', *Journal of World History*, VI/2 (1995), p. 209.

47 J. A. Cole, *The Potosi Mita* (Stanford, CA, 1985).

48 M. A. Peterson, 'The World in a Shilling', in *Early Modern Things*, ed. Findlen, pp. 252–73.

49 P. Bakewell, 'Introduction', and R. C. West, 'Aboriginal Metallurgy and Metalworking in Spanish America', both in *Mines of Silver and Gold in the Americas*, ed. P. Bakewell (Aldershot, 1997), pp. xv–xvi and 42–73.

50 A.J.R. Russell-Wood, 'Technology and Society: The Impact of Gold Mining on the Institution of Slavery in Portuguese America', *Journal of Economic History*, XXXVII (1977), pp. 59–83.

51 J. Newell, 'Exotic Possessions: Polynesians and the Eighteenth-century Collections', *Journal of Museum Ethnography*, XVII (2005), pp. 75–88.

52 Flynn and Giráldez, "Silver Spoon", p. 205.

53 A. G. Frank, *ReOrient: Global Economy in the Asian Age* (Berkeley, CA, 1997), p. 165, in R. Markley, 'Riches, Power, Trade and Religion: The Far East and the English Imagination, 1600–1720', *Renaissance Studies*, XVII/3 (2003), pp. 494–516 (p. 503).

54 See T. Brook, *The Confusions of Pleasure* (Berkeley, CA, 1998); C. Clunas, *Superfluous Things* (Cambridge, 1991); S. R. Graubard, 'Early Modernities', *Daedalus*, CXXVII/3 (1998); L. Jardine and J. Brotton, *Global Interests* (London, 2000), pp. 60–62 and 183–5.

55 M. Drelichman, 'All that Glitters: Precious Metals, Rent-seeking and the Decline of Spain', *European Review of Economic History*, IX/3 (2005), pp. 313–36.

56 Barrionuevo, *Avisos de Madrid*, pp. 83–4, in B. E. Hamann, 'The Mirrors of Las Meninas', *Art Bulletin*, XCII/1–2 (2010), pp. 26–7.

57 Flynn and Giráldez, "Silver Spoon", pp. 209–14.

58 J. Hwang Degenhardt, 'Cracking the Mysteries of "China"', *Studies in Philology*, CX/1 (2013), pp. 132–67.

59 S. R. Pendey, 'Portuguese Tin-glazed Earthenware in Seventeenth-century New England', *Historical Archaeology*, XXXIV/4 (1999), pp. 58–77.

60 J. Needham, *Science and Civilisation in China*, vol. V, pt 12 (Cambridge, 2008).

61 R. Finlay, 'The Pilgrim Art', *Journal of World History*, IX/2 (1998), pp. 151–5.

62 Ibid., pp. 155–7.

63 L. Y. Andaya, *The World of Maluku* (Honolulu, HI, 1993), and M. W. Helms, 'Essay on Objects', in *Implicit Understandings*, ed. S. B. Schwartz (Cambridge, 1994), pp. 162–3; Finlay, 'Pilgrim', pp. 155–7.

64 Ibid., pp. 167–76.

65 In fact, it was a mix of loess and kaolin, fired at over 1,300°C.

66 *The Travels of Marco Polo*, trans. R. Latham (Harmondsworth, 1987), p. 238.

67 *Pseudodoxia epidemica* (II, v, 7), in *Browne*, ed. Killeen, p. 208.

68 M. Kemp, 'Wrought by no Artist's Hand', in *Reframing the Renaissance*, ed. C. Farago (New Haven, CT, 1995), pp. 175–96.

69 Gaspar da Cruz, in *South China in the Sixteenth Century*, ed. C. R. Boxer (London, 1953), pp. 126–7.

70 Franciscus de Retza, in A.S.H. Breure and S. R. de Heer, 'From a Domestic Commodity to a Secret of Trade', *Basteria*, LXXIX/4–6 (2015), p. 83.

71 In other words, they went from the simple 'existential' stage to an 'existential-reproductive-sentient' stage without going through the 'existential-reproductive' stage. H. Hirai, 'Kircher's Chymical Interpretation of the Creation and Spontaneous Generation', in *History of Alchemy and Chemistry*, ed. L. Principe (New York, 2007), pp. 77–88. M. T. Walton, 'Genesis and Chemistry in the Sixteenth Century', in *Reading the Book of Nature*, ed. A. G. Debus and M. T. Walton (Kirksville, MO, 1998), pp. 1–14.

72 Cicero, *De oratorem* (II, vi, 23), in L. van Hogendorp Propseretti, '"Conchas Legere" Shells as Trophies of Repose in Northern European Humanism', *Art History*, IX/3 (2006), p. 395.

73 John Tradescant, *Musaeum Tradescantianum, or A Collection of Rarities Preserved at South Lambeth* (London, 1656).

74 M. Carruthers, *The Craft of Thought* (Cambridge, 1998), pp. 1–10.

75 Propseretti, 'Shells', p. 397.

76 Preface to Thomas Moufet, *The Theatre of Insects* (London, 1658), in K. W. Scoular, *Natural Magic* (Oxford, 1965), p. 87.

77 Aurelian Townshend, *Albion's Triumph* (230–32), cited in S. Orgel and R. Strong, *Inigo Jones: The Theatre of the Stuart Court* (Berkeley and Los Angeles, CA, 1973), p. 59.

78 Apuleius, *Apologia*, wrote about the oyster's chequer work. See B. Stafford, 'Characters in Stones, Marks on Paper', *Art Journal*, XLIV (1984), p. 233.

79 *Religio Medici* (II, 2), in *Browne*, ed. Killeen, p. 63; Sir Walter Raleigh, *The History of the World* (I, i, 1), in *The Works of Walter Raleigh*, ed. W. Oldys and T. Birch (Oxford, 1829), vol. II, p. 3.

80 I. Wray, 'Some Observations Concerning the Odd Turn of Some Shell-snailes', *Philosophical Transactions*, IV (1669), pp. 1011–16.

81 Propseretti, 'Shells', p. 405.

82 A. Cutler, *The Seashell on the Mountaintop* (New York, 2004).

83 Manfredus Septalius, 'Some Observations . . . Shells Found upon In-land Mountains', *Philosophical Transactions*, II (1666–7), p. 493.

84 K. Leonhard, 'Shell Collecting', *Early Modern Zoology*, *Intersections*, VII (2007), pp. 209–10.

85 Leonhard, 'Collecting', p. 181.

86 R. Kuroda et al., 'Chiral Blastomere Arrangement Dictates Zygotic Left–Right Asymmetry', *Nature*, CDLXII (December 2009), pp. 790–94.

87 P. T. Nicholson and I. Shaw, eds, *Ancient Egyptian Materials and Technology* (Cambridge, 2000), pp. 332–3.

88 N. Green, 'Ostrich Eggs and Peacock Feathers: Sacred Objects as Cultural Exchange between Christianity and Islam', *Al-Masaq*, XVIII/1 (2006), pp. 40–48.

89 G. Galavaris, 'Some Aspects of the Symbolic Use of Lights in the Eastern Church', *Byzantine and Modern Greek Studies*, IV (1978), p. 76.

90 Green, 'Ostrich', p. 30.

91 William Durandus, *The Symbolism of Churches and Church Ornaments*, trans. J. M. Neale and B. Webb (London, 1906), p. 62, in Green, 'Ostrich', p. 36.

92 Green, 'Ostrich', p. 65.

93 D. W. Brisson, 'Piero della Francesca's Egg Again', *Art Bulletin*, LXII/2 (1980), pp. 284–6.

94 M. P. Stark, 'Mounted Bezoar Stones, Seychelles Nuts and Rhinoceros Horns: Decorative Objects as Antidotes in Early Modern Europe', *Studies in the Decorative Arts*, XI/1 (2003–4), pp. 69–94.

95 This is one of the few shells to have its outer surface intact – it was not polished down or engraved to the mother-of-pearl. As Sir William Paston knew, the colour of turbans was significant, and green turbans were only worn by those directly descended from the Prophet Muhammad.

96 Georg Eberhard Rumphius, *The Ambronese Curiosity Cabinet* (Amsterdam, 1705), p. 137, in Leonhard, 'Collecting', p. 212.

97 N. Bryson, *Looking at the Overlooked* (London, 1990), p. 121.

98 M. A. Gemery, 'Emigration from the British Isles to the New World', *Research in Economic History*, V (1980), pp. 179–231. E. A. Wrigley and R. S. Schofield, *The Population History of England* (Cambridge, 1981).

99 M.-L. Hinkkanen and D. Kirby, *The Baltic and North Seas* (London, 2000), p. 39.

100 Thomas Nashe, *Lenten Stuffe* (1599), in *The Works of Thomas Nashe*, ed. R. B. McKerrow and A. H. Bullen (London, 1904), vol. III, p. 156.

101 Ibid., pp. 221 and 185–6.

102 H. S. Turner, 'Nashe's Red Herring: Epistemologies of the Commodity in "Lenten Stuffe" (1599)', *Journal of English Literary History*, LXVIII/3 (2001), pp. 529–61.

103 Georgius Agricola, *De re metallica* (1556), ed. H. C. and L. H. Hoover (New York, 1950).

104 E. Bergvelt, 'The Paston Treasure and its Netherlandish/Continental Inspiration', in *Microcosm*, ed. Moore, Flis and Vanke.

105 J. Welu, 'Vermeer's *Astronomer*: Observations on an Open Book', *Art Bulletin*, LXVIII/2 (1986), p. 263.

106 S. D. Thomas, *The Last Navigator* (London, 1987), p. 4; G. Irwin, *The Prehistoric Exploration and Colonisation of the Pacific* (Cambridge, 1992), pp. 78–83; M. Spriggs, *The Island Melanesians* (Oxford, 1997), p. 29.

107 J. Banks, *The Endeavour Journal, 1768–71*, ed. J. C. Beaglehole (Sydney, 1962), vol. I, p. 368, in Irwin, *Prehistoric*, p. 14.

108 Thomas, *Last*, pp. 239–49.

109 D. Lewis, *We, the Navigators* (Honolulu, HI, 1994), pp. 252–6.

110 Thomas, *Last*, pp. 261–7 and 272–85.

111 Lewis, *Navigators*, pp. 123–5, 256, 126–33, 224–5.

112 T. Gladwin, *East is a Big Bird* (Cambridge, MA, 1970), p. 183.

113 J. Bennett, *Navigation: A Very Short Introduction* (Oxford, 2017). C. Ginzburg, *Clues, Myths and the Historical Method* (Baltimore, MD, 2013).

114 Thomas Mun, *England's Treasure by Forraign Trade*, in C. H. Wilson, *Profit and Power: A Study of England and the Dutch Wars* (London, 1957), p. 19.

115 E. A. Honig, 'Making Sense of Things: On the Motives of Dutch Still Life', RES: *Anthropology and Aesthetics*, XXXIV (1998), pp. 180–82.

116 Ibid., pp. 166–83.

117 J. de Vries and A. van der Woude, *The First Modern Economy: Success, Failure and Perseverance of the Dutch Economy, 1500–1815* (Cambridge, 1997).

118 H. J. Cook, *Matters of Exchange: Commerce, Medicine and Science in the Dutch Golden Age* (New Haven, CT, 2007).

119 S. Dupre, 'Trading Luxury Glass, Picturing Collections and Consuming Objects of Knowledge in Early Seventeenth-century Antwerp', *Intellectual History Review*, XX/1 (2010), p. 70.

120 Ibid., p. 69.

121 J. Harris, 'The Practice of Community: Humanist Friendship during the Dutch Revolt', *Texas Studies in Literature and Language*, XLVII (2005), p. 315, in Dupre, 'Trading Luxury Glass', p. 68 (n. 119).

122 D. W. Meinig, *The Shaping of America* (New Haven, CT, 1986); U. Lamb and W. Storey, 'The Globe Encircled and the World Revealed', *Annals of Science*, LIV/6 (1997), pp. 141–52.

123 J.H.L., *Address upon the Death of William Paston*, Sloane MS 1009, British Library, London, vol. I, fol. 136. Based on the translation by David Money, with thanks to Michael Hunter and Nathan Flis. M. Hunter and N. Flis, 'Mecoena's Face: A Portrait of Sir William Paston, First Baronet', in *Microcosm*, ed. Moore, Flis and Vanke.

124 'Account of Athanasii Kircheri China Illustrata', *Philosophical Transactions*, II (1666–7), pp. 484–8; P. Findlen, ed., *Athanasius Kircher: The Last Man Who Knew Everything* (New York, 2004).

five Red and White Elixirs

1 8 April 1663, in J. Agnew, ed., *The Whirlpool of Misadventures: Letters of Robert Paston, 1663–79* (Norwich, 2017), pp. 39–40.

2 Two and a half thousand titles were sold when the Paston's library was eventually dispersed. About one-third were published after Sir Robert's death, but we can have very little confidence about exactly how many of the other two-thirds were actually his. Mark Purcell, in A. Moore, N. Flis and F. Vanke, eds, *The Paston Treasure: Microcosm of the Known World* (New Haven, CT, 2018).

3 N. O. Brown, *Hermes the Thief: The Evolution of a Myth* (New York, 1947).

4 However, see M. Lister, 'An Extract of a Letter of Mr Martin Lister

concerning the First Part of his Tables of Snails', *Philosophical Transactions*, IX (1674), pp. 96–100.

5 A. Roy, 'Rubens's "Peace and War"', *National Gallery Technical Bulletin*, XX (1999), pp. 89–95. The painting's title means 'The Goddess of Wisdom, Arts and Trade, Protects Peace from War.' Minerva and Hermes shared roles.

6 Homer called merchants 'professional boundary crossers'. Brown, *Hermes*, p. 44.

7 Ibid., pp. 32–8, 10–19.

8 M. Govier, 'The Royal Society, Slavery and the Island of Jamaica', *Notes and Records of the Royal Society of London*, LIII/2 (1999), pp. 203–17.

9 Samuel Hartlib, *Ephemerides*, 1655, pt 4 (13 August–31 December), in M. Greengrass, M. Leslie and M. Hannon, *The Hartlib Papers*, HRI Online Publications, Sheffield, 2013, www.hrionline.ac.uk/hartlib.

10 J. Needham, *Science and Civilisation in China*, vol. V, pt 7 (Cambridge, 1986).

11 P. T. Hoffman, 'Prices, the Military Revolution and Western Europe's Comparative Advantage in Violence', *Economic History Review*, LXIV/1 (2011), pp. 39–59.

12 D. N. Livingstone, 'Science, Magic and Religion: A Contextual Reassessment of Geography in the Sixteenth and Seventeenth Centuries', *History of Science*, XXVI (1988), p. 290.

13 A century later, the Ordnance Office said the mix should be 75 per cent, 15 per cent and 10 per cent respectively. S. H. Mauskopf, 'The Crisis of English Gunpowder', in *Materials and Expertise in Early Modern Europe*, ed. U. Klein and E. C. Spary (Chicago, IL, 2010), p. 295.

14 D. Cressy, 'Saltpetre, State Security and Vexation in Early Modern England', *Past and Present*, CCXII (2011), p. 85, and B.H.StJ. O'Neil, 'Stefan von Haschenperg: An Engineer to Henry VIII', *Archaeologia*, XCI (1945), pp. 137–55.

15 Govier, 'Slavery', p. 213.

16 Cressy, 'Saltpetre', p. 88.

17 J. A. Mendelsohn, 'Alchemy and Politics in England, 1649–1665', *Past and Present*, CXXXV (1992), pp. 30–78 (p. 30).

18 *I Henry IV* (I, iii, 60–61).

19 A. R. Williams, 'The Production of Saltpetre in the Middle Ages', *Ambix*, XX/2 (1975), pp. 125–33.

20 Cressy, 'Saltpetre', pp. 104, 107, 94–6, 98 and 84.

21 Thomas Henshaw, 'The History of Making Gun-powder', in Tho. Sprat, *The History of the Royal Society of London* (London, 1667), ed. J. I. Cope and H. W. Jones (St Louis, MO, 1958).

22 NRO BL/Y/1/60, in Agnew, *Whirlpool*, p. 132.

23 NRO BL/Y/1/57, 34 and 57, ibid., pp. 127, 101 and 127.

24 In the New World, this fluidity was expressed by relating apparently solid silver and gold to the tears and sweat of the moon and sun. An equivalent European expression of Aristotelian matter's liquidity will be considered in the final chapter.

25 T. Nummedal, 'Words and Works in the History of Alchemy', *Isis*, CII/2 (2011), pp. 350–71.

26 NRO BL/Y/1/60, in Agnew, *Whirlpool*, p. 132.

27 S. Wilkin, ed., *Sir Thomas Browne's Works* (London, 1835), vol. I, p. 411.

28 Ibid., vol. I, p. 412.

29 Thomas Browne, *Pseudodoxia epidemica* (III, 22), in *Thomas Browne*, ed. K. Killeen (Oxford, 2014), pp. 298–300.

30 *Pseudodoxia* (II, 5), ibid., pp. 200–202.

31 Pliny, *Natural History* (x, i), trans. H. Rackham (London, 1967), vol. v, pp. 292–3.

32 *The Saga of Thidrek of Bern* (§67), trans. E. R. Haymes (New York, 1988), pp. 46–7.

33 F. Viré, 'Na'ām', *Encyclopaedia of Islam*, 2nd edn (Leiden, 1993), online version at www. referenceworks.brillonline.com/browse/ encyclopedia-of-islam-2.

34 D. Willen, W. Soedel and V. Foley, 'Wayland the Smith', *Historical Metallurgy*, x/2 (1976), pp. 84–6.

35 L. Stewart and S. Schaffer, 'Vigani and After', in *The 1702 Chemistry Chair at Cambridge: Transformation and Change*, ed. M. D. Archer and C. D. Haley (Cambridge, 2004), pp. 31–55.

36 L. Levy Peck, *Consuming Splendor* (Cambridge, 2005), p. 337.

37 *Philosophical Transactions* (1665–78), vol. XII, pp. 935–6, vol. I, pp. 362–3, vol. VI, pp. 2196–7, vol. III, pp. 796–7, vol. XII, pp. 1052–6, vol. VI, pp. 2132–6, vol. XVI, pp. 24–32, vol. IV, pp. 1080–83, and vol. I, pp. 45–6.

38 MS Osborn fb255, Beinecke Library, Yale University, New Haven, CT, p. 5. For mosaic gold, see S. Bucklow, *The Alchemy of Paint* (London, 2009), pp. 103–4.

39 S. Bucklow, *The Riddle of the Image* (London, 2014), pp. 11–41.

40 For example, the metal copper was governed by the planet Venus and therefore had venereal qualities. Might such qualities have contributed to the use of copper coils as intrauterine contraceptive devices?

41 Brown, *Hermes*, p. 44.

42 Cennino Cennini, *The Craftsman's Handbook* (New York, 1960), pp. 24–5, 30, 33–4.

43 S. Edelstein, 'Cornelius Drebbel', in *Dictionary of Scientific Biography*, ed. C. C. Gillispie (New York, 1970–86), vol. IV, pp. 183–5. L. E. Harris, *The Two Netherlanders* (Cambridge, 1961), and J. R. Partington, *A History of Chemistry* (London, 1961), vol. II, pp. 321–4. V. Keller, 'How to Become a Seventeenth Century Natural Philosopher', in *Silent Messengers*, ed. S. Dupré and C. Lüthy (Berlin, 2011), pp. 125–52.

44 J. Kirby, M. Spring and C. Higgitt, 'The Technology of Eighteenth- and Nineteenth-century Red Lake Pigments', *National Gallery Technical Bulletin*, XXVIII (2007), pp. 69–95.

45 Analysis of the lake pigments indicated the presence of phosphorus that came from coagulated wool proteins. Other pigments in the curtain were red lead and red earths.

46 In another Hermetic piece of boundary crossing, the linseed oil was modified, inks were made and printed books became possible.

47 B. Mühlethaler and J. Thissen, 'Smalt', in *Artists' Pigments*, ed. A. Roy
     (Washington, DC, 1993), vol. II, pp. 113–30.
48 E. W. FitzHugh, 'Orpiment', in *Artists' Pigments*, ed. E. W. FitzHugh
     (Washington, DC, 1997), vol. III, pp. 47–80.
49 H. Kühn, 'Lead Tin Yellow', in *Artists'*, ed. Roy, pp. 83–112.
50 Bucklow, *Alchemy*, pp. 103–4.
51 Ibid., pp. 75–108.
52 P. M. Rattansi, 'Paracelsus and the Puritan Revolution', *Ambix*, XI/1
     (1963), p. 26.
53 S. J. Linden, 'Alchemy and Eschatology', *Ambix*, XXI/3 (1984), p. 120.
54 M. C. Jacob, 'Millenarianism and Science in the Late Seventeenth
     Century', *Journal of the History of Ideas*, XXXVII (1976), pp. 335–341.
     D. Bilak, 'Alchemy and the End Times', *Ambix*, LX/4 (2013),
     pp. 390–414.
55 John Wilkin, *Discovery of a New World* (London, 1640), in
     M. Nicolson, 'Cosmic Voyages', *Journal of English Literary
     History*, VII/2 (1940), pp. 103–4.
56 Geoffrey Chaucer, 'The Canon's Yeoman's Tale' (I), in *The Canterbury
     Tales*, trans. N. Coghill (Harmondsworth, 1975), p. 472.
57 J. A. Mendelsohn, 'Alchemy and Politics in England, 1649–1665',
     Past and Present, CXXXV (1992), p. 33.
58 H. Breger, 'Elias Artista – A Precursor of the Messiah in the Natural
     Sciences', in *1984: Science between Utopia and Dystopia*,
     ed. E. Mendelson and H. Novotny (Dordrecht, 1984), pp. 49–72.
59 F. E. Manuel, *The Religion of Isaac Newton* (Oxford, 1974), p. 19.
60 A. M. Roos, 'The Chymistry of "The Learned Dr Plot"', *Osiris*, XXIX/1
     (2014), p. 89. The particular 'dragon' to which he referred was a
     potentially explosive mixture of nitric acid and alcohol that could
     be obtained whilst distilling vitriol, saltpetre and spirit of wine in
     the production of a 'very pleasing' medicinal 'sweet spirit of niter'.
61 G. Monger, 'Dragons and Big Cats', *Folklore*, CIII/2 (1992), pp. 203–6.
     Sir Robert would also have seen the dragon that was paraded
     annually through Norwich in his childhood and after the
     Restoration. M. C. McClendon, 'A Moveable Feast: St George's
     Day Celebrations and Religious Change in Early Modern
     England', *Journal of British Studies*, XXXVIII/1 (1999), pp. 1–27.
62 Breger, 'Elias', p. 64.
63 E. K. Chambers, *The Elizabethan Stage* (Oxford, 2009), vol. III,
     pp. 423–4.
64 See F. A. Yates, *Giordano Bruno and the Hermetic Tradition* (Chicago,
     IL, 1964), *The Art of Memory* (Chicago, IL, 1966), and *Theatre of the
     World* (Chicago, IL, 1969).
65 J. Shanahan, 'Ben Jonson's "Alchemist" and Early Modern Laboratory
     Space', *Journal for Early Modern Cultural Studies*, VIII/1 (2008),
     pp. 35–66. P. H. Smith, 'Laboratories', in *Early Modern Science*,
     ed. K. Park and L. Daston (Cambridge, 2006), pp. 290–305.
66 T. Birch, ed., *The Works of the Honourable Robert Boyle* (London, 1999),
     vol. II, p. 30, cited in Shanahan, 'Jonson's', p. 57.

67 S. Shapin, 'The House of Experiment in Seventeenth Century England', *Isis*, LXXIX/3 (1988), pp. 399–40.

68 *The Diary of Samuel Pepys*, ed. R. Latham and W. Matthews (Berkeley, CA, 2000), vol. V, p. 33.

69 W. E. Knowles-Middleton, 'What did Charles II call the Fellows of the Royal Society?', *Notes and Records of the Royal Society of London*, XXXII (1977), pp. 13–17.

70 P. Findlen, *Possessing Nature* (Oakland, CA, 1994), p. 292.

71 Shapin, 'House', pp. 373–404.

72 L. Dalston, *Things that Talk* (New York, 2004).

73 *The Merchant of Venice* (I, iii, 94).

74 Sir Philiberto Vernatti, 'A Relation of the Making of Ceruss', *Philosophical Transactions*, XII (1677– 8), pp. 935–6.

75 I. Hacking, *The Emergence of Probability* (Cambridge, 2006).

76 L. Principe, 'Robert Boyle's Alchemical Secrecy', *Ambix*, XXXIX (1992), p. 63.

77 W. Newman, 'From Alchemy to Chemistry', in *The Cambridge History of Science*, ed. K. Park and L. Dalston (Cambridge, 2006), p. 511.

78 2 September 1671, in Agnew, *Whirlpool*, p. 133.

79 Osborn MS fb255, p. 40.

80 Ibid., p. 5.

81 A. Marshall, *Intelligence and Espionage in the Reign of Charles II* (Cambridge, 1994).

82 H. N. Davies, 'Bishop Goodwin's "Lunatique language"', *Journal of the Warburg and Courtauld Institutes*, XXX (1967), pp. 296–316.

83 P. Gouk, *Music, Science and Natural Magic in Seventeenth-Century England* (New Haven, CT, 1999), pp. 117–35. P. Brett, 'Edward Paston (1550–1630): A Norfolk Gentleman and His Musical Collection', *Transactions of the Cambridge Bibliographical Society*, IV/I (1964), pp. 51–69.

84 Basil Valentine, *Révélations des mystères des teintures essential des sept métaux* (1668) and Henry More, *Opera theological* (1675), in Gouk, *Music*, pp. 150–51.

85 They are lead white, copper green, lead tin yellow and mercury sulphide.

86 29 May and 7 June 1666, in Agnew, *Whirlpool*, pp. 65 and 67.

87 16 July 1670, ibid., p. 100.

88 1671, ibid., pp. 107–8.

89 The phrase comes from Paracelsus and was an assessment of wood, but was related to the 'chiromancy' of all matter. See Paracelsus, 'Liber de imaginibus', in M. Baxandall, *The Limewood Sculptors of Renaissance Germany* (New Haven, CT, 1995), p. 32.

90 *The Gentle Craft* (1596–8) and *The Shoemaker's Holiday* (1599), in U. Rublack, 'Matter in the Material Renaissance', *Past and Present*, CCXIX (2013), p. 74.

91 Shapin, 'House', pp. 375–95.

92 C. Webster, *The Great Instauration* (London, 1975), pp. 302–5.

93 16 January 1668/9, *Pepys*, ed. Latham and Matthews, vol. IX, p. 416.

94 Stewart and Schaffer, 'Vigani', pp. 31–5.
95 P. E. Spargo, 'Investigating the Site of Newton's Laboratory in Trinity College Cambridge', *South African Journal of Science*, CI (2005), pp. 315–21. The soil included high concentrations of cobalt and lead; medium of arsenic and tin; and low of mercury, silver and gold. All were above background levels.
96 24 April 1676, in Agnew, *Whirlpool*, p. 221.
97 D. N. Livingstone, *Putting Science in its Place: Geographies of Scientific Knowledge* (Chicago, IL, 2003).
98 R. Ilffe, 'Material Doubts: Hooke, Artisan Culture and the Exchange of Information in 1670s London', *British Journal for the History of Science*, XXVIII/3 (1995), pp. 314–18; L. Dalston, 'The Ideal and Reality of the Republic of Letters', *Science in Context*, II (1991), pp. 367–86.
99 R. Barbour, *Sir Thomas Browne: A Life* (Oxford, 2013), pp. 373 and 287; Wilkin, *Browne*, vol. I, pp. 409, 413 and 463–7.
100 N. H. Clulee, *John Dee's Natural Philosophy: Between Science and Religion* (London, 1988).
101 Keynes (4, 293), in A. Kitch, 'The Ingendred Stone: The Ripley Scrolls and the Generative Science of Alchemy', *Huntington Library Quarterly*, LXXVIII/1 (2015), p. 95.
102 MS 3777, Wellcome Library, London, fol. 18r–v.
103 A. Rankin, *Panaceia's Daughters* (Chicago, IL, 2013).
104 8 June 1669, in Agnew, *Whirlpool*, p. 85.
105 Samuel Hartlib, *Ephemerides* (1649), in D. R. Dickson, 'Thomas Henshaw and Sir Robert Paston's Pursuit of the Red Elixir: An Early Collaboration between Fellows of the Royal Society', *Notes and Records of the Royal Society of London*, LI/1 (1997), p. 58.
106 C. H. Hull, ed., *The Economic Writings of Sir William Petty* (Cambridge, 1899), vol. I, p. 105, in P. Slack, 'Material Progress', *Economic History Review*, new ser., LXII/3 (2009), p. 587.
107 Sloane MS 2222, British Library, London.
108 Dickson, 'Collaboration', p. 62.
109 *Aubrey's Brief Lives*, ed. A. Powell (London, 1949), pp. 142–4.
110 Dickson, 'Collaboration', p. 63.
111 Ibid., p. 69.
112 8 April 1663, in Agnew, *Whirlpool*, p. 39.
113 Bucklow, *Alchemy*, pp. 75–108.
114 B. Zorach, *Blood, Milk, Ink, Gold* (Chicago, IL, 2007).
115 1671, in Agnew, *Whirlpool*, pp. 107–8.
116 Osborn MS fb255, p. 43.
117 5 November 1663, in Agnew, *Whirlpool*, p. 44.
118 They are, respectively, lead acetate or $Pb(CH_3COO)_23H_2O$, potassium nitrate or KNO_3 and potassium carbonate or K_2CO_3. Saltpetre in 2 September 1671, in Agnew, *Whirlpool*, p. 133. Potash in 2 January 1672, ibid., p. 140.
119 Using modern chemical notation, the chemistry underlying the first version of the alchemical transformation would have been $Pb(CH_3COO)23H_2O + HgCl_2 \rightarrow Hg + PbCl_2 + 2CH_3COOH$.

120 Basic lead carbonate or $2PbCO_3Pb(OH)_2$.

121 C. Merchant, 'The Violence of Impediments: Francis Bacon and the Origins of Experimentation', *Isis*, XCIX/4 (2008), pp. 731–60.

122 A. Pickering, *The Mangle of Practice: Time, Agency and Science* (Chicago, IL, 1995).

123 P. J. Willis, '"Tongues in Trees": The Book of Nature in "As You Like It"', *Modern Language Studies*, XVIII/3 (1988), pp. 65–74.

124 5 August 1671, in Agnew, *Whirlpool*, p. 125.

125 L. Kassel, 'Secrets Revealed: Alchemical Books in Early Modern England', *History of Science*, XXIX (2001), pp. 61–87.

126 Ellinor Bergvelt, '*The Paston Treasure* and its Continental Inspiration', in *Microcosm*, ed. Moore, Flis and Vanke.

127 Michael Maier, *Atalanta fugiens* (Oppenhein, 1617).

128 G. Richardson, 'A Norfolk Network within the Royal Society', *Notes and Records of the Royal Society of London*, LVI/1 (2002), pp. 27–39.

129 An alchemist who gave due weight to both meanings of *surreverence* would have seen the chemical properties of bird droppings as mere flickering projections into the material realm of eternal spiritual realities. They knew that St Francis spoke to the birds and they would have interpreted Sigurd's tale guided by images like the bestiary's peridexion tree, which had a dragon at its base and birds in its branches. Overcoming the dragon would allow ascent of the tree and access to divine sources of inspiration.

130 *The Saga of Thidrek of Bern* (§58), trans E. R. Haymes (New York, 1988), p. 40. Actually, dwarves (or subterranean elves or sprites) still nominally feature in modern metallurgy. Porcelain's blue glaze is the oxide of a metal – cobalt – whose name is derived from a particularly mischievous type encountered in German mines through the Middle Ages.

131 Ibid. (§77–9), pp. 53–5. In this old Nordic myth, Wayland's feather-clad appearance was compared with two birds. It is perhaps significant that neither was indigenous and one was the ostrich.

132 Henshaw had advised him to 'set down what trials you make . . . for memory is frail': 19 June 1669, in Agnew, *Whirlpool*, p. 87.

six The Scattering

1 B.T.J. Dobbs, *The Janus Face of Genius* (Cambridge, 1991), pp. 53–88.

2 K. Ellison, 'Digital Scholarship as Handwork and Brainwork', *Journal for Early Modern Cultural Studies*, XIII/4 (2013), p. 30.

3 Add. MS 27447, British Library, London, fols 303–4, in J. Agnew, 'Appendix 1', in *The Whirlpool of Misadventures: Letters of Robert Paston, 1663–79*, ed. J. Agnew (Norwich, 2017), p. 386.

4 3 April 1676, in Agnew, *Whirlpool*, p. 205.

5 J. Agnew, 'Introduction', ibid., p. 6, citing *The Life of Edward Earl of Clarendon . . . written by Himself* (Oxford, 1827), vol. II, pp. 309–15.

6 R. W. Ketton-Cremer, *Norfolk Portraits* (London, 1944), p. 29.

7 29 November 1664, in Agnew, *Whirlpool*, p. 46.

8 Ketton-Cremer, *Portraits*, pp. 31–2.

9   7 June and 22 September 1666, in Agnew, *Whirlpool*, pp. 66 and 76.

10 Ketton-Cremer, *Portraits*, p. 33.

11 D. E. van Zandt, 'The Lesson of the Lighthouse: Government or Private Provision of Goods', *Journal of Legal Studies*, XXII/1 (1993), pp. 47–72.

12 21 August 1669, in Agnew, *Whirlpool*, p. 97.

13 Ibid., pp. 8–10, 84.

14 17 March–21 June 1671, ibid., pp. 108–23.

15 Ibid., pp. 138–9.

16 29 August 1671, ibid., pp. 10, 131.

17 John Hildeyard, *Sermon Preached . . . at the Funeral of the Earl of Yarmouth* (1683), in Ketton-Cremer, *Portraits*, p. 26.

18 L. L. Knoppers, 'Opening the Queen's Closet: Henrietta Maria, Elizabeth Cromwell and the Politics of Cookery', *Renaissance Quarterly*, LX/2 (2007), pp. 464–99.

19 Robert May, *The Accomplisht Cook, or The Art and Mystery of Cookery* (London, 1660), p. 3.

20 S. McTighe, 'Foods and the Body in Italian Genre Paintings', *Art Bulletin*, LXXXVI/2 (2004), pp. 301–23.

21 R. Falkenburg, 'Matters of Taste: Pieter Aertsen's Market Scenes, Eating Habits and Pictorial Rhetoric in the Sixteenth Century', in *The Object as Subject*, ed. A. W. Lowenthal (Princeton, NJ, 1996), pp. 15–16.

22 K. Albala, *Eating Right in the Renaissance* (Oakland, CA, 2002), pp. 236–9.

23 William Vaughan, *Directions for Health Both Natural and Artificial* (1600), cited ibid., p. 41.

24 Ketton-Cremer, *Portraits*, pp. 10–11.

25 Ibid., pp. 12–14.

26 18 September 1671, in Agnew, *Whirlpool*, p. 136.

27 Hildeyard, *Sermon*, p. 25; ibid., p. 10.

28 Ketton-Cremer, *Portraits*, pp. 17–19.

29 R. W. Ketton-Cremer, *Norfolk Assembly* (London, 1957), p. 33.

30 Agnew, *Whirlpool*, pp. 138–9.

31 Ibid., p. 11.

32 28 January 1665, ibid., p. 51.

33 Ibid.

34 J. Daly, 'Cosmic Harmony and Political Thinking in Early Stuart England', *Transactions of the American Philosophical Society*, LXIX/7 (1979), p. 19. The text at the top of the illustrated section of the Ripley Scroll alludes to this elemental cycling. It reads: '+ you must make water of ye erthe and erthe of the eyre and eyere of the fyere and fyere of ye erthe.'

35 *Pseudodoxia epidemica* (III, 25), in *Thomas Browne*, ed. K. Killeen (Oxford, 2014), pp. 307–13.

36 Albala, *Eating*, p. 218.

37 M. Visser, *The Rituals of Dinner* (New York, 1991).

38 Humphrey Brooke, ΥΤΙΕΙΝΗ, *or A Conservatory of Health* (London, 1650), in Albala, *Eating*, p. 218.

39 Brooke, *Conservatory*, p. 255; ibid., p. 222.

40 17 and 19 April, 5, 10, 12 and 17 May 1676, in Agnew, *Whirlpool*, pp. 214, 215, 229, 230, 231 and 235. Gout remedies in MS Osborn fb255, Beinecke Library, Yale University, New Haven, CT, pp. 32, 33, 37 and 38.

41 George Wither, *The Nature of Man* (London, 1636), p. 126.

42 William Harvey, *De motu locali animalium* (1627), in J. Riskin, 'The Restless Clock', in *Early Modern Things*, ed. P. Findlen (London, 2013), p. 86.

43 *Richard II* (v, v, 42–3).

44 Browne said he was born under Saturn and had a 'piece of the leaden planet' in him: *Religio Medici* (II, 11), in *Browne*, ed. Killeen, p. 77.

45 E. Leong, 'Making Medicines in the Early Modern Household', *Bulletin of the History of Medicine*, LXXXII/1 (2008), pp. 145–68. See also A. Rankin, *Panaceia's Daughters* (Chicago, IL, 2013).

46 Today, oil of hypericum is used to treat depression and has been shown to be as effective as standard anti-depressants with fewer adverse side-effects. On the other hand, the medicinal effects of hart's horn water (MS Osborn fb255, p. 72) are not recognized.

47 W. Pagel, 'Paracelsus', in *Dictionary of Scientific Biography*, ed. C. C. Gillispie (New York, 1970–86), vol. X, pp. 304–13.

48 Ketton-Cremer, *Assembly*, p. 214.

49 W. Schleiner, 'Jaques and the Melancholy Stag', *English Language Notes*, XVII/3 (1980), pp. 175–9.

50 Giovanni Paolo Lomazzo, *A Tracte Containing the Artes of Curious Paintinge Carvinge and Building* (III, xi), trans. R. Haydocke (Farnborough, 1970), p. 112.

51 Robert Burton, 'Synopsis of the Second Partition', *Anatomy of Melancholy* (Philadelphia, PA, 1883), p. 268.

52 Agnew, *Whirlpool*, pp. 12–13.

53 Ibid., p. 11.

54 Ketton-Cremer, *Portraits*, p. 37.

55 Agnew, *Whirlpool*, p. 12.

56 If the *Paston Treasure* was painted shortly after the death of Sir Robert's father, then the silver platter may have gone to his stepmother.

57 H. Clifford, 'A Commerce with Things', in *Consumers and Luxury*, ed. M. Berg and H. Clifford (Manchester, 1999), p. 158.

58 B. de Munck, 'Artisans, Productions and Gifts: Rethinking the History of Material Culture in Early Modern Europe', *Past and Present*, CCXXIV (2014), p. 59.

59 Clifford, 'Commerce', p. 154.

60 Macro-XRF by Dr Francesco Paolo Romano and Claudia Caliri of the University of Catania.

61 These would not have been visible to Sir Robert. Just as pigments can fade, paint can become more transparent. Changes of mind, or *pentimenti*, therefore slowly emerge over time.

62 V. L. Slater, 'Continuity and Change in English Provincial Politics: Robert Paston in Norfolk, 1675–1683', *Albion*, xxv/2 (1993), pp. 193–216.
63 Ibid., p. 204.
64 31 March 1676, in Agnew, *Whirlpool*, pp. 201–2.
65 Ibid., pp. 198–9.
66 Ketton-Cremer, *Assembly*, p. 212.
67 *The Pack of Autolycus, or Strange and Terrible News*, ed. H. E. Rollins (Port Washington, NY, 1969), p. 208.
68 G. Parker, *Global Crisis: War, Climate Change and Catastrophe in the Seventeenth Century* (New Haven, CT, 2013).
69 Ibid., p. 112.
70 J. de Vries, 'The Crisis of the Seventeenth Century', *Journal of Interdisciplinary History*, xliv/3 (2014), pp. 369–77.
71 J. Cowie, *Climate Change: Biological and Human Aspects* (Cambridge, 2013), pp. 173–6.
72 Add. MS 36988, British Library, London, fol. 220, in Agnew, *Whirlpool*, p. 25.
73 *Religio Medici* (II, 4), in *Browne*, ed. Killeen, p. 67.
74 R. W. Ketton-Cremer, *Forty Norfolk Essays* (Norwich, 1961), p. 94.
75 V. Janković, *Reading the Skies* (Manchester, 2000), pp. 56–9.
76 Archdeacon Prideaux, 1693, in Ketton-Cremer, *Portraits*, p. 54.
77 Richard Gough, *The History of Myddle*, ed. D. Hey (Harmondsworth, 1981), pp. 217–23.
78 Ossulston *v.* Yarmouth, in R. B. Comyn, *A Treatise on the Law of Usury* (London, 1817), p. 147, in J. Agnew, 'The Bankrupt Bibliophile', in *A Verray Parfit Praktisour*, ed. L. Clark and E. Danbury (Woodbridge, 2017), p. 160.
79 Agnew, 'Bibliophile', pp. 153–74.
80 Ketton-Cremer, *Portraits*, pp. 55–6.
81 *The Daily Courant*, in Agnew, 'Bibliophile', p. 174.
82 Ketton-Cremer, *Assembly*, pp. 214–15.
83 W. L. Spiers, 'The Note-book and Account Book of Nicholas Stone', *Walpole Society*, VII (1919), p. 69.
84 Ketton-Cremer, *Assembly*, pp. 217–18.
85 Clifford, 'Commerce', pp. 159–60.
86 Ibid., pp. 161–2.
87 Agnew, 'Bibliophile', p. 174.
88 Maurice Howard and Edward Town, 'The Development of Oxnead: From Tudor House to Nicholas Stone', in *The Paston Treasure: Microcosm of the Known World*, ed. A. Moore, N. Flis and F. Vanke (New Haven, CT, 2018).
89 D. Woodward, 'Swords into Ploughshares: Recycling in Pre-Industrial England', *Economic History Review*, xxxviii/2 (1985), pp. 180–86.
90 M. Aston, 'English Ruins and English History', *Journal of the Warburg and Courtauld Institutes*, xxxvi (1973), pp. 231–55.

seven Repentance

1 Cited in E. Pasztory, *Thinking with Things* (Austin, TX, 2005), p. 82.
2 As Browne said, the 'glory of one state depends on the ruin of another': *Religio Medici* (I, 17), in *Thomas Browne*, ed. K. Killeen (Oxford, 2014), p. 21.
3 C. Booker, *The Seven Basic Plots* (London, 2004).
4 As Browne said, 'To be ignorant of evils to come and forgetfull of evils past is a mercifull provision of nature': *Hydriotaphia or Urne Buriall* (v), in *Browne*, ed. Killeen, p. 545.
5 Modern science's condemnation of alchemy rests on its attempts to impose an unbridgeable gulf between the experimenter and the experiment. Science moved the goalposts – a typically Hermetic trick – to exclude the human from its view of the world. Sir Robert would have found the move utterly pointless if not completely incomprehensible.
6 MS Add. 6968, Cambridge University Library, partially transcribed in F. Worship, *Account of a MS Genealogy of the Paston Family in the Possession of His Grace the Duke of Newcastle* (Norwich, 1852), and in *Norfolk Archaeology*, IV (1855), pp. 1–55.
7 24 April 1676, in J. Agnew, ed., *The Whirlpool of Misadventures: Letters of Robert Paston, 1663–79* (Norwich, 2017), p. 220.
8 J. B. Hochstrasser, *Still Life and Trade* (New Haven, CT, 2007), pp. 252–60.
9 C. W. Bynum, 'Wonder', *American Historical Review*, CII/1 (1997), pp. 1–26; P. G. Grant, ed., *Wonders, Marvels and Monsters in Early Modern Culture* (Cranbury, NJ, 1999).
10 E. S. de Beer, 'The Earliest Fellows of the Royal Society', *Notes and Records of the Royal Society*, VII/2 (1950), p. 185.
11 In fact, the mathematician Gödel demonstrated that systems cannot be closed, but in practice the new scientific knowledge became treated as if it could provide a complete view of reality.
12 N. Bryson, *Looking at the Overlooked* (London, 1990), p. 120.
13 J. Sheehan, 'Sacred and Profane: Idolatry, Antiquarianism and the Polemics of Distinction in the Seventeenth Century', *Past and Present*, CXCII (2006), pp. 35–66.
14 Of course, like all political interventions, the idea had unforeseen consequences. And the conscious seventeenth-century desacralization of the everyday lies at the root of, amongst other things, the modern ecological crisis.
15 5 August 1671, in Agnew, *Whirlpool*, p. 125.
16 24 February 1678/9, ibid., p. 378.
17 Appropriately, shells' order was expressed in their Aristotelian *morph* or alchemical 'fixity', whilst their disorder was expressed in their matter, *hyle* or 'volatility'.
18 F. Kermode, 'Introduction', in *The Arden Shakespeare: The Tempest* (London, 1984), pp. xxvi–xxxiv.
19 *The Tempest* (I, ii, 399–404).

20 B. J. Sokol, *A Brave New World of Knowledge* (Cranbury, NJ, 2003), pp. 30–47.

21 He may even have had a tenuous link to Prospero since it has been suggested that Shakespeare's character may have been based on Dr John Dee, the father of Browne's friend and neighbour Dr Arthur Dee. See W. H. Sherman, *John Dee: The Politics of Reading and Writing in the English Renaissance* (Amhurst, MA, 1995), pp. 51–2. It has also been suggested that Prospero may have been based on Cornelius Drebbel, the inventor of cochineal tin lakes. R. Grudin, 'Rudolf II of Prague and Cornelis Drebbel: Shakespearean Archetypes?', *Huntington Library Quarterly*, LIV/3 (1991), pp. 181–205.

22 *Religio Medici* (II, I), in *Browne*, ed. Killeen, p. 61.

23 This text is full of serious jokes. For example, amongst the lost books he describes is Solomon's *De umbris idaerum*, a treatise on the shadows cast by our thoughts. This sounds funny, but Browne had lived through the consequences of radically differing ideas about government, he had heard about the consequences of European ideas on the New World, and he could imagine the consequences of the new sciences' mechanistic ideas. Browne had read Plato's parable of the cave, and Solomon's missing book was a sad admission that a history written in the light of wisdom did not exist. The power of the idea is such that, even though Solomon's book did not exist, one of the shadows it cast might be *A First Encyclopedia of Tlön*.

24 *Hydroitaphia or Urne-Buriall* (V), in *Browne*, ed. Killeen, p. 543.

25 25 March 1678, in Agnew, *Whirlpool*, p. 328.

26 *The Tempest* (Epilogue, 15–16).

27 E. Spiller, *Science, Reading and Renaissance Literature, 1580–1670* (Cambridge, 2004).

28 H. Grootenboer, *The Rhetoric of Perspective* (Chicago, IL, 2005), p. 10; B. Latour and S. Woolgar, *Laboratory Life: The Social Construction of Scientific Facts* (Beverly Hills, CA, 1979); L. Daston, 'Fear and Loathing of the Imagination in Science', *Daedalus*, CIIVII/I (1998), pp. 74–7; S. Shapin and S. Schaffer, *Leviathan and the Air-Pump* (Princeton, NJ, 1985), p. 225.

29 E. Panofsky, 'Galileo as a Critic of the Arts', *Isis*, XLVII/I (1956), p. 10.

30 'The Description of an Instrument Invented Divers Years Ago by Dr Christopher Wren, for Drawing the Outlines of Any Object in Perspective', *Philosophical Transactions*, IV (1669), pp. 898–9.

31 Our familiarity with cameras has made us turn history on its head. The problem 'was not how to make a picture that looked like the image produced by the camera, it was how to make a machine that produced an image like the ones [artists] painted': J. Snyder, 'Picturing Vision', *Critical Inquiry*, VI/3 (1980), p. 512.

32 Hilliard's insight has been elaborated upon by today's theorists. For example, amongst others, Nicholas Mirzoeff explores the political implications of perspective, which is 'not important because it shows us how we "really" see . . . but because it allows us to order and control

what we see': *An Introduction to Visual Culture* (London, 1999), p. 40.
See also W.J.T. Mitchell, *Iconology* (Chicago, IL, 2002).

33 C. A. Johnston, 'Heavenly Perspectives, Mirrors of Eternity: Thomas
Traherne's Yearning Subject', *Criticism*, XLIII/4 (2001), p. 386.

34 H. Wölfflin, *Principles of Art History*, trans. M. D. Hottinger (New
York, 1950).

35 D. Ashton, ed., *Picasso on Art* (New York, 1972), p. 21.

36 P. Smith, 'Cézanne's "Primitive" Perspective, or the "View from
Everywhere"', *Art Bulletin*, XCV/1 (2013), pp. 102–19.

37 J. Gasquet, *Cézanne*, p. 122, in Smith, 'Cézanne', p. 110.

38 Apollinaire, *Les Peintres Cubistes*, p. 69, ibid., p. 107.

39 Cited in G. B. Madison, *The Phenomenology of Merleau-Ponty*
(Athens, OH, 1981), p. 82; M. Merleau-Ponty, *The Phenomenology of
Perception*, pp. 67–9, in Smith, 'Cézanne', p. 103.

40 A. D. Milner and M. A. Goodale, *The Visual Brain in Action* (Oxford,
1995), pp. 88–92, in Smith, 'Cézanne', p. 103. Cézanne's interest
in the tactile aspect of visual scenes was a response to the novel
phenomenon of department store windows which allowed
people to look but not touch: ibid., p. 116. One wonders what he
would have made of online shopping.

41 Smith, 'Cézanne', pp. 112–13.

42 R. Barbour, *Sir Thomas Browne: A Life* (Oxford, 2013), p. 470.

43 T. Hughes, 'Sir Thomas Browne's Knighthood', *Norfolk Archaeology*,
XLIII (1998–9), pp. 326–7. *The Diary of John Evelyn*, ed. E. S. de
Beer (Oxford, 1955), vol. III, p. 594.

44 *Religio Medici* (II, 9), in *Browne*, ed. Killeen, p. 73.

45 J. S. Morrill, 'William Dowsing, Bureaucratic Puritan', in *Public Duty
and Private Conscience in Seventeenth-century England*, ed. J. S. Morrill,
P. Slack and D. Woolf (Oxford, 1993), p. 188.

46 *The Journal of William Dowsing*, ed. T. Cooper (Woodbridge, 2003);
M. Aston, *England's Iconoclasts* (Oxford, 1988).

47 *Pseudodoxia epidemica* (V, 5), in *Browne*, ed. Killeen, pp. 373–6.

48 K. Killeen, 'The Politics of Painting: *Pseudodoxia Epidemica* and
Iconoclasm', in *Sir Thomas Browne: The World Proposed*, ed. R. Barbour
and C. Preston (Oxford, 2008), pp. 188–205.

49 Ibid., p. 198.

50 8 June 1669, in Agnew, *Whirlpool*, p. 85.

51 K. Murphy, '"A Likely Story": Plato's *Timaeus* in the *Garden of Cyrus*',
in *Sir Thomas Browne*, ed. Barbour and Preston, p. 242.

52 Ibid., p. 243.

53 C. Preston, 'Unriddling the World', *Critical Survey*, V/3 (1993),
p. 263.

54 *The Tempest* (I, i, 29–30).

55 X-rays of the painting show that the girl's head was always intended
to overlap the lobster and plate. There is no evidence of her being an
afterthought that partially obscures a complete lobster.

56 J. Kepler, *Harmonices mundi* (V, vi, 207), illustrated in J. Hollander,
The Untuning of the Sky (New York, 1970), pp. 242–3.

57 The downward-moving ostrich egg covered in mother-of-pearl and the star-tortoise shell only made their appearance in the painting after the silver platter had been overpainted. The X-ray shows that original version would have been a rising crescendo with a big finish.

58 J. C. Kassler, 'Music as a Model in Early Modern Science', *History of Science*, xx (1982), pp. 103–39.

59 Murphy, 'Likely', p. 253.

60 *Religio Medici* (1, 16), in *Browne*, ed. Killeen, p. 18.

61 Plato, *Timaeus* (29d), trans. R. G. Bury (London, 1966), p. 53.

62 'Preface', *Garden*, in *Browne*, ed. Killeen, p. 551.

63 L. Salerno, 'Seventeenth-century English Literature on Painting', *Journal of the Warburg and Courtauld Institutes*, xiv/3–4 (1951), p. 241.

64 Aristotle said that if the tragic hero is pure evil, then the audience can have no empathy with his fate, but if he is pure good, then the audience can have no empathy with divine justice. With all his faults, Sir Robert qualifies as a tragic hero. Aristotle, *Poetics* (xiii, ii, 3), trans. S. Halliwell (London, 1995), pp. 69–71.

65 *Religio Medici* (1, 16), in *Browne*, ed. Killeen, p. 19.

66 Preston, 'Unriddling', p. 268. The word was Samuel Taylor Coleridge's.

67 T. C. Singer, 'Sir Thomas Browne's "Emphaticall Decussation, or Fundamentall Figure"', *English Literary Renaissance*, xvii (1987), p. 102.

68 Killeen, ed., *Browne*, p. xviii.

69 J. G. Turner, 'Ralph Austen', *Oxford Dictionary of National Biography*, www.oxforddnb.com, October 2006.

70 Thomas Fuller, *The History of the Worthies of England*, ed. P. A. Nuttall (London, 1840), vol. iii, p. 487.

71 J. Bartos, 'The Spiritual Orchard: God, Garden and Landscape in the Seventeenth Century', *Garden History*, xxxviii/2 (2010), pp. 177–93.

72 *Garden* (iv), in *Browne*, ed. Killeen, pp. 583–5.

73 Ibid., p. 590.

74 P. Smith, 'Science and Taste: Painting, Passions and the New Philosophy in Seventeenth Century Leiden', *Isis*, xc/3 (1999), p. 438.

75 Nicolas Le Febvre, *A Discourse on Sir Walter Rawleigh's Great Cordial*, trans. Peter Belon (London, 1664).

76 Osborn ms fb255, Beinecke Library, Yale University, New Haven, ct, p. 67.

77 Dante, *The Divine Comedy: Paradiso* (xxxiii, 145), trans. C. H. Sisson (Oxford, 1993), p. 499.

78 Madison, *Merleau-Ponty*, pp. 77–80.

79 Sir Robert knew that 'where your treasure is, there will your heart be also' and that, unlike earthly treasures, 'neither moth nor rust doth corrupt' spiritual treasure (Matthew 6:19–21).

80 S. Stewart, *On Longing: Narratives of the Miniature, the Gigantic, the Souvenir, the Collection* (Durham, nc, 1992).

81 For example, the shell cup that lies on the table by the servant has a patch on the rim of the base that reflects the lobster. However, since the lobster and its reflection were both painted in the vermilion that

faded, it is no longer visible and is evident only through scientific analysis of mercury's presence.

82 F. H. Cook, *Hua-Yen Buddhism: The Jewel Net of Indra* (University Park, PA, 1977).

83 Nicholas of Cusa, *Of Learned Ignorance* (II, 5), trans. G. Heron (London, 1954), p. 83.

84 J. F. Adkins, 'Neoplatonism in Marvell's "On a Drop of Dew" and "The Garden"', *Bulletin of the Rocky Mountain Modern Language Association*, XXVIII/4 (1974), pp. 77–92. Dante, *Paradiso* (XXIX, 143–50), p. 481.

85 Laozi, *Daodejing* (25), trans. E. Ryden (Oxford, 2008), p. 53.

86 I. Weinryb, 'Living Matter: Materiality, Maker and Ornament in the Middle Ages', *Gesta*, LII/2 (2013), pp. 113–32.

87 *A Midsummer's Night's Dream* (II, i, 103).

88 Pliny, *Natural History* (XXXIII, 95), trans. H. Rackham (London, 1967), vol. IX, p. 73.

89 It is no coincidence that the Chinese chose silver for their currency since they associated the lunar metal with *yin*, the Far Eastern equivalent of *sylva* and *hyle*.

90 H. L. Kessler, 'The Eloquence of Silver', in *L'Allégorie dans l'art du Moyen Age: Formes et fonctions*, ed. C. Heck (Turnhout, 2011), p. 50.

91 Paracelsus, 'Liber de imaginibus', in M. Baxandall, *The Limewood Sculptors of Renaissance Germany* (New Haven, CT, 1995), p. 32.

92 *Garden* (IV), in *Browne*, ed. Killeen, p. 591.

93 The shell upon which it was engraved is the painting's most obviously helical form. The helix combines the circular movement of the heavens with linear earthly movement, like the snake on Hermes' caduceus – symbol of alchemy.

94 Apollodorus, *The Library* (III, ix, 2), trans. R. Hard (Oxford, 2008), pp. 116–17.

95 19 August 1671, in Agnew, *Whirlpool*, p. 128.

96 *Religio Medici* (I, 34), in *Browne*, ed. Killeen, p. 37. The *Paston Treasure* purposefully defied established visual convention in order to give equal weight to, and maximum contact between, the things it depicted. Giving equal weight to, and suggesting intercourse between, the material and spiritual is most appropriate for a *pronk-vanitas*.

97 This is why comedies often focus their narratives on their protagonists' worldly travails that precede union and end abruptly upon union, implying that 'they lived happily ever after', the posthumous state of all blessed souls.

98 E. DeMarrais and J. Robb, 'Art Makes Society', *World Art*, III/1 (2013), pp. 3–22.

99 J. A. Welu, 'Vermeer: His Cartographic Sources', *Art Bulletin*, LVII/4 (1975), p. 543.

100 Sir Walter Raleigh, *The History of the World* (II, xxiii, 4), in *The Works of Sir Walter Raleigh . . .*, ed. W. Oldys and T. Birch (Oxford, 1829), vol. IV, p. 684.

101 Like perspective pictures, they also imply control over what they
represent. See V.-P. Herva, 'Maps and Magic in Renaissance Europe',
Journal of Material Culture, XV (2010), pp. 323–43.

102 Jan and Caspar Luiken, cited in J. Welu, 'Vermeer's "Astronomer":
Observations on an Open Book', *Art Bulletin*, LXVIII/2 (1986), p. 267.

103 J. Brooks and J. Wainwright, 'Dialogues in the *Paston Treasure*', in
The Paston Treasure: Microcosm of the Known World, ed. A. Moore,
N. Flis and F. Vanke (New Haven, CT, 2018); I. Payne, 'Robert
Ramsey', *Oxford Dictionary of National Biography*, www.
oxforddnb.com, October 2006.

104 Dante, *Paradiso* (XXVI, 106–7), p. 466.

105 E. Turnor, *Collections for the History of the Town and Soke of Grantham*
(London, 1806), p. 173, n. 2, in S. Schaffer, 'Newton on the Beach',
History of Science, XLVII (2009), p. 243.

106 See, for example, P. A. Jorgensen, 'Much Ado about Nothing',
Shakespeare Quarterly, V/3 (1954), pp. 287–95, and G. Calmann, 'The
Picture of Nobody', *Journal of the Warburg and Courtauld Institutes*,
XXIII/1–2 (1960), pp. 60–104. Sir Robert probably knew of ceramic
tobacco jars in the shape of a man with a head, arms and legs but no
torso. They were made in London in the 1670s and were so popular
that they prompted Chinese imitations. Their appeal lay in exchanges
such as: 'Who's got the tobacco? . . . Nobody's got the tobacco', in
Calmann, 'Nobody', p. 97.

107 Laozi, *Daodejing*, II, p. 25.

108 Anon., *The Cloud of Unknowing* (68), trans. C. Wolters
(Harmondsworth, 1978), pp. 142–3.

109 *Religio Medici* (1, 9), in *Browne*, ed. Killeen, p. 12.

110 Sir Robert lived through a period of iconoclasm caused by a failure
to recognize that whilst the symbol and symbolized may be essentially
the same, they are materially different. He may have appreciated the
faded version of his picture as a reminder of that difference.

Epilogue

1 Sir Walter Raleigh, *The History of the World* (1, ii, 5), in *The Works of
Sir Walter Raleigh . . .*, ed. W. Oldys and T. Birch (Oxford, 1829), vol. II,
p. 60.

2 E.M.W. Tillyard, *The Elizabethan World Picture* (Harmondsworth,
1972), p. 63.

3 Jonathan Swift, *The Accomplishment of the First of Mr Bickerstaff's
Predictions* (London, 1708), p. 3.

4 Craftsmen had been validated by all members of society through
their performance in traditional Passion plays. Scientists achieved
validation by performing their own honed improvisations to the
Society.

5 Before the rise of magic, the traditional sciences sought knowledge
in order to better conform the will to nature. Scientific practice
externalized its focus, inverting the earlier internalization of religious

practice. Michael Hunter has described the intellectual shift as less
a decline in magic and more a 'rise in schizophrenia': *Robert Boyle:
Scrupulosity and Science* (Woodbridge, 2000), p. 244.

6 R. Janko, *Homer, Hesiod and the Hymns* (Cambridge, 1982), pp. 140–43.

7 D. Graeber, *Towards an Anthropological Theory of Value: The False
Coin of Our Own Dreams* (Basingstoke, 2001). Given contemporary
understanding of perspective as an ideology and its connection with
capitalism, it is interesting that Sir Robert's *Paston Treasure* eschewed
the colonizing control of space implied by rational, single-point,
linear perspective. For example, D. E. Cosgrove claims that the 'visual
power' of perspective 'complements the real power humans exert over
land as property', in 'Prospect, Perspective and the Evolution of the
Landscape Idea', *Transactions of the Institute of British Geographers*,
new ser., x/1 (1985), p. 45.

8 T. Elliott and T. Rossio, *Pirates of the Caribbean: Dead Man's Chest*,
dir. G. Verbinski (Walt Disney Pictures, 2006).

9 F. Heal, *Hospitality in Early Modern England* (Oxford, 1990).

10 M. Mauss, *The Gift*, trans. J. I. Guyer (Chicago, IL, 2016).

11 *The Diaries of Lady Anne Clifford*, ed. D.J.H. Clifford (Stroud, 1990),
p. 102.

12 *The Correspondence of Lady Katherine Paston, 1603–1627*, ed. R.
Hughey (Norwich, 1941), p. 62.

13 William Harrison, *The Description of England*, ed. G. Edelen
(Washington, DC, 1994), p. 255.

14 F. Heal, 'Food Gifts, the Household and the Politics of Exchange
in Early Modern Europe', *Past and Present,* CXCIX (2008), pp. 41–70.

15 *Paston Letters* (1, 36), in R. M. Faurot, 'From Records to Romance',
Studies in English Literature, V/4 (1965), p. 681.

16 P. Fumerton, 'Exchanging Gifts: The Elizabethan Currency of
Children and Poetry', *Journal of English Literary History*, LIII/2 (1986),
p. 250.

17 Ibid., pp. 241–78.

18 Ibid., p. 252.

19 M. E. Lamb, 'Taken by the Fairies: Fairy Practices and the Production
of Popular Culture in "A Midsummer Night's Dream"', *Shakespeare
Quarterly*, LI/3 (2000), pp. 285–304.

20 *The Winter's Tale* (III, iii, 70–74).

21 L. L. Peck, *Court Patronage and Corruption in Early Stuart England*
(London, 1990).

22 25 March 1665, in J. Agnew, ed., *The Whirlpool of Misadventures: Letters
of Robert Paston, 1663–79* (Norwich, 2017), p. 61.

23 John Dryden, *Annus mirabilis* (London, 1667).

24 H. Liebersohn, *The Return of the Gift* (Cambridge, 2011).

25 B. Malinowski, *Argonauts of the Western Pacific* (London, 1922).

26 J. Parry, 'The Gift, the Indian Gift and the "Indian Gift"', *Man*, XXI/3
(1986), pp. 453–73. It is, for example, significant that today America,
the country with a great investment in the market economy, also has
a thriving philanthropic culture.

27 S. Pumfrey, 'Ideas above his Station: A Social Study of Hooke's Curatorship of Experiments', *History of Science*, XXIX (1991), pp. 1–44.

28 L. Jardine, 'Dr Wilkins's Boy Wonders', *Notes and Records of the Royal Society of London*, LVIII/1 (2004), pp. 107–29.

29 To Hooke, 5 February 1675, online facsimile at http://digitallibrary. hsp.org/index.php/Detail/Object/Show/object_id/9285. It is in keeping with the motto that Newton simply rephrased Bernard of Chartres and it is in keeping with his character that he did not credit Bernard.

30 A. M. Roos, 'The Chymistry of "The Learned Dr Plot" (1640–96)', *Osiris*, XXIX/1 (2014), p. 95.

31 For example, the human genome is in the public domain because international teams of scientists worked together to prevent the information being patented by 'volatile' multinational corporations. The concept of 'intellectual property' turns such gifts into commodities.

32 Fulmerton, 'Exchanging', pp. 241 and 266.

33 Ralph Waldo Emerson, 'Gifts', in *The Collected Works of Ralph Waldo Emerson*, vol. III: *Essays, Second Series*, ed. J. Slater, A. R. Ferguson and J. F. Carr (Cambridge, MA, 1983), p. 94.

34 Craft skills were transmitted by embodied practices, accompanied by now lost oral traditions and very sparse written manuals. Studying physical processes and the compositions of crafted objects can supplement the written evidence to throw light on the extent to which guilds' religious functions were linked to ways of making objects. My research in the conservation studio is partly driven by a desire to address such questions.

35 Karel van Mander, *Schilder-Boeck*, cited in L. Silver and P. H. Smith, 'Splendour in the Grass', in *Merchants and Marvels*, ed. P. H. Smith and P. Findlen (New York, 2002), p. 44.

36 Cited in Lin Yutang, *From Pagan to Christian* (London, 1960), p. 92. Laozi, *Daodejing* (14), trans. E. Ryden (Oxford, 2008), p. 31.

37 De Munck, B., 'Artisans, Productions and Gifts: Rethinking the History of Material Culture in Early Modern Europe', *Past and Present*, CCXXIV (2014), p. 63. G. Warwick, 'Gift Exchange and Art Collecting', *Art Bulletin*, LXXIX/4 (1997), pp. 630–46.

38 She also gave the shell cup that was depicted lying on the table, held by the servant's left hand.

Select Bibliography

Agnew, J., ed., *The Whirlpool of Misadventures: Letters of Robert Paston, 1663–79* (Norwich, 2017)

Agricola, G., *De re metallica*, ed. H. C. and L. H. Hoover (New York, 1950)

Barbour, R., *Sir Thomas Browne: A Life* (Oxford, 2013)

Barbour, R., and C. Preston, eds, *Thomas Brown: The World Proposed* (Oxford, 2008)

Bennett, H. S., *The Pastons and their England* (Cambridge, 1922)

Blomefield, F., *An Essay towards a Topographical History of the County of Norfolk* (London, 1805–10)

Brown, N. O., *Hermes the Thief: The Evolution of a Myth* (New York, 1947)

Bryson, N., *Looking at the Overlooked* (London, 1990)

Bucklow, S., *The Alchemy of Paint* (London, 2009)

Carruthers, M., *The Craft of Thought* (Cambridge, 1998)

Daly, J., 'Cosmic Harmony and Political Thinking in Early Stuart England', *Transactions of the American Philosophical Society*, LXIX/7 (1979)

Davis, N., ed., *Paston Letters and Papers of the Fifteenth Century* (Oxford, 1971–6)

—, *The Paston Letters: A Selection in Modern Spelling* (Oxford, 1983)

De Munck, B., 'Artisans, Productions and Gifts: Rethinking the History of Material Culture in Early Modern Europe', *Past and Present*, CCXXIV (2014), pp. 39–74

Dixon, D. R., 'Thomas Henshaw and Sir Robert Paston's Pursuit of the Red Elixir: An Early Collaboration between Fellows of the Royal Society', *Notes and Records of the Royal Society of London*, LI/1 (1997), pp. 57–76

Dobbs, B.T.J., *The Janus Face of Genius* (Cambridge, 1991)

Evelyn, John, *The Diary of John Evelyn*, ed. E. S. de Beer (Oxford, 1955)

Findlen, P., ed., *Early Modern Things* (London, 2013)

Fumerton, P., 'Exchanging Gifts: The Elizabethan Currency of Children and Poetry', *Journal of English Literary History*, LIII/2 (1986), pp. 241–78

Gough, R., *The History of Myddle*, ed. D. Dey (Harmondsworth, 1981)

Gouk, P., *Music, Science and Natural Magic in Seventeenth-century England* (New Haven, CT, 1999)

Habib, I., *Black Lives in the English Archives, 1500–1677* (London, 2008)

Hart, V., *Art and Magic in the Court of the Stuarts* (London, 1994)

Hughey, R., ed., *The Correspondence of Lady Katherine Paston, 1603–27*
   (Norwich, 1941)
Janković,V., *Reading the Skies* (Manchester, 2000)
Jardine, L., and J. Brotton, *Global Interests* (London, 2000)
Ketton-Cremer, R. W., *Norfolk Portraits* (London, 1944)
—, *Norfolk Assembly* (London, 1957)
Killeen, K., ed., *Thomas Browne* (Oxford, 2014)
Klein, U., and E. C. Spary, eds, *Materials and Expertise in Early Modern
   Europe* (Chicago, IL, 2010)
Lewis, D., *We, the Navigators* (Honolulu, HI, 1994)
Manuel, F. E., *The Religion of Isaac Newton* (Oxford, 1974)
Mauss, M., *The Gift*, trans. J. I. Guyer (Chicago, IL, 2016)
Merrifield, M. P., *Original Treatises on the Arts of Painting*
   (New York, 1967)
Moore, A., N. Flis and F. Vanke, *The Paston Treasure: Microcosm of the Known
   World* (New Haven, CT, 2018)
Peacham, H., *The Compleat Gentleman*, ed. V. B. Heltzel (Ithaca, NY, 1962)
Pepys, Samuel, *The Diary of Samuel Pepys*, ed. R. Latham and W. Matthews
   (Berkeley, CA, 2000)
Richmond, C., *The Paston Family in the Fifteenth Century: The First Phase*
   (Cambridge, 1990)
—, *The Paston Family in the Fifteenth Century: Fastolf's Will* (Cambridge,
   1996)
—, *The Paston Family in the Fifteenth Century: Endings* (Manchester, 2000)
Roberts, L., S. Schaffer and P. Dear, eds, *The Mindful Hand: Inquiry
   and Invention from the Later Renaissance to Early Industrialization*
   (Amsterdam, 2007)
The Saga of Thidrek of Bern, trans. E. R. Haymes (New York, 1988)
Shapin, S., and S. Schaffer, *Leviathan and the Air-Pump* (Princeton, NJ, 1985)

Acknowledgements

The conservators with whom I worked on the *Paston Treasure* were Dani Leonard, Lucy Wrapson and the late Renate Woudhuysen. The project was overseen by Ian McClure. The painting's conservation was funded by grants from numerous charities including the Silver Society, Goldsmiths' Company and Schroder Foundation. I undertook the scientific analysis with Jeremy Skepper (SEM) and Francesco Paolo Romano and Claudia Caliri (Macro-XRF). Documentary photography, investigative imaging and assembly of X-ray and Macro-XRF data was undertaken by Chris Titmus.

Work on the book started at Stanford during a visit that was made possible by a gift from Diana Bowes – in memory of her grandmother, Ruth Garland Bowes – for which I am most thankful. I would like to thank the following for their hospitality and support at the Stanford Humanities Center: Caroline Winterer, fellow visitor Günter Blamberger and especially Kelda Jamison, who made all the difference. I would also like to thank Paula Findlen, Katheryn Starkey, Elaine Treharne, Susan Roberts-Manganelli, Curt Frank, Marissa Galvez and Christina Smith. Special thanks to Fabio Barry, who very generously thought that a stint on the farm would help my work. He was right, and I am most grateful for his efforts in arranging my visit as well as his great company in San Francisco.

At the same time, the Yale Center for British Art decided to feature the *Paston Treasure* in an exhibition and invited me to contribute to their research. I would like to thank all those involved, including Amy Meyers, Lisa Ford, Elisabeth Fairman, Sarah Welcome and Belene Day. In workshops organized by Yale, I met and benefited from discussions with Jean Agnew, Esther Chadwick, Maurice Howard, Michael Hunter, Simon Jervis, Andrew Moore, Victor Morgan, Mark Purcell, Edward Town and Annabel Westman. Special thanks are due to Nathan Flis who expertly coordinated, and contributed much to, the research. It was a great pleasure to work with Jessica David, with whom I had many fruitful discussions about the details of the painting process. Jessica also very kindly shared the digital reconstructions that she made – impressions of the painting's changing appearance during stages of its production.

The Yale Center for British Art project was undertaken in collaboration with the Norwich Castle Museum. I would like to thank all the Museum staff, and especially Francesca Vanke, for their support of the project and for granting access to the painting that allowed its examination by Macro-XRF.

Many offered information and encouragement through the process of research and to them I give my thanks. They include Alison Ayres and Ken Eglen, Lucy Care (of Paston Heritage Society), Anuschka Fux, Kaja Kollandsrud, Aileen Ribeiro and Elizabeth Wells. Whilst I was writing, a historian of science steeped in the ways of the 'invisible college' treated me to coffee. Amongst other things, Simon Schaffer reminded me how 'probability' had changed, told me about Newton's anagram, and pointed out the Janus nature of the 'shoals' encountered by Yarmouth's fishermen. Early modern historian Ulinka Rublack read a nearly final draft and very generously clarified and refined many details whilst encouraging me to engage with the characters. I thank them both most sincerely for their help. My wife, Tara, read more drafts than I care to admit and her insightful comments were invaluable in shaping the book. I am deeply grateful for her guidance. Of course, the book's shortcomings remain my own. It was a pleasure to work with Martha Jay and Aimee Selby at Reaktion, and, finally, I am very grateful to Michael Leaman at Reaktion for introducing the aids gently, then giving me free rein.

Photo Acknowledgements

The author and publishers wish to express their thanks to the below sources of illustrative material and/or permission to reproduce it. Some locations are given here for reasons of brevity.

Courtesy the author: (Hamilton Kerr Institute, Fitzwilliam Museum, Cambridge): pp. 8, 14, 144, 137 (top and foot); from [Thomas Browne], *Hydriotaphia, Urne-buriall, or, A Discourse of the Sepulchrall Urnes lately found in Norfolk. Together with The Garden of Cyrus, or The Quincunciall, Lozenge, or Net-work Plantations of the Ancients, Artificially, Naturally, Mystically Considered ... By Thomas Browne D. of Physick* (London, 1658): p. 224 (photo reproduced by permission of the Syndics of the Fitzwilliam Museum, Cambridge); Cambridge University Library, Department of Manuscripts and University Archives: p. 129 (Francis Sandeford, *Genealogy of Robert Paston, Lord Yarmouth* [1674], MS Add 6968 – photo reproduced by kind permission of the Syndics of Cambridge University Library); digital reconstructions by Jessica David, Yale Center for Studies in British Art, New Haven, Connecticut: pp. 134 (top and foot), 135 (top); from [Robert Farley], *Lychnocausia sive Moralia facum emblemata. Lights Morall Emblems. Authore Roberto Farlæo Scoto-Britanno ...* (London, 1638): p. 90 (photo reproduced by kind permission of the Syndics of Cambridge University Library); Fitzwilliam Museum, Cambridge: pp. 60 (P142–1947, *Robert Paston, 1st Earl of Yarmouth*, Edward Lutterell, *c.* 1680), 120 (MS 276*, gift of James W. L. Glaisher, 1914); photos reproduced by permission of the Syndics of the Fitzwilliam Museum, Cambridge: pp. 60, 120; Norwich Castle Museum and Art Gallery, Norwich, Norfolk: pp. 130–31 (photo Chris Titmus, Hamilton Kerr Institute, Fitzwilliam Museum, Cambridge, reproduced by kind permission of the Norfolk Museums Service); from [John Partridge, Henry Coley (*sic*), John Tanner and William Andrews], *The Great and Wonderful Prophecies of Mr. Partridge, Mr. Coly, Mr. Tanner and Mr. Andrews, Predicting what may befall this Climate of England And other kingdoms, for this year 1689, With the Account of the memorable* Eclipses, *and their Signification, with other remarkable matters worthy of Note* (London, 1689) – photo by the London Metropolitan Archive, by kind permission of the Guildhall Library, London: p. 36; Dr Paolo Romano and Claudia Caliri: pp. 139, 140 (digital assembly by Chris Titmus, Hamilton Kerr Institute, Fitzwilliam Museum, Cambridge); Tate, London:

pp. 132–3, 138 (digital assembly by Chris Titmus, Hamilton Kerr Institute, Fitzwilliam Museum, Cambridge); photos Chris Titmus (Hamilton Kerr Institute, Fitzwilliam Museum, Cambridge), reproduced by kind permission of the Norfolk Museums Service: pp. 135 (foot), 136 (top and foot), 141, 142, 143 (top and foot), 192; from Sylvanus Urban, *The Gentleman's Magazine*, XXI, new series [176] (London, January–June 1844): p. 168 (photo reproduced by permission of Yale Center for British Art, New Haven, Connecticut – Paul Mellon Collection).

Index